Mohammad Salehin makes an innovative contribution to understanding the role of non-governmental organisations in the development process. Based on fieldwork in Bangladesh, Salehin shows how secular NGOs offering micro-credit to small enterprises have taken on a role akin to a parallel state in rural areas. More recently, Islamic NGOs have provided a new challenge. Both secular and Islamic NGOs prefer to give credits to women, as they are seen as more reliable in repaying debts. But in an unconventional analysis of gender relations, Salehin argues that Islamic NGOs are more sensitive than secular organisation to traditional structures, and therefore tend to strengthen the position of women rather than isolating them. This leads to a new form of neoliberal social management, which Salehin refers to as 'pious governmentality'.

Stephen Castles, *Professor, Research Chair in Sociology, The University of Sydney, Australia*

Through extensive field research, Mohammad Musfequs Salehin gives us a unique account of the relationship between Islamic NGOs, the state and the lives of rural women and men. In arguing for a new form of governmentality that emerges in the context of neoliberalism – 'pious' or 'sacralized governmentality' – Mohammad demonstrates the strategies that civil society and subaltern groups use both to resist and make claims on the state. *Islamic NGOs in Bangladesh* makes an important contribution to the field of both development studies and religion and gender. In particular, Mohammad's foregrounding of the experience of rural women contributes to our understanding of the relationship between governmentality and the production of Muslim women's subjectivities.

Laura Beth Bugg, *Assistant Professor, Department for the Study of Religion, University of Toronto*

This is a groundbreaking study of a new form of governmentality, pious governmentality, supported by international donors. The examination of how religious forms of social regulation produce and reproduce subjectivities, particularly the subjectivity of Muslim women, is original and pertinent. The topic is also a critical contribution to the policy field, concerning the role of NGOs in neoliberal governing practices.

Randi Gressgård, *Professor of Gender Studies, University of Bergen*

# Islamic NGOs in Bangladesh

NGOs (non-governmental organizations) have emerged in both a development and aid capacity in Bangladesh, providing wide-reaching public services to the country's population living in extreme poverty. However, resistance to and limitations of NGO-led development, in conjunction with Bangladesh's social transformation, has led to a new religious-based NGO development practice.

Looking at the role of Islamic NGOs in Bangladesh, the book investigates new forms of neoliberal governmentality supported by international donors. It discusses how this form of social regulation produces and reproduces subjectivities, particularly Muslim women's subjectivity, and has combined religious and economic rationality, further complicating the boundaries and the relationship between Islam, modernity and development. The book argues that both secular and Islamic NGOs target women in the name of empowerment but more importantly as the most reliable partners to meet their debt obligations of microfinancing schemes, including *shari'a*-based financing. The targeted women, in turn, experience Islamic NGOs as less coercive and more sensitive to their religious environment in the rural village community than are secular NGOs.

Providing a comparative study of the role of religious and secular NGOs in the implementation of neoliberal policies and development strategies, this book will be a significant addition to research on South Asian Politics, Development Studies, Gender Studies and Religion.

**Mohammad Musfequs Salehin** is a Visiting Researcher at the Centre for Women's and Gender Research (SKOK), University of Bergen, Norway.

## Routledge contemporary South Asia series

1 **Pakistan**
Social and cultural transformations in a Muslim nation
*Mohammad A. Qadeer*

2 **Labor, Democratization and Development in India and Pakistan**
*Christopher Candland*

3 **China–India Relations**
Contemporary dynamics
*Amardeep Athwal*

4 **Madrasas in South Asia**
Teaching terror?
*Jamal Malik*

5 **Labor, Globalization and the State**
Workers, women and migrants confront neoliberalism
*Edited by Debdas Banerjee and Michael Goldfield*

6 **Indian Literature and Popular Cinema**
Recasting classics
*Edited by Heidi R.M. Pauwels*

7 **Islamist Militancy in Bangladesh**
A complex web
*Ali Riaz*

8 **Regionalism in South Asia**
Negotiating cooperation, institutional structures
*Kishore C. Dash*

9 **Federalism, Nationalism and Development**
India and the Punjab economy
*Pritam Singh*

10 **Human Development and Social Power**
Perspectives from South Asia
*Ananya Mukherjee Reed*

11 **The South Asian Diaspora**
Transnational networks and changing identities
*Edited by Rajesh Rai and Peter Reeves*

12 **Pakistan–Japan Relations**
Continuity and change in economic relations and security interests
*Ahmad Rashid Malik*

13 **Himalayan Frontiers of India**
Historical, geo-political and strategic perspectives
*K. Warikoo*

14 **India's Open-Economy Policy**
Globalism, rivalry, continuity
*Jalal Alamgir*

15 **The Separatist Conflict in Sri Lanka**
Terrorism, ethnicity, political economy
*Asoka Bandarage*

16 **India's Energy Security**
*Edited by Ligia Noronha and Anant Sudarshan*

17 **Globalization and the Middle Classes in India**
The social and cultural impact of neoliberal reforms
*Ruchira Ganguly-Scrase and Timothy J. Scrase*

18 **Water Policy Processes in India**
Discourses of power and resistance
*Vandana Asthana*

19 **Minority Governments in India**
The puzzle of elusive majorities
*Csaba Nikolenyi*

20 **The Maoist Insurgency in Nepal**
Revolution in the twenty-first century
*Edited by Mahendra Lawoti and Anup K. Pahari*

21 **Global Capital and Peripheral Labour**
The history and political economy of plantation workers in India
*K. Ravi Raman*

22 **Maoism in India**
Reincarnation of ultra-left wing extremism in the twenty-first century
*Bidyut Chakrabarty and Rajat Kujur*

23 **Economic and Human Development in Contemporary India**
Cronyism and fragility
*Debdas Banerjee*

24 **Culture and the Environment in the Himalaya**
*Arjun Guneratne*

25 **The Rise of Ethnic Politics in Nepal**
Democracy in the margins
*Susan I. Hangen*

26 **The Multiplex in India**
A cultural economy of urban leisure
*Adrian Athique and Douglas Hill*

27 **Tsunami Recovery in Sri Lanka**
Ethnic and regional dimensions
*Dennis B. McGilvray and Michele R. Gamburd*

28 **Development, Democracy and the State**
Critiquing the Kerala model of development
*K. Ravi Raman*

29 **Mohajir Militancy in Pakistan**
Violence and transformation in the Karachi conflict
*Nichola Khan*

30 **Nationbuilding, Gender and War Crimes in South Asia**
*Bina D'Costa*

31 **The State in India after Liberalization**
Interdisciplinary perspectives
*Edited by Akhil Gupta and K. Sivaramakrishnan*

32 **National Identities in Pakistan**
The 1971 war in contemporary Pakistani fiction
*Cara Cilano*

33 **Political Islam and Governance in Bangladesh**
*Edited by Ali Riaz and C. Christine Fair*

34 **Bengali Cinema**
'An other nation'
*Sharmistha Gooptu*

35 **NGOs in India**
The challenges of women's empowerment and accountability
*Patrick Kilby*

36 **The Labour Movement in the Global South**
Trade unions in Sri Lanka
*S. Janaka Biyanwila*

37 **Building Bangalore**
Architecture and urban transformation in India's Silicon Valley
*John C. Stallmeyer*

38 **Conflict and Peacebuilding in Sri Lanka**
Caught in the peace trap?
*Edited by Jonathan Goodhand, Jonathan Spencer and Benedict Korf*

39 **Microcredit and Women's Empowerment**
A case study of Bangladesh
*Amunui Faraizi, Jim McAllister and Taskinur Rahman*

40 **South Asia in the New World Order**
The role of regional cooperation
*Shahid Javed Burki*

41 **Explaining Pakistan's Foreign Policy**
Escaping India
*Aparna Pande*

42 **Development-induced Displacement, Rehabilitation and Resettlement in India**
Current issues and challenges
*Edited by Sakarama Somayaji and Smrithi Talwar*

43 **The Politics of Belonging in India**
Becoming Adivasi
*Edited by Daniel J. Rycroft and Sangeeta Dasgupta*

44 **Re-Orientalism and South Asian Identity Politics**
The oriental Other within
*Edited by Lisa Lau and Ana Cristina Mendes*

45 **Islamic Revival in Nepal**
Religion and a new nation
*Megan Adamson Sijapati*

46 **Education and Inequality in India**
A classroom view
*Manabi Majumdar and Jos Mooij*

47 **The Culturalization of Caste in India**
Identity and inequality in a multicultural age
*Balmurli Natrajan*

48 **Corporate Social Responsibility in India**
*Bidyut Chakrabarty*

49 **Pakistan's Stability Paradox**
Domestic, regional and international dimensions
*Edited by Ashutosh Misra and Michael E. Clarke*

**50 Transforming Urban Water Supplies in India**
The role of reform and partnerships in globalization
*Govind Gopakumar*

**51 South Asian Security**
Twenty-first century discourse
*Sagarika Dutt and Alok Bansal*

**52 Non-discrimination and Equality in India**
Contesting boundaries of social justice
*Vidhu Verma*

**53 Being Middle-class in India**
A way of life
*Henrike Donner*

**54 Kashmir's Right to Secede**
A critical examination of contemporary theories of secession
*Matthew J. Webb*

**55 Bollywood Travels**
Culture, diaspora and border crossings in popular Hindi cinema
*Rajinder Dudrah*

**56 Nation, Territory, and Globalization in Pakistan**
Traversing the margins
*Chad Haines*

**57 The Politics of Ethnicity in Pakistan**
The Baloch, Sindhi and Mohajir ethnic movements
*Farhan Hanif Siddiqi*

**58 Nationalism and Ethnic Conflict**
Identities and mobilization after 1990
*Edited by Mahendra Lawoti and Susan Hangen*

**59 Islam and Higher Education**
Concepts, challenges and opportunities
*Marodsilton Muborakshoeva*

**60 Religious Freedom in India**
Sovereignty and (anti) conversion
*Goldie Osuri*

**61 Everyday Ethnicity in Sri Lanka**
Up-country Tamil identity politics
*Daniel Bass*

**62 Ritual and Recovery in Post-Conflict Sri Lanka**
Eloquent bodies
*Jane Derges*

**63 Bollywood and Globalisation**
The global power of popular Hindi cinema
*Edited by David J. Schaefer and Kavita Karan*

**64 Regional Economic Integration in South Asia**
Trapped in conflict?
*Amita Batra*

**65 Architecture and Nationalism in Sri Lanka**
The trouser under the cloth
*Anoma Pieris*

**66 Civil Society and Democratization in India**
Institutions, ideologies and interests
*Sarbeswar Sahoo*

**67 Contemporary Pakistani Fiction in English**
Idea, nation, state
*Cara N. Cilano*

68 **Transitional Justice in South Asia**
A study of Afghanistan and Nepal
*Tazreena Sajjad*

69 **Displacement and Resettlement in India**
The human cost of development
*Hari Mohan Mathur*

70 **Water, Democracy and Neoliberalism in India**
The power to reform
*Vicky Walters*

71 **Capitalist Development in India's Informal Economy**
*Elisabetta Basile*

72 **Nation, Constitutionalism and Buddhism in Sri Lanka**
*Roshan de Silva Wijeyeratne*

73 **Counterinsurgency, Democracy, and the Politics of Identity in India**
From warfare to welfare?
*Mona Bhan*

74 **Enterprise Culture in Neoliberal India**
Studies in youth, class, work and media
*Edited by Nandini Gooptu*

75 **The Politics of Economic Restructuring in India**
Economic governance and state spatial rescaling
*Loraine Kennedy*

76 **The Other in South Asian Religion, Literature and Film**
Perspectives on Otherism and Otherness
*Edited by Diana Dimitrova*

77 **Being Bengali**
At home and in the world
*Edited by*
*Mridula Nath Chakraborty*

78 **The Political Economy of Ethnic Conflict in Sri Lanka**
*Nikolaos Biziouras*

79 **Indian Arranged Marriages**
A social psychological perspective
*Tulika Jaiswal*

80 **Writing the City in British Asian Diasporas**
*Edited by Seán McLoughlin, William Gould, Ananya Jahanara Kabir and Emma Tomalin*

81 **Post-9/11 Espionage Fiction in the US and Pakistan**
Spies and 'terrorists'
*Cara Cilano*

82 **Left Radicalism in India**
*Bidyut Chakrabarty*

83 **"Nation-State" and Minority Rights in India**
Comparative perspectives on Muslim and Sikh identities
*Tanweer Fazal*

84 **Pakistan's Nuclear Policy**
A minimum credible deterrence
*Zafar Khan*

85 **Imagining Muslims in South Asia and the Diaspora**
Secularism, religion, representations
*Claire Chambers and Caroline Herbert*

**86 Indian Foreign Policy in Transition**
Relations with South Asia
*Arijit Mazumdar*

**87 Corporate Social Responsibility and Development in Pakistan**
*Nadeem Malik*

**88 Indian Capitalism in Development**
*Barbara Harriss-White and Judith Heyer*

**89 Bangladesh Cinema and National Identity**
In search of the modern?
*Zakir Hossain Raju*

**90 Suicide in Sri Lanka**
The anthropology of an epidemic
*Tom Widger*

**91 Epigraphy and Islamic Culture**
Inscriptions of the early Muslim rulers of Bengal (1205–1494)
*Mohammad Yusuf Siddiq*

**92 Reshaping City Governance**
London, Mumbai, Kolkata, Hyderabad
*Nirmala Rao*

**93 The Indian Partition in Literature and Films**
History, politics, and aesthetics
*Rini Bhattacharya Mehta and Debali Mookerjea-Leonard*

**94 Development, Poverty and Power in Pakistan**
The impact of state and donor interventions on farmers
*Syed Mohammad Ali*

**95 Ethnic Subnationalist Insurgencies in South Asia**
Identities, interests and challenges to state authority
*Edited by Jugdep S. Chima*

**96 International Migration and Development in South Asia**
*Edited by Md Mizanur Rahman and Tan Tai Yong*

**97 Twenty-First Century Bollywood**
*Ajay Gehlawat*

**98 Political Economy of Development in India**
Indigeneity in transition in the state of Kerala
*Darley Kjosavik and Nadarajah Shanmugaratnam*

**99 State and Nation-Building in Pakistan**
Beyond Islam and security
*Edited by Roger D. Long, Gurharpal Singh, Yunas Samad, and Ian Talbot*

**100 Subaltern Movements in India**
Gendered geographies of struggle against neoliberal development
*Manisha Desai*

**101 Islamic Banking in Pakistan**
Shariah-compliant finance and the quest to make Pakistan more Islamic
*Feisal Khan*

**102 The Bengal Diaspora**
Rethinking Muslim migration
*Claire Alexander, Joya Chatterji, and Annu Jalais*

**103 Mobilizing Religion and Gender in India**
The role of activism
*Nandini Deo*

**104 Social Movements and the Indian Diaspora**
*Movindri Reddy*

**105 Identity Politics and Elections in Malaysia and Indonesia**
Ethnic engineering in Borneo
*Karolina Prasad*

**106 Religion and Modernity in the Himalaya**
*Edited by Megan Adamson Sijapati and Jessica Vantine Birkenholtz*

**107 Devotional Islam in Contemporary South Asia**
Shrines, journeys and wanderers
*Edited by Michel Boivin and Rémy Delage*

**108 Women and Resistance in Contemporary Bengali Cinema**
A freedom incomplete
*Srimati Mukherjee*

**109 Islamic NGOs in Bangladesh**
Development, piety and neoliberal governmentality
*Mohammad Musfequs Salehin*

# Islamic NGOs in Bangladesh

## Development, piety and neoliberal governmentality

**Mohammad Musfequs Salehin**

Routledge
Taylor & Francis Group
LONDON AND NEW YORK

First published 2016 by Routledge

2 Park Square, Milton Park, Abingdon, Oxfordshire OX14 4RN
711 Third Avenue, New York, NY 10017

*Routledge is an imprint of the Taylor & Francis Group, an informa business*

First issued in paperback 2018



*British Library Cataloguing in Publication Data*
A catalogue record for this book is available from the British Library

*Library of Congress Cataloging in Publication Data*
Names: Salehin, Mohammad Musfequs, author.
Title: Islamic NGOs in Bangladesh : development, piety and neoliberal governmentality / Mohammad Musfequs Salehin.
Description: Abingdon, Oxon ; New York, NY : Routledge, 2016. | Series: Routledge contemporary South Asia series ; 109 | Includes bibliographical references and index.
Identifiers: LCCN 2015031449| ISBN 9781138844452 (hardback) | ISBN 9781315730356 (ebook)
Subjects: LCSH: Economic development–Bangladesh. | Economic development–Religious aspects–Islam. | Non-governmental organizations–Bangladesh. | Islam and civil society–Bangladesh. | Islam–Bangladesh.
Classification: LCC HC440.8 .S338 2016 | DDC 361.7/5095492–dc23
LC record available at http://lccn.loc.gov/2015031449

ISBN: 978-1-138-84445-2 (hbk)
ISBN: 978-1-138-34755-7 (pbk)

Typeset in Times New Roman
by Wearset Ltd, Boldon, Tyne and Wear

**Dedicated to**
**My parents, Samina and Nubaid**

# Contents

# Illustrations

## Figure



## Tables

# Acknowledgements

Since 2009, many people have provided me with help and support in various ways which has enabled me to complete the research upon which the book is based. First and foremost, I am greatly indebted to Professor Stephen Castles at the University of Sydney and Dr Laura Beth Bugg at the University of Toronto for their intellectual stimulation, encouraging advice and careful readings of many drafts, and constructive feedback on the earlier version.

My heartfelt thanks, of course, go to the Centre for Women's and Gender Research (SKOK) for offering me a Visiting Researcher position where I reworked the manuscript. During the manuscript's preparation, I have been indebted to many more people. Among them, I must mention Randi Elin Gressgård, Michael Humphrey and Christine M. Jacobsen who have either read one or more chapters or given invaluable insight into my book.

I would like to acknowledge my debt to the Government of Australia for awarding me an Endeavour Award to conduct the research which forms the basis of the book. I also gratefully acknowledge Maryellen Galbally's editorial assistance on the earlier version of the manuscript. I also thank Sophie Iddamalgoda at Routledge for her continuous and prompt support throughout the publication process. An earlier version of Chapter 5 was published as 'Religion, Gender Relations and Islamic NGOs in Rural Bangladesh' in *Australian Sociological Association (TASA) Annual Conference 2011 Proceedings: Local lives/global networks*, edited by Steven Threadgold, Emma Kirby and John Germov, University of Newcastle, Australia, ISBN: 978-0-646-56779-2 and reprinted by permission of the publishers from 'Piety, Gender Relations and Muslim Women's Empowerment: The Case of Islamic NGOs in Bangladesh' in *Islam and Development: Exploring the Invisible Aid Economy*, edited by Matthew Clarke and David Tittensor (Farnham: Ashgate, 2014), pp. 173–196. Copyright © 2014. I thank them for granting me the permission to reproduce the chapter.

Finally, my family members have been loving and supportive through the long years of this project. My wife Samina Shirajee, through her moral support, constructive criticism and keen interest in my research, and also through other practical help, has sustained me during the last crucial years of writing what has been a long-drawn-out process of finishing this work. Last, but not in the least, I will never forget the love and affection of my young son Nubaid, who has always been the source of inspiration to do something better and for humanity.

# Glossary of acronyms and non-English terms

| | |
|---|---|
| *adarsha* | Ideal |
| *amol* | Practice (in relation to Islamic practice) |
| AMWAB | Association of Muslim Welfare Agencies in Bangladesh |
| *apoman* | Humiliation |
| ASA | Association for Social Advancement |
| *babsya* | Business |
| *bae-purdha* | Literally, unveiled or without *purdah*; also means immodesty |
| BAL | Bangladesh Awami League |
| *barakat* | Blessing |
| BDT | Bangladeshi Taka; Taka is the monetary unit of Bangladeshi currency |
| *bedeshi* | Foreigners |
| *bhi* | Brother |
| *bigha* | Unit of measurement for land |
| BNP | Bangladesh Nationalist Party |
| *boro* | Big/great |
| *boyan* | Speech (usually related Islamic speech/lecture) |
| BRAC | Bangladesh Rural Advancement Committee |
| *burqa* | Traditional veil for women |
| CARE | One of the major NGOs in the world |
| CARITAS | One of the leading Catholic NGOs |
| CCDB | Christian Commission for Development in Bangladesh |
| CEDAW | Convention to Eliminate All Forms of Discrimination Against Women |
| *chanachur* | A traditional snack |
| *charitraban* | A person of good character |
| *choto* | Small/little |
| *chowki* | Cot |
| *daner Taka* | Money from donation |
| DANIDA | Danish International Development Agency |
| *Da'wa* | Literally means call/invitation and refers to the practice of urging others towards Islam |

| | |
|---|---|
| DDVE | Development Dialogue on Values and Ethics |
| *deen* | Religion |
| DFID | Department for International Development of the UK Government |
| *dharma* | Religion |
| *dharmic* | Religious |
| *du'aa* | Request/supplication (to Allah) |
| *dumba* | Arabian lambs |
| *eid-ul-fitar* | Feast of breaking the fast, a religious festival marking the end of Ramadan |
| *Fael Khair* | Benevolent philanthropist |
| FBO | Faith-based organization |
| FGDs | Focus group discussions |
| *Gali-galaj* | Name-calling |
| GB | Grameen Bank |
| *Gush* | Bribe |
| *Hadiths* | Sayings of the Prophet of Islam |
| Hajj | Pilgrimage to Mecca |
| *halal* | Approved (in Islam) |
| *Haram* | Prohibited (in Islam) |
| *Hasana* | Beautiful/good deed that pleases Allah |
| HDI | Human Development Index |
| *hijab* | Veil |
| *hojur* | Used as a term of respect, particularly for religious scholars |
| *ibadat* | Worship |
| IBF | Islami Bank Foundation |
| IDB | Islamic Development Bank |
| *ijjat* | Honour |
| Imam | Prayer leader |
| *iman* | A believer's faith in the metaphysical aspects of Islam |
| IMF | International Monetary Fund |
| Islami | Bengali word for anything Islamic |
| *jaghra-bibad* | Strife |
| *jumma* | Obligatory Friday afternoon congregational prayer |
| *kawmi madrasah* | Largest *madrasah* education system in Bangladesh |
| *khas land* | State-owned land |
| *khati* | Pure |
| *khutba* | Sermon |
| *kistee* | Instalment |
| *lojja* | Shame |
| MACCA | Masjid Council for Community Advancement |
| *madrassah* | Islamic educational institutions |
| MDGs | Millennium Development Goals |
| *mohajan* | Money lenders |
| *mohorana* | Bride-money |

| | |
|---|---|
| *monajat* | An Islamic tradition to ask for mercy and forgiveness of God |
| *moulivis* | An honorific Islamic religious title for religious scholars |
| *mowulana* | A title for graduates of *madrassah* |
| *mukti* | Freedom, salvation |
| Mullah | A title for Islamic clergy, an Islamic leader or a local mosque leader |
| *Murabha* | A type of Islamic financing system |
| *muri* | Puffed rice |
| *Musharaka* | A type of Islamic financing system |
| *nakphul* | Nose pin |
| NGO | Non-governmental organization |
| NORAD | Norwegian Agency for Development Cooperation |
| NRMs | New religious movements |
| *panjabi* | A traditional dress for men |
| *para/mahalla* | Neighbourhood |
| *Parshi* | Neighbours |
| *polli* | Rural |
| *porojibi* | Parasite (usually used to mention someone who lives on others) |
| *purdha* | Veil, modesty |
| *Quard-Hasana* | A type of Islamic financing system |
| *rahamat* | Clemency |
| Ramadan | Islamic month of fasting |
| RCTR | Rational Choice Theory in Religion |
| RDS | Rural Development Scheme (of Islami Bank Bangladesh Ltd) |
| *reen* | Credit |
| *riba* | Arabic word for interest |
| RNGO | Religious non-governmental organization |
| *roktochusa* | Bloodsucker |
| *rukun* | Member (usually referring to Jamaat-e-Islam's members) |
| *sadaqa* | Voluntary charity |
| *saheb* | Gentleman |
| *salam* | A Muslim greeting |
| *samity* | Association; it stands for the NGO and its different centres related to microcredit (e.g. *Islami samity*, BRAC *samity*, etc.) |
| *samman* | honour |
| SAP | Structural Adjustment Programme |
| *sarkar* | Government |
| *shami-sheba* | Serving her husband |
| *shari'a* | Islamic law |
| *sheba* | Serve |
| *shud* | Interest |

| | |
|---|---|
| Sida | Swedish International Development Cooperation Agency |
| *Sidr* | Very severe cyclonic storm that hit Bangladesh on 15 November 2007 |
| *Sunna* | Standards of behaviour/deeds set by the Prophet |
| *swab* | Reward gained from the performance of good deeds and piety |
| *tabligh* | An Islamic 'pietistic' movement with a large following in Bangladesh |
| *talaq* | Divorce |
| *talim* | Literally means teaching, used mainly to mean a congregation of Muslim women in a certain place where a woman makes a speech on the Quran and *Hadith* |
| *ugrapanthi* | Extremist/fundamentalist |
| *ummah* | Community of Muslims |
| UNDP | United Nations Development Program |
| USAID | United Sates of America International Development Aid |
| *usila* | Medium |
| *uttam* | Better |
| *Vater khota* | Shaming for eating |
| *Vhita* | Homestead |
| *viru* | Fearful |
| *waz-mahfil* | Gatherings of Muslims where religious scholars give lectures on Islam and societal issues |
| WID | Women in Development |
| *zakat* | Compulsory alms giving for eligible Muslim, one of the five pillars of Islam |
| *zulm* | Oppression |

# Introduction

This book investigates the relationship between religion, the state, neoliberal development, Muslim women and secular and religious NGOs in Bangladesh. With one-third of its population living in extreme poverty, NGOs have emerged in both a development and aid capacity (UNFPA, 2011). This aid is wide-reaching, with the NGO sector in Bangladesh now providing a large portion of public services (e.g. health care, education, credit) both in urban and rural areas. This shift has been understood as the establishment by NGOs as a type of parallel state, with few mechanisms for accountability, and as a threat to the state's legitimacy (White, 1999). A shift in sovereignty, from state to non-state actors, has become one of the most significant issues for development practice (Karim, 2008, p. 8) in Bangladesh. Hence Bangladesh has experienced the emergence of non-state actors and their role in the relocation of authority, and the subsequent erosion of state sovereignty and the emergence of new forms of governance, in which the state is only one actor among others.

Yet NGO-led development practice confronted resistance from religious elites (e.g. local Imam, Mullahs) and rural people in the 1990s. This resistance, deemed by many scholars as an 'Islamic fundamentalist' backlash against the NGO movement (Ahmad, 2009a; Naher, 2010; Rafi and Chowdhury, 2000; Shehabuddin, 1999, 2008), has had an immense impact on the way academics have understood the problems of NGOs in Bangladesh and brings an 'alternative' to the existing models of development. During the 1980s and 1990s, Bangladesh underwent the adoption of Structural Adjustment Programmes (SAPs), privatization, the growth of an export-oriented industry, rural–urban female labour migration, and the privatization of education, all of which may be termed a period of 'social transformation' (Castles, 2001, p. 15; 2010, p. 12). In the context of such a 'social transformation' a new type of NGO based on a particular religious faith emerged in development practices. This was the beginning of Islamic faith-based development in Bangladesh.

Bangladesh is a Muslim majority state where around 90 per cent of people are adherents of Islam (Bangladesh Bureau of Statistics, 2011). Around 73 per cent of people in Bangladesh live in rural areas and have endured immense changes in their social, economic, and organizational lives (Lewis and Hossain, 2008). NGO intervention was one of the intervening factors in such 'social transformation'. All

NGOs, including religious NGOs (RNGOs), have targeted the rural economy due to the virtual absence of the state in the rural economy (Karim, 2008, p. 12). Development NGOs were given free rein to grow and expand their rural outreach with Western aid and transnational actors. Western aid organizations also preferred the NGO sector as their aid allies. It enabled them to bypass the bureaucracy and corruption of the Bangladeshi state, and to directly reach targeted segments of the rural population (Karim, 2004). Over time, this developed into a lattice of dependent relationships between aid organizations, Western capital and transnational actors, NGOs and the Bangladeshi state. Thus it is essential to examine the nature of the Bangladeshi state.

For Hamza Alavi (1972, p. 62), Bangladesh, as a 'post-colonial state', represents an 'over-developed state' while Sarah White (1999), following Joel Migdal (1988), terms it a 'weak state' in a 'strong society'. She examines the capacity of the state to '*penetrate* society, *regulate* social relationships, *extract* resources and appropriate or use resources in determined ways' (Migdal, 1988, p. 4, emphasis in original). The main argument behind Bangladesh as a 'weak state' in a 'strong society' is the failure of the government's repeated attempts through successive regimes to reorganize local administration, prohibit dowry and effectively redistribute *khas*[1] land. For Peter Davis and Allister McGregor (2000, p. 56), the state in Bangladesh is a 'patron state' where there is a significant presence of bureaucratic power supported by a latent military threat. David Lewis (2004, p. 308) argues that 'the state nevertheless remains weak in terms of citizen accountability, its capacity to provide social welfare or ensure an independent judiciary, to collect taxes or to represent the interest of the poor', all of which may lead to what Geof Wood (1997) terms a 'state without citizens'. Therefore, Wood (2009, pp. 79–92) argues that due to patronage relationships and an ideology of structural adjustment, the Bangladeshi state has abandoned its 'responsibilities for service provision and citizen accountability through the "franchising out" of certain key state functions to NGOs and the private sector, which now cater – inadequately – to the citizens as "consumers"' (Lewis, 2004, p. 308).

It is of course relevant to ask in what way development or specifically economic development, which is built on an understanding of progress through science and technology, should be based on religion generally or on a particular faith (Bornstein, 2005, p. 1). Yet development is multifaceted and value-laden (Törnquist, 1999, p. 7), and the connection between faith and development became, as Katherine Marshall and Lucy Keough (2004, p. 1) argue, 'fragile and intermittent at best, critical and confrontational at worst'. Being strongly influenced by the 'secularization thesis',[2] development studies has traditionally neglected the role of religion and faith in the lives of the poor throughout the world (Clarke, 2008, p. 17). The thesis suggests that 'religious institutions, actions and consciousness lose their social significance' over time as societies modernize (Wilson, 1982, p. 149). However, many scholars (e.g. Clarke, 2011; Haynes, 2007; Marshall, 2001; Rakodi, 2012) have argued for the continued importance and even revival of religious practice. Thus, with the launch of a small 'Directorate on Faith' within the World Bank in 1997, faith leaders and policy makers were brought together to examine the impact of religion in international politics and development (Clarke, 2009, p. 386). Moreover, in the context of post-colonial societies like Bangladesh, as Ashis Nandy (1998) maintains, 'the hegemonic language of secularism' is no more than a Western import transplanted onto a traditional society of the Global South that has exhausted all its possibilities (Kolluri and Mir, 2002). In the same vein, Peter Berger (1999, p. 11) argues: '[M]odernity, for fully understandable reasons, undermines all the old certainties; uncertainty is a condition that many people find very hard to bear; therefore, any movement ... that promises to provide or to renew certainty has a ready market.'

It may be argued that the withdrawal of the state in service provision and the failure of secular NGO-led development practice pave the way for religion and faith-based organizations (FBOs) in the development practices of Bangladesh. Since development as a dominant ideology appears strongly secular, often undermining and sidelining religion, we require a clearer understanding of the importance of religion and faith-based NGOs in development practice. It is imperative to see that the potential for a religiously coded practice of governmentality builds upon the idea of 'neoliberal governmentality' which puts agents other than the state in a position of exerting power over social life (Arif, 2008, p. 671; Atia, 2012). This book points specifically to the work of religious non-governmental organizations (e.g. through humanitarian aid or *shari'a*-based microfinance programmes) which, in the context of inadequate or absent state intervention in rehabilitative efforts, provide humane relief, both long term and immediate, especially to those populations whose insecure categorization renders them both threatening and threatened. Critical understanding is required to see whether these humanitarian and other activities of RNGOs are channelled as religiously motivated aid to populations which are already marked out as bearers of that same religiously coded community identity since secular (state-sponsored) aid cannot or will not be available. Therefore, it is crucial to see how religious non-governmental organizations (RNGOs) in Bangladesh with their transnational ties have reshaped the secular neoliberal 'development model', thereby generating a new form of governmentality.

RNGOs, particularly Islamic NGOs, emerged in the 1990s – the decade of the adoption of the World Bank and IMF's Structural Adjustment Programmes (SAPs). However, Islamic NGOs, which in many cases still maintain religious and traditional norms, attempted to make a separate space in the civil society in Bangladesh (D'Costa, 2007, p. 220). Religious-inspired NGOs (RNGOs) in Bangladesh have been very successful in the mobilization of humanitarian aid in a transparent and efficient manner. Moreover, Islamic microfinance (which is based on *shari'a* and does not charge any interest on credit which is *haram* or prohibited in Islam), contrary to the microcredit programme of the largest (secular) NGOs (which charge high interest), has become very successful among the poor people of Bangladesh. At present, there are no correct and complete data on the number and extent of their activities, though, according to AMWAB (Association of Muslim Welfare Agencies in Bangladesh), there are more than 300 organizations working under and in cooperation with them (Association of

Muslim Welfare Agencies in Bangladesh, n.d.a, p. 7; n.d.b). Muslim Aid, one of the largest UK-based Islamic NGOs working in Bangladesh, maintains that they are working in more than 1,433 villages with a total of 51,466 beneficiaries of Islamic microfinance (Muslim Aid, 2010, pp. 6, 13), while the Islamic Bank Foundation (IBF) maintain that their aid reached 719 villages in 2009 with their microfinance under the *Fael Khair* programme.[3]

In this book I seek to address the questions: What are the ideological frameworks that inform Islamic NGOs and in what ways do these frameworks inform the practice of Islamic NGOs in Bangladesh? In what ways do Islamic and secular NGOs govern the people of rural villages in Bangladesh, particularly in relation to Islamic NGOs' activities in disaster relief and Islamic microfinance? What are the transnational links that NGOs, particularly Islamic NGOs, use, and in what ways do these transnational links shape the activities of Islamic NGOs in Bangladesh? What is the role of Islamic NGOs in the changing gender ideology around the role of women in Bangladesh? And in what ways do secular NGOs become coercive, what is the nature of such coercive practices, and what alternatives can Islamic NGOs provide to coercive practices?

In seeking answers to the above questions, this book produces new knowledge on the nexus between religion and development. Research and subsequent publications on NGOs are abundant since the inception of some of the large Bangladeshi NGOs, such as BRAC. Recently, a considerable number of research projects and publications on gender and NGO interventions and their relation to the practice of Islam have been carried out (Naher, 2005; Shehabuddin. 1999, 2008; White, 2009, 2012). Other literature has explored religious or faith-based NGOs in Bangladesh to demonstrate their role in development, yet these are incomplete because they lack a detailed and critical scrutiny of RNGOs (see e.g. Ahmad, 2009a; D'Costa, 2007), and thus provide a simplistic understanding of the nexus between religion and development. However, some recent works have advanced an 'emerging Islamic model of development' to explore the intricate relationship between religion and development through the efforts of Islamic NGOs (e.g. Mesbahuddin, 2010, p. 224), though they do not provide a critical perspective on Islamic NGOs and development. Hardly any major research work on the role of RNGOs, and particularly Islamic NGOs in the polity of Bangladesh, has as yet been conducted. This book is intended to make a contribution towards the study of the relationship between the development initiatives of Islamic NGOs and changes in the 'development discourse/model' in general, and the governance and gender relations structure in particular, in Bangladesh. Moreover, consideration of the role of religion and development is under-researched in the field of development studies and the empirical evidence base is limited. This book adds to this empirical evidence base by considering the role of religious (Islamic) NGOs (RNGOs) in Bangladesh.

The book provides a sociological analysis of the relationship between development practices of RNGOs over the lives of rural people in Bangladesh and addresses a gap in the existing literature on religion and development. It analyses the role of Islamic NGOs in changing governance and ideological structure in the rural villages of Bangladesh, and hence addresses the issue of multilevel governance which may be used to understand and generalize the social theories of governance. Therefore, it is important to look at the practice of a new form of governmentality which I call 'pious governmentality' (as a distinct variant of neoliberal governmentality). I define pious governmentality as an assemblage of the techniques and practices of governance that integrate the neoliberal principles of accountability and transparency, as well as that of 'personal responsibility' and 'self-care' by the entrepreneurial, competitive and rational economic-individual with that of religious values and piety.

Piety as a virtue in Islam has been reconfigured as a technology of regulation under pious neoliberalism. It is therefore important to see how Islamic NGOs are governing and redefining piety in order to construct the 'ideal woman' as well as one who is a successful entrepreneur. This book, therefore, systematically develops its argument about the role of religious (Islamic) NGOs in promoting new forms of governmentality supported by diverse international donors focused on neoliberal development strategies and its unequivocal impact on the changing gender relations in rural Bangladesh. This form of social regulation produces and reproduces subjectivities, particularly Muslim (women) subjectivity, and has combined religious and economic rationality and further complicated the boundaries and the relationship between Islam, modernity and development. Therefore, development discourses and their related technologies (of accountability, self-reliance, entrepreneurship, rational economic beings, individualization of responsibility) are now coupled with the religious obligations and Islamic principles of justice for the solution of poverty in rural Bangladesh. This hybrid form of neoliberalism works rather better with FBOs, and therefore contradicts the discourses that bring forward a binary opposition between Muslims and the West and Islam and neoliberal development.

At the conceptual level, I base my definition of religious NGOs on that of Julia Berger (2003). Berger defined religious NGOs as:

> Formal organizations whose identity and mission are self-consciously derived from the teachings of one or more religious or spiritual traditions and which operates on a nonprofit, independent, voluntary basis to promote and realize collectively articulated ideas about the public good at national and international level.
>
> (Berger, 2003, p. 16)

Thus I define and use those formal organizations as Islamic NGOs in this book whose mission, vision (either latent or manifest) and activities are rooted in the teachings of Islam, including any subsect of Islam. While labelling those NGOs as Islamic, I mainly considered their social service provision, motivation (financial gains, personal and political gains) and organizational structure.[4] The aim is not to enter into the debate about whether or how the concepts of religion and faith and Islam and Muslim are distinct from each other, leading to the use of religion and faith interchangeably throughout the book.

I use the concept of neoliberal development to understand the pre-eminence of the development trajectory in Bangladesh in terms of a form of 'governmentality', a term first introduced by Michel Foucault (1991). To expand the conceptual framework for analysis, I rely on two other concepts: 'neoliberal governmentality' (Foucault, 1991; Ong, 2006, p. 13; Rose *et al.*, 2006) and 'transnational governmentality' (Ferguson and Gupta, 2002, p. 989). Neoliberalism, as I understood it in the context of this book, is not an abstract ideology within development theory, but rather a practice of development based on rational calculation and market logic. Thus, following Foucault (1991), I understand 'neoliberal governmentality' as a technology of development crafted to the logic of market rationality to govern the conduct of a population, which, in this book, is poor rural women, through reconfiguring rural finance and development. This book also looks at the transnational organizations and linkages; thus I also use the term 'transnational governmentality' – a concept, following Foucault, developed by James Ferguson and Akhil Gupta (2002). I define 'transnational governmentality', in the context of this research, as a form of conduct and strategies by the transnational NGOs, mainly through the 'grassroots' over the lives of the rural masses. Empirically, the book is based on qualitative field data collected between July 2010 and February 2011 mainly in the Bagerhat, Satkhira and Manikganj districts, which were the main districts to receive aid from Islamic NGOs after disasters, and also the regions to have model villages (e.g. Bagerhat and Manikganj). However, interviews were also conducted with NGO officials at their head offices located in Dhaka, the capital of Bangladesh.

## Overview of the book

After introducing the topic, its significance and setting out the context in the Introduction, this book provides an analysis of the emergence of religion in the context of state retreat and the growth of transnational religious networks and projects, especially from the diaspora outlined in Chapter 1. It also introduces a key idea about new religious movements producing a new religious subject which becomes the basis of 'pious neoliberalism'. An important sociological insight is the recognition that neoliberal development, as an expression of economic globalization, is compatible with the expansion of secular as well as Islamic modes of self-governmentality.

Chapter 2 provides a historical context to development and state formation, especially the long-standing role of civil society organizations and the impetus for the growth of NGOs. The role of NGOs as an integral part of the state-building process binding people to the nation and state highlights a strong governmental dimension to the role of NGOs, even among grassroots organizations. The strong focus of NGOs on microcredit reflects the importance of the Grameen Bank in shaping NGO orientation, the priority given to the micro-entrepreneurial model of development and the opportunities for NGO funding in this field. The reference to the 'shadow state' refers to the emergence of NGOs' interdependent corporate capital, donors, the state, and other civil society actors. The NGO field is constructed as the agent of neoliberal governmentality – 'the subjection of the population by non-state actors'. Echoing the literature on decentralization and neoliberal governmentality, this chapter makes the important point that the NGOs' 'de-clientization' of individuals from previous dependent relationships is actually replaced by new forms of dependency (i.e. women targeted from microcredit because of their 'positive vulnerability', making them easier to manipulate).

Chapter 3 provides an outline of the new Islamic NGOs that emerged in Bangladesh in the 1990s. It provides details about their no-interest microcredit arrangements (Islamic *shari'a*-based) by introducing Islamic practice of *zakat* into the transnational NGO field. In addition to the appeal of 'no-interest loans' and the rapid growth in the participation of clients, the book points to the importance of cultural sensitivity towards women in the success of Islamic NGOs. I argue that the single greatest resistance to secular NGOs is the impact of their women's empowerment programmes. Yet, at the same time, Islamic NGOs avoid reference to their Islamic identity, arguing instead that their services and programmes are for everyone. The defensive strategy of Islamic NGOs in a national political environment hostile to the politicization of Islam and in a transnational environment, shaped by the 'war on terror', points to the transnational scalar articulation of governance. This links to the following chapter's exploration of neoliberal and sacralized forms of governmentality.

Chapter 4 presents an analysis of the merging of Islamic practice, Islamic subjectivity and neoliberal forms of self-responsibility to call it pious or sacralized governmentality. The focus on Islamic *shari'a*-based microcredit programmes demonstrates how market principles are combined with Islamic morality to reinforce debt obligations. In the case of Islamic NGOs, the logic of the interdependence of finance and faith is revealed in a fascinating anecdote about the woman who believed that if the cows she bought with credit died, she would not have to repay the debt because Allah had willed it. Interestingly, the Islamic NGO officials confirmed her view, saying that she would not have to repay the loan because it reinforced her belief (i.e. credit fortified belief). The secular NGOs make a similar observation, suggesting that microcredit schemes are as much about instilling new modes of governmentality as poverty reduction. Both secular and religious NGOs seek to use neoliberal principles to generate a self-regulating society, targeting women as the linchpin to engender responsibility and obligation.

The chapter also reveals the gap between neoliberal discourse and the individual disciplined by indebtedness and managed by enterprise. It shows how narrowly the exchange relationship of neoliberalism is conceived (i.e. the relationship between the lender, the debtor and her support group). The ready availability of microcredit, often as a result of NGO officials needing to meet targets for disbursement of funds, results in clients taking multiple loans from other NGO to pay the debt of the original NGO lender, and, worse still, borrowing from money lenders. The chapter suggests that the neoliberal microcredit model is in practice embedded in multiple networks of exchange, obligation, sanctions (such as harassment by NGOs, gender shaming), and hence self-regulation. This view opens up a complex understanding of how (*shari'a*-based) microcredit works in practice.

Chapter 5 provides an analysis of secular development perspectives on intervention through gender policies against 'patriarchy' and the alternative strategies which have worked through Islamic institutions and authorities. One of the central themes of the chapter is the ambiguous character of the state gender policy and its instrumentalist attitude towards gender. Hence the continued issue of 'fatwas' to regulate women's behaviour, especially in rural communities, was targeted to protect women from indiscriminate authority but also to diminish the authority of local Islamic officials. Yet one theme remains: women are targeted as agents to preserve tradition or change it, highlighting the politicized nature of gender in development policy. Islamic NGOs seem to open up greater opportunities for change and the empowerment of women within the conservative structures of rural Muslim communities.

Chapter 6 highlights the coercive character of neoliberal governance as implemented through NGO microcredit schemes. The rhetoric of women's empowerment, the alleviation of poverty and engendering entrepreneurialism as the best path to significant social improvement is accompanied by coercive sanctions to fulfil loan repayment obligations. Cooperation and decision making conceal the experience of coercion and harm experienced in the NGOs' demands for the repayment of loans. The chapter reveals the importance of close-up investigation of the implementation of neoliberal governance, and the harm individuals who fail to repay loans experience. It provides insights into the way neoliberal policies shape social relations within specific cultural contexts. This chapter shows that abstract ideas about self-organization in response to market logic are only part of the microcredit development story. Social engineering through coercive women's groups, creating surveillance and shaming mechanisms embedded in cultural institutions of gender obligations, all become knotted into the instrumental objective of ensuring the repayment of loans and accounting targets. Pious governmentality however rests upon religious as well as upon economic sanctions.

Chapter 7 summarizes the main argument of the book to show how, in the domain of the hegemonic secular development practices of NGOs, Islamic NGOs have emerged as a new frontier of development in Bangladesh and produce a hybrid form of neoliberalism.

## Notes

1 The land that belongs to the government and, in most cases, the land which emerges due to the changes in the course of the river coastal system, is known as *khas* land.

2 Although Peter Berger was one of the main proponents of the secularization thesis in the 1960s, he apologizes and says he was wrong. Rather, he argues that theorists of 'secularization' who have been saying that religion must inevitably decline in the modern world are wrong. Today, much of the world is more religious than ever before. See Berger (1999).

3 Since there was no formal report available during my fieldwork, the statistics of the Islami Bank Foundation were collected during interviews with the high officials of Islami Bank Bangladesh Ltd and the Islamic Bank Foundation.

4 I am aware of the distinction between religion and faith and Islamic and Muslim.

## References


Ahmad, M. M. (2009a). For God's Sake: The Religious Non-governmental Organizations in Bangladesh. In F. C. Khan, A. Ahmad and M. Quddus (eds), *Recreating the Commons? NGOs in Bangladesh* (pp. 183–206). Dhaka: The University Press.

Ahmad, M. M. (2009b). New Threat to Development: The Non-governmental Organizations – Fundamentalist Conflict in Bangladesh. In F. C. Khan, A. Ahmad and M. Quddus (eds), *Recreating the Commons? NGOs in Bangladesh* (pp. 129–148). Dhaka: The University Press.

Alavi, H. (1972). The State in Post-colonial Societies: Pakistan and Bangladesh. *New Left Review, 74*(1), 59–81.

Arif, Y. (2008). Religion and Rehabilitation: Humanitarian Biopolitics, City Spaces and Acts of Religion. *International Journal of Urban and Regional Research, 32*(3), 671–689. doi: 10.1111/j.1468-2427.2008.00804.x.

Association of Muslim Welfare Agencies in Bangladesh. (n.d.a). About AMWAB. Retrieved 4 July 2009 from www.amwab.org/.

Association of Muslim Welfare Agencies in Bangladesh. (n.d.b). *Annual Report 2008* (p. 32). Dhaka: Association of Muslim Welfare Agencies in Bangladesh.

Atia, M. (2012). 'A Way to Paradise': Pious Neoliberalism, Islam, and Faith-based Development. *Annals of the Association of American Geographers, 102*(4), 808–827.

Bangladesh Bureau of Statistics. (2011). *Statistical Pocketbook of Bangladesh 2010*. Dhaka: Ministry of Planning.

Berger, J. (2003). Religious Nongovernmental Organizations: An Exploratory Analysis. *Voluntas: International Journal of Voluntary and Nonprofit Organizations, 14*(1), 15–39.

Berger, P. L. (1999). *The Desecularization of the World: Resurgent Religion and World Politics*. Washington, D.C.: Ethics and Public Policy Center.

Bornstein, E. (2005). *The Spirit of Development: Protestant NGOs, Morality, and Economics in Zimbabwe*. Stanford, CA: Stanford University Press.

Castles, S. (2001). Studying Social Transformation. *International Political Science Review, 22*(1), 13–32.

Castles, S. (2010). Understanding Global Migration: A Social Transformation Perspective. *Journal of Ethnic and Migration Studies, 36*(10), 1565–1586.

Clarke, G. (2008). Faith-based Organizations and International Development. In G. Clarke and M. Jennings (eds), *Development, Civil Society and Faith-based Organizations: Bridging the Sacred and the Secular*. New York: Palgrave Macmillan.

Clarke, G. (2009). Religion and International Development. In J. Haynes (ed.), *Routledge Handbook of Religion and Politics* (pp. 385–402). New York: Routledge.

Clarke, M. (2011). *Development and Religion: Theology and Practice*. Cheltenham: Edward Elgar.

D'Costa, B. (2007). Faith, NGOs and the Politics of Development in Bangladesh. In H. James (ed.), *Civil Society, Religion and Global Governance: Paradigms of Power and Persuasion* (pp. 219–238). London: Routledge.

Davis, P.R. and McGregor, J.A. (2000). Civil Society, International Donors and Poverty in Bangladesh. *Journal of Commonwealth and Comparative Politics, 38*(1), 47–64.

Ferguson, J. and Gupta, A. (2002). Spatializing States: Toward an Ethnography of Neoliberal Governmentality. *American ethnologist, 29*(4), 981–1002.

Foucault, M. (1991). The Foucault Effect: Studies in Governmentality: With Two Lectures by and an Interview with Michel Foucault. In G. Burchell, C. Gordon and P. Miller (eds),

*The Foucault Effect: Studies in Governmentality: With Two Lectures by and an Interview with Michel Foucault* (pp. 87–104). Chicago, IL: University of Chicago Press.

Haynes, J. (2007). *Religion and Development: Conflict or Cooperation?* Basingstoke: Palgrave Macmillan.

Karim, L. (2004). Democratizing Bangladesh State, NGOs, and Militant Islam. *Cultural Dynamics, 16*(2–3), 291–318.

Karim, L. (2008). Demystifying Micro-credit: The Grameen Bank, NGOs, and Neo-liberalism in Bangladesh. *Cultural Dynamics, 20*(1), 5–29. doi: 10.1177/0921374007088053.

Kolluri, S. and Mir, A. (2002). Redefining Secularism in Postcolonial Contexts: An Introduction. *Cultural Dynamics, 14*(1), 7–20.

Lewis, D. (2004). On the Difficulty of Studying 'Civil Society': Reflections on NGOs, State and Democracy in Bangladesh. *Contributions to Indian sociology, 38*(3), 299–322.

Lewis, D. and Hossain, A. (2008). A Tale of Three Villages: Power, Difference and Locality in Rural Bangladesh. *Journal of South Asian Development, 3*(1), 33–51.

Marshall, K. (2001). Development and Religion: A Different Lens on Development Debates. *Peabody Journal of Education, 76*(3–4), 339–375.

Marshall, K. and Keough, L. (2004). *Mind, Heart, and Soul in the Fight Against Poverty.* Washington, D.C.: World Bank.

Mesbahuddin, T. (2010). Religion in Development: An Islamic Model Emerging in Bangladesh. *Journal of South Asian Development, 5*(2), 221–241.

Migdal, J.S. (1988). *Strong Societies and Weak States: State–Society Relations and State Capabilities in the Third World.* Princeton, NJ: Princeton University Press.

Muslim Aid. (2010). *Annual Report 2009: Microfinance and SME Programme* (p. 48). Dhaka: Muslim Aid.

Naher, A. (2005). *Gender, Religion and Development in Rural Bangladesh.* PhD thesis, Heidelberg University, Germany.

Naher, A. (2010). 'Defending Islam and Women's Honour against NGOs' in Bangladesh. *Women's Studies International Forum, 33*(4), 316–324. doi: 10.1016/j.wsif.2010.02.005.

Nandy, A. (1998). The Twilight of Certitudes: Secularism, Hindu Nationalism and Other Masks of Deculturation. *Postcolonial Studies, 1*(3), 283–298. doi: 10.1080/13688799889969.

Ong, A. (2006). *Neoliberalism as Exception: Mutations in Citizenship and Sovereignty.* Durham, NC: Duke University Press.

Rafi, M. and Chowdhury, A. R. (2000). Human Rights and Religious Backlash: The Experience of a Bangladeshi NGO. *Development in Practice, 10*(1), 19–30.

Rakodi, C. (2012). A Framework for Analysing the Links between Religion and Development. *Development in Practice, 22*(5–6), 634–650. doi: 10.1080/09614524.2012.685873.

Rose, N., O'Malley, P. and Valverde, M. (2006). Governmentality. *Annual Review of Law and Social Science, 2*(1), 83–104. doi: 10.1146/annurev.lawsocsci.2.081805.105900.

Shehabuddin, E. (1999). Contesting the Illicit: Gender and the Politics of Fatwas in Bangladesh. *Signs, 24*(4), 1011–1044.

Shehabuddin, E. (2008). *Reshaping the Holy: Democracy, Development, and Muslim Women in Bangladesh.* New York: Columbia University Press.

Törnquist, O. (1999). *Politics and Development: A Critical Introduction.* London: Sage.

UNFPA. (2011). *State of the World's Population 2011*. New York: UNFPA.

White, S. (2009). Beyond the Paradox: Religion, Family and Modernity in Contemporary Bangladesh. In *Religions and Development (RaD) Research Programme*. University of Bath, UK.

White, S. (2012). Beyond the Paradox: Religion, Family and Modernity in Contemporary Bangladesh. *Review of Modern Asian Studies*, FirstView: 1–30. doi:10.1017/S0026749X12000133.

White, S.C. (1999). NGOs, Civil Society, and the State in Bangladesh: The Politics of Representing the Poor. *Development and Change*, *30*(2), 307–326.

Wilson, B.R. (1982). *Religion in Sociological Perspective*. Oxford: Oxford University Press.

Wood, G. (1997). States Without Citizens: The Problem of the Franchise State. In D. Hulme and M. Edwards (eds), *NGOs, States and Donors: Too Close for Comfort* (pp. 79–92). London: Macmillan.

Wood, G. (2009). Clashing Values in Bangladesh: NGOs, Secularism and the Ummah. In F. C. Khan, A. Ahmad and M. Quddus (eds), *Recreating the Commons? NGOs in Bangladesh* (pp. 43–80). Dhaka: The University Press.

# 1 Development, religion and faith-based NGOs

This chapter focuses on the discourse of development and the issue of religion from both a sociology and development studies perspective. It is argued that development discourse has long avoided the issue of religion as one of its major concerns in spite of religion being represented as the 'inner core of life' in the Global South; for example, Bangladesh. Until recently, religion was considered as 'distinct' or 'other'. This, I argue, is due to the dominance of 'modernization and secularization' followed by a new form of 'governmentality' – 'neoliberal governmentality' in development practice. At the turn of the new Millennium, particularly after 9/11, religion and fundamentalism have reappeared in the academic discussion but still bear a negative connotation. However, increasing exploration of the role of religion in development has been visible since the last decade of the twentieth century. Since the research about the engagement of religion in development practices is still in its early stages, it affords this book more opportunity to contribute to the debate on faith-based development.

## Crisis in development theory and discourse

Scholars argue that development, as a concept and a discourse, is an 'unstable term' (Edelman and Haugerud, 2005, p. 1). Development in general used to be considered as economic progress and growth measured in GDP which in time also included improvements in well-being, living standards and opportunities. Development, for Amartya Sen, is freedom, meaning development is the 'process of expanding the real freedoms that people enjoy' (Sen, 1999, p. 3). Despite the debate about the aim of development, for many, development equates to Westernization; for example, Latouche argues that 'development has been and still is the *Westernization of the world*' (Latouche, 1993, p. 160, emphasis in original). For Arturo Escobar (2012, p. 4), development is exogenous and is based on the Western model of industrialization which led to the total restructuring of the 'underdeveloped societies' to establish a 'kingdom of abundance' which, on the contrary, 'produced its opposite: massive underdevelopment and impoverishment, untold exploitation and oppression'. In many developing countries, including Bangladesh, development discourse is dominated by foreign donors and NGOs, and revolves around the ideology that Bangladeshi society needs to be modernized through privatizing public services by the NGOs, the empowerment of women and transforming ordinary individuals into entrepreneurs and rational economic beings (this was championed by all the major NGOs; for example, the Grameen Bank, BRAC). Therefore, development in the Global South was seen as a linear, rational progress in the economy and public psyche to follow a Rostowian idea of going through certain stages of development. Yet this idea ultimately failed, as development in the context of the Global South is more complex. Critical approaches to development include post-development deals with the dark side of development. For example, dependency theories deal with the question of global inequality, and alternative development approaches focus on the lack of popular participation in development (Pieterse, 2010, p. 100). To understand the idea of development and the process of development, this book focuses on the evolution of development as a process; for example, from modernization to dependency to world system to neoliberalism and to a human development approach.

In the progress of development theories Marc Edelman and Angelique Haugerud (2005, p. 5) explain three different historical phases to locate a certain benchmark in thinking about development. For them, the first phase, spanning from the fifteenth to the late eighteenth century, includes attempts to understand development that equates to the rise of industrial capitalism and related social transformation. In the second phase of development theory which emerges in the late 1900s, the focus shifts towards a narrower development theory about 'how the economies of the colonies of Britain, France, Portugal and other European powers, colonies comprising some 28 per cent of the world's population, might be transformed and made more productive as decolonization approached' (Leys, 1996, p. 5, cited in Edelman and Haugerud, 2005, p. 6). The third phase of development began in the 1970s. This phase accompanied a series of policy changes that led to the weakening of state capacities to promote national economic development which has come to be known as economic neoliberalism (Edelman and Haugerud, 2005, p. 7). In the above-mentioned phases of development theory, different modes of development emerged. Thus one of the most significant events (in the second phase) was the establishment of Bretton Woods financial institutions (e.g. the World Bank and IMF) in 1944. Other significant components of development during this period were the introduction of a system of fixed currency exchange rates, and the institutionalization of national economic planning to promote growth. Notions of development in this phase were dominated by John Maynard Keynes who underlined the centrality of state sovereignty where supranational institutions (e.g. the World Bank, IMF) would assist the nation state in achieving development. However, Ferguson (1990) termed these institutions 'anti-politics machines'. This was due to the adoption of a technocratic and universalizing approach in their engagement with underdeveloped countries in ways that tended to obscure the political character of many development problems and the local and national political struggle of these poor countries. In the third phase (neoliberalism), the significant mode of development promoted a set of reforms in the poorer countries to promote growth otherwise known as structural adjustment, emphasizing the reduction of state expenditure on social welfare. Before moving to discuss neoliberalism in detail, I will focus on modernization, dependency and world system theories in brief.

### *From modernization, dependency, world system to human development*

Modernization has been one of the most important theoretical frames for development ascribed in the developing countries, with the assumption that developing countries would follow the path of the developed Western countries. Among the modernization theorists, W. W. Rostow represents the main figure. Modernization theorists, particularly Rostow (1960), have proposed a stage theory which claims that all societies will eventually pass through the same stages. These stages are as follows:

1 Traditional society
2 A pre-take-off period
3 Take-off stage
4 Drive to maturity
5 The age of high mass consumption.

For modernization theorists,

> development was a question of instilling the 'right' orientations – values and norms – into the cultures of the non-Western world so as to enable its people to partake of the modern wealth-creating economic and political institutions of the advanced West.
>
> (Portes, 1997, p. 230)

Simply put, modernization theorists ask traditional societies to 'advance' to the model of modern industrial societies (Eisenstadt, 1974). Disregarding whether these traditional societies are similar or not, modernization theory predicted that such orientations would lead to changes in all aspects of social, economic and cultural life. For example, it would lead to changes in 'demographic behaviour (a decline in fertility), in political culture (the emergence of democracy), and in social patterns (reduced social inequality through a "trickle-down" of the new wealth)' (Castles, 2001, p. 16). However, modernization theorists, particularly Rostow, have been highly criticized for their pro-Western bias. His stage theory was criticized for his emphasis on economic measures of progress in terms of GNP growth and his stress on the 'traditional' values, and institutions and subsequent neglect of structures of exploitation. Moreover his assumption that all societies would pass through the same historical trajectory, albeit at different places, is over-generalized (Edelman and Haugerud, 2005, p. 16). Thus, by the 1960s, modernization theories had failed to bring expected changes in the South; for example, in Africa, Latin America or Asia, economic growth was slow and inequality had increased (Castles, 2001, p. 17).

Since this book involves religion, I focus rather more on the cultural dimensions of modernization theory, and on secularization, which goes hand in hand with modernization. Modernization theories predict a necessary decline of traditional values and religious beliefs and practices with rapid industrial growth. One of the proponents of a secularization paradigm, Bruce (2002, p. 3) sees

> Secularization as a social condition that manifests in (a) the declining importance of religion for the operation of non-religious roles and institutions such as those of the state and the economy; (b) a decline in the social standing of religious roles and institutions; and (c) a decline in the context to which people engage in religious practices, display beliefs of a religious kind, and conduct other aspects of their lives in a manner informed by such beliefs.

In response to the critique of modernization theory, dependency theory emerged particularly in Latin America with the efforts of Cardoso, Andre Gunder Frank, Paul Baran and others. Frank (1969) has argued that there has been a 'development of underdevelopment' in the Third World as a consequence of emerging relationships among political-economic formations which began with the expansion of capitalism. Hence it was a deliberate process designed to perpetuate exploitation outside the West. Thus dependency theorists argue that import substitution strategies would help to overcome inequality which would increase national economic and political autonomy (Castles, 2001). However, Alejandro Portes (1997, p. 231) argues that the dependency school failed to predict the 'erratic performance of import-substitution models of development'. For example, Latin American countries had not been very successful in using this import substitution approach.

Yet, of the existing sociological perspectives, as Portes (1997, p. 232) argues, world system theorist Immanuel Wallerstein, as its founder, came closest to predicting the general trend of events during the past few decades with the introduction of the idea of a world 'system of stratification' which is composed of core, semi-peripheral and peripheral countries (Wallerstein, 1974, pp. 403–405). Wallerstein (1984, p. 11) argues that 'it has been the world-system then and not the separate "societies" that has been "developing", to show that national development has become an "irrelevant concept"' (Castles, 2001, p. 17), and 'only one world system' (Pieterse, 1988, p. 252) has emerged through increasing flows of trade, investment, labour, etc. In this world economy, countries could gain ascendancy based on economic, political or military strength due to which 'less-developed countries could not achieve autonomy (as proposed by dependency theory); rather they had to insert themselves in global economic chains to avoid marginalization' (Castles, 2001, p. 17). Yet, critics argue that world system theory failed to recognize the outcome of diverse local initiatives, local responses, and social struggles that sought varying relationships in the international system (Edelman and Haugerud, 2005, p. 12).

With the end of the post-war economic boom in the 1970s, the limitations of state-led development became clear, leading to invoking the neoclassical economic theory with an ascendency of the market and a reduced role of the state or public sector (Castles, 2001, p. 17; Edelman and Haugerud, 2005, p. 13). Therefore, this approach to development, otherwise known as neoliberalism (which I discuss in detail in the latter part of this chapter), became dominant in the 1980s and 1990s where the state could still function in providing infrastructure (e.g. roads) and securing order (e.g. preventing civil unrest), while the regulation of economic activity was to be left entirely to the market (Castles, 2001, p. 17). Yet, this approach to development brought devastating consequences (e.g. increased inequality) to many poor countries in Africa and Asia with the policy prescription known as the Structural Adjustment Programme (SAP).

Stephen Castles (2001, p. 18) argues that 'the key notions of development theories – "developed," "underdeveloped," "modernization," "dependency" – all became problematic'. One of the main arguments for this problem is that economic growth became the main focus in approaching development, particularly following the Second World War. Therefore, the United Nations Development Programme (UNDP) introduced the idea of 'Human Development' to promote individual well-being to replace the dominance of the growth rate of per capita GDP as the sole measure of development (UNDP, 1990). Therefore, human development is about putting people at the centre of development that would enable them to realize their potential, widen their choices (created by expanding human capabilities and functioning) and to enjoy the freedom to lead lives which they value (UNDP, 1990). The first Human Development Report also introduced the Human Development Index (HDI) which it claims 'captures the three essential components of human life: longevity, knowledge, and basic income for decent living standard' (UNDP, 1990). Therefore, the shift from economic growth to development with a human face replaces a top-down approach with a bottom-up approach to enhance people's 'choices' and 'capabilities', and has frequently been referred to in the World Bank's policies and documents (Castles, 2001, p. 20). Yet, religion as one of the main signifiers in development was still missing. Neglecting religion in mainstream development literature has made it difficult to frame a generally accepted conceptual design for the analysis of the relationship between religion and development, which, due to disciplinary boundaries and engagement, has made it more complex (Rakodi, 2007, p. 17). In the section that follows, I discuss the evolution of religion in development theories and discourse.

## Development and religion: from negligence to incorporation

Although religion has been one of the important issues of analysis among the founding fathers of sociology such as Emile Durkheim, Max Weber and Karl Marx, there has been a long silence in sociology when considering the phenomenon of religion. As Malcolm Hamilton argues, 'sociological studies of religion are generally seen as being towards the fringes of the discipline' (Hamilton, 1998, p. 1, cited in Tomalin, 2007, p. 2). This is partly because sociology was dominated by or was a product of modernism, which saw the progress of society with an increasing loss of the significance of religion or faith. Thus Grace Davie (2007, p. 4), based on James Beckford's (1989, 2003) idea of 'insulation and isolation' of the sociology of religion from sociology, has mentioned that

> main stream sociology has been increasingly inclined to ignore both religion itself and the sociological debate that surrounds this ... sociologists of religion have withdrawn from mainstream sociological discussion, concentrating instead on the specificities of their own subject matter, whether empirically or theoretically.

This is, as Davie argues, the result of an 'over-preoccupation' with secularization (Davie, 2007, p. 4). However, Berger (1999) argues that theorists of 'secularization' who have been saying that religion must inevitably decline in the modern world are wrong; rather the reality is that the modern world is 'as furiously religious as ever' (Berger, 1999, p. 2) through 'de-secularization', a process where religion is no longer seen as privatized and isolated from the public sphere. For millions of souls around the world religion is fundamental to their lives and hence represents an 'inner core of life' for making sense of people's everyday lives, livelihood, death and survival.

A recent study by the World Value Survey, Pew Forum and Gallup suggests that religion is crucial in the lives of people. It gives meaning to many things, enabling them to survive and continue their lives and livelihoods. Table 1.1 shows the importance of religion in people's lives around the world.

To make it clear that the importance of religion can no longer be ignored, a summary of survey results from Gallup and Pew Forum is presented in Table 1.2.

Since religion is still important for large segments of the world's population, it is not necessarily easy to argue that 'secularization is a universal, desirable, and irreversible trend' (Deneulin and Rakodi, 2011, p. 46) throughout the world. The neglect of religion both in academic scholarship and at a policy level reflects historical and cultural contexts of decolonization (Deneulin and Rakodi, 2011, p. 45). Therefore, development initiatives from international aid agencies seek a proper understanding of the importance of religion in the lives of these people and require a development paradigm to navigate religion, religious customs and actors while framing the development of such areas. However, in recent years, especially after the fall of dominant development agendas led by modernization and neoliberalism, some of the world's largest financial and aid institutions and academic actors have taken religion seriously. Thus, in the following discussion I will present a glimpse of the 'inclusion and exclusion' of religion in development from academics and research, to policy and institution, to practice (Lunn, 2009).

In the 1980s, one of the most important and influential academic journals in development studies, *World Development*, dedicated an entire issue to the role of religion in development (Rakodi, 2007, p. 1). In this special edition, its editors and contributors (especially Goulet) advanced the claim that 'religion should be

*Table 1.1* The importance of religion in life based on religious denomination

| *N* = 2,622 | *Religious denomination* | | | | | | | | |
|---|---|---|---|---|---|---|---|---|---|
| | | *Total (%)* | *Evangelical (%)* | *Jehovah witnesses (%)* | *Muslim (%)* | *Other (%)* | *Protestant (%)* | *Roman Catholic (%)* | *Seven-Day Adventist (%)* |
| Religion important | Very important | 45.0 | 57.1 | 66.7 | – | 26.7 | 44.7 | 43.3 | 69.6 |
| | Important | 51.0 | 39.4 | 30.3 | 100.0 | 66.7 | 42.4 | 52.9 | 21.7 |
| | Not at all important | 4.1 | 3.5 | 3.0 | – | 6.7 | 12.9 | 3.8 | 8.7 |
| | Total | 2,622 (100) | 226 (100) | 33 (100) | 1 (100) | 15 (100) | 85 (100) | 2,239 (100) | 23 (100) |

Source: Based on the data available at World Values Survey Online Databank at www.wvsevsdb.com/wvs/WVSAnalizeQuestion.jsp (accessed 5 January 2012).

*Table: 1.2* Global distribution of the importance of religion in life

| *% of respondents who* | *Total* | *Western Europe* | *Eastern Europe* | *West Africa* | *SE Asia* | *North America* | *Latin America* | *Middle East* |
|---|---|---|---|---|---|---|---|---|
| **Gallup International Millennium Survey** | | | | | | | | |
| 'Give God high importance'[a] | 63 | 49 | 49 | 97 | 47 | 83 | 87 | NA |
| 'Belong to any religious denomination' | 87 | 88 | 84 | 99 | 77 | 91 | 96 | NA |
| 'Attend religious services regularly'[b] | 32 | 20 | 14 | 82 | 27 | 47 | 35 | NA |
| **Gallup Voice of the People 2005**[c] | | | | | | | | |
| 'Consider themselves to be a religious person' | 66 | 60 | 65 | 91[d] | 50[e] | 71 | 82 | 79 |
| **Pew Forum** | | | | | | | | |
| Say that 'religion is very important to their lives' | NA | 21 | 19 | 87[f] | 93[g] | NA | 55[h] | 81 |

Source: Deneulin and Rakodi (2011, p. 47).

Notes
NA Not available.
a 7–10 on a scale of 1–10.
b Once a week or more.
c Gallup.
d All Africa.
e Asia Pacific.
f Sub-Saharan Africa.
g Asia Pacific.
h South America.

seen as the moral base of society rather than one of several dimensions comprising society' (Lunn, 2009, p. 946), as 'full human development is not possible without regards for essential religious values' (Goulet, 1980, p. 488).[1] However, since then, there has not been any sustained interest in the issue of religion in development which could be deemed worthy of mention until the 2000s. As late as the last decade of the last Millennium through to the beginning of the new Millennium, a number of academic writings and reports have appeared.[2] An article published in *Development in Practice* by Kurt Ver Beek in 2000 mentioned that 'for most of the "south", spirituality is integral to their understanding of the world and their place in it, and so is central to the decisions that they make about their own and their communities' development' (Ver Beek, 2000, p. 31), and 'religious beliefs, symbols, practices and mysteries their primary source of meaning' (Goulet, 1980, p. 482). A search through three prominent development journals (*World Development*, *Journal of Development Studies* and *Journal of Developing Areas*) during the period from 1982 to 1998 reveals a very rare reference to the role of religion or spirituality in development. As a result of this avoidance, as Ver Beek (2000, p. 31) argues, inferior research and less effective programmes have been produced, and ultimately fail to 'provide participants with opportunities to reflect on how their development and their spirituality will and should shape each other'. This avoidance of religion in theory formation and academic discussion may be attributed to a lasting 'legacy of the period of modernism, comprising the modernisation thesis and its antithesis based on neo-Marxist concepts' (Lunn, 2009, p. 939).

As I have discussed in the earlier section of this chapter, modernism, comprising a modernization and secularization thesis, regarded religion as antithetical to development, which equated with economic progress measured in terms of GDP. This was accompanied by 'rational' belief, which, as I argued, would replace 'traditional' or religious belief. From this perspective religion was seen as an impediment to economic progress and would subsequently lose its significance in society. Thus 'there exists an international intelligentsia which is indeed heavily secularized' (Berger, 2009, p. 70) and advocated long-lasting plausibility of a secularization theory. This led to a legitimation of the marginalization of religion in academic scholarship in development studies. Therefore, 'Sociological theory not only shares in the marginalization of religion as a topic of inquiry, it has helped to produce it' (Calhoun, 1999, p. 237), because 'classical sociologists made the secularization argument so basic to theorizing about religion that it displaced attempts to understand the actual meaning and organizational significance of religion in the contemporary society' (Ebaugh, 2002, p. 387).

Another reason behind ignoring religion lies with the positivist stance of social science in the twentieth century which introduced an anti-religious bias both in research and organization. This was due to, as Helen Ebaugh (2002, p. 388) maintains, the fact that religion 'involves transcendent, non-empirical realities in the lives of people it is frequently seen as outside the purview of the objective, value-free world of science, despite the fact that religious variables are central in explanations of human behaviour'. With the constitutional separation of church and state in the West, religion has moved from the public to the private realm and has led many Westerners to feel uncomfortable talking about religion in public, something which is a private or personal matter (Lunn, 2009, p. 940).

There are three different motivating factors, as Ver Beek (2000) argues, for avoiding the topic of spirituality/religion in development theory and practice. The first factor is the presence of a 'scientific/materialistic' bias and a 'respect' towards local traditions that might have led the researchers and practitioners to sideline religion. The second factor is the dichotomizing perspective of the sacred and the secular in Northern society which led to the personal discomfort and fear of charges of improper use of funds for the promotion of religion and encouraged researchers to avoid religion. The third motivating factor is the lack of precedent and of models and a theory for addressing religion which 'may convince some that spirituality is not a legitimate research topic ... or is either inappropriate or that their attempts to address the topic might cause conflict with supervisors, funders, or participants' (Ver Beek, 2000, p. 40).

It is not only the academician, researcher or the theoretical model that tends to avoid religion in discussions. International financial institutions and donor agencies have not paid attention to bridging the gap between religion and development (Marshall, 2001). In this context, Gerard Clarke (2007, p. 79) notes that Western official donors were highly influenced by the secularization thesis and thus considered the relationship between faith and the activities of faith-based organizations with development as antagonistic. A recent search of the web pages of the United Nations, The UK Government Department for International Development (DFID) and the World Bank by Leah Selinger (2004, p. 525) has found very few articles that addressed religion and development. However, those articles that did address religion and development 'often avoid involving religion in the construction and critique of development strategy' (Selinger, 2004, p. 525). Ver Beek (2000) found that many of the largest development agencies in the USA (e.g. USAID, CARE, Catholic Relief Services) have extensive policies and programme guidelines to deal with certain important and sensitive issues like gender, indigenous issues, land reforms, the environment and violence against women. However, there was no policy on religion and spirituality, as Ver Beek argues.

Moving beyond academic, policy and aid agencies, the same is true for development practice. Although the past few decades have seen the exponential growth of NGOs in the form of civil society and 'effective' development partners in the Global South (e.g. in Bangladesh), religious NGOs or faith-based NGOs or spiritual organizations have been sidelined and marginalized (Hefferan, 2007, p. 888), and hence were not included in the definition of NGOs. Religious NGOs, as Berger (2003, p. 16) argues, 'represent unique hybrid of religious beliefs and socio-political activism at all levels of society'. Still, faith-based or religious NGOs have been ignored due to, as Berger (2003, p. 17) maintains, 'a lack of agreement about what constitutes a "RNGO" legally, sociologically, and in a non-western context'. Other factors include the disinclination of RNGOs to refer to themselves in religious terms due to the negative connotations associated with religions; the use of religious references faces legal obstacles when it comes to public funding and resulted in RNGOs not referring to the religion to which they adhered.

Moreover, this tendency has its roots in the long-standing trend in the social and political sciences' literature to overlook the role of religion and religious actors in the public sphere (Berger, 2003, p. 17). Moreover, trends in preferential treatment from the donor and the NGOs themselves for particular 'religious' beneficiaries (e.g. Christian) have made the scenario even more complex. This also relates to the history of colonization and missionary activities in the South. Therefore, for Christian missionaries who were active throughout the centuries around the world, their mission was connected to the colonial state and to imperialism (Lunn, 2009, p. 943). Many of the Islamic-inspired NGOs who are new to the mission of development tend to be adherents to a particular 'variant' of Islam (e.g. Wahhabism), and hence are considered to be tied up with militant organizations and the spread of radical Islam. In spite of such accusations against some religious NGOs, it is obvious that they constitute the major provider of public goods in the poorer regions of Africa, Asia and many parts of the world. One estimate suggests that religious NGOs in Uganda provide half of the total health care services (Lunn, 2009, p. 943) and in Sub-Saharan Africa, as the World Bank estimates, 50 per cent of all health care and education was provided by the faith groups and faith-based or religious NGOs (Wolfensohn, 2004).

## The changing context: return of religion and prominence of FBOs

Despite the long prevailing ignorance about and suppression of religion, it is coming back to academics and policy makers and researchers who deal with 'development' which, as Clarke and Jennings (2008, p. 2) maintain, is a shift from 'estrangement to engagement'. Therefore, the silence over religion, as sociologist Ver Beek (2000) once declared as a 'development taboo', has been broken, and talking about the use of religion in development has almost become, as Emanuel De Kadt (2009, p. 784) maintains, 'the fashion'. In academic circles, religion has been gaining importance in its analyses since the turn of the twenty-first century. Several journals have chosen religion and development as the topic of their special issues. These journals include *Gender and Development* (with the theme 'Gender, religion and spirituality', vol. 7, no. 1, March 1999), *Cultures and Development* (with the theme 'The spirituality of social commitment', nos 35/36, 1999), and *Development* (with the theme 'Development and religion'. vol. 46, no. 4, 2003).

A number of books and edited volumes have appeared over the past few years on religion and development. These include *Religion and Development: Theology and Practice* by Matthew Clarke (2011), *Spiritual Economy: Islam, Globalization and the Afterlife of Development* by Daromir Rundnyckyj (2010), *The Spirit of Development; Protestant NGOs, Morality, and Economics in Zimbabwe* by Erica Bornstein (2005), *Acting on Faith: Religious Development Organizations in Northwestern Argentina, Development, Civil Society and the Faith-based Organizations: Bridging the Sacred and the Secular* by Gerard Clarke and Michael Jennings (2007), *Religion and Development: Conflict or Cooperation* by Jeffery Hynes (2007), and *Religion and Development: Towards an Integrated Approach* by Philip Quarles van Ufford and Matthew Schoffeleers (1988). A significant amount of academic literature (which is radical and challenging) on religion and development is also emerging from beyond the Western academics (Lunn, 2009, p. 941). Therefore, there has been significant growth whether in the form of academic conferences, seminars and round-table discussions, or in the form of books, journals or periodicals dealing with the issue of religion in relation to 'development' or any aspect of it.

As early as 1998, the World Bank had established a dialogue between faith leaders and development agencies. The then president of the World Bank James D. Wolfensohn and the then Archbishop of Canterbury George Carey launched a World Faiths Development Dialogue on Values and Ethics to a regular discussion on the issue of faith and development. Therefore a small unit of the World Bank Development Dialogue on Values and Ethics (DDVE) has been its focal point on the intersection of faith and development since 2000. By the end of the 1990s, a major study sponsored by the World Bank entitled 'Voices of the Poor' that included a study of 60,000 people in 50 different countries around the world emphasized the non-material aspect of well-being which, in turn, added to the importance of the role of religion in development and particularly the work of FBOs. In 2005, the UK Department for International Development (DFID) received a major grant for a research programme about religions and development managed by the University of Birmingham. In the UK between 2007 and 2012, £12 million was invested by two research councils, the AHRC (Arts and Humanities Research Council) and the ESRC (Economic and Social Research Council) in the largest-ever funded research programme on 'Religion and Society' headed by Professor Linda Woodhead.[3] Since the beginning of this new Millennium, many development funding agencies (e.g. DANIDA, NORAD, Sida, DFID, the World Bank and UN agencies) have extended their partnership with the FBOs and faith communities in order to achieve the Millennium Development Goals (MDGs) (Deneulin and Rakodi, 2011, p. 45).

Ebaugh (2002, p. 389) mentions developments in four theoretical areas that have, in fact, brought religion back into the social sciences discourse, namely social movements, civic culture, globalization and rational choice theory. The first area of interest for Ebaugh (2002, p. 390) is globalization, which prompted scholars to include religion in their analysis. The works of Wallerstein (1983), Featherstone (1990), and Basch and colleagues (1994) were in the forefront, referring to the role of religion and religious systems in advancing as well as hindering the global process. Globalization has made religion easier to access whether in its old or new form. In the area of the sociology of religion, the idea of globalization advanced by a sociologist of religion, namely Robertson (1985, 1992) (who once argued that globalization was a complex process with religious implications), prompted many social scientists to engage with globalization in relation to religion. Therefore, Beckford (2000, p. 941) argues that ideas about globalization or 'glocalization' were behind the 'innovative and challenging ways' of thinking about religion and the religious phenomenon in society. Many scholars argue that religious responses to globalization (e.g. Iranian Islam even before the Revolution of 1979 (Beyer, 1994), various forms of fundamentalism (Brouwer *et al.*, 1996; Kurti, 1997), and the tensions between Hindus and Muslims in India as well as in the Indian Diaspora (Bhatt, 1997) thwart globalization. Yet universalistic responses to globalization are apparent in New Age Spiritualities and various New Religious Movements (NRM). Whether the responses to religion are universalistic or particularistic, religions can be used, as Beckford (2000, p. 491) suggests, to mediate between the local and the global.

In the 1970s and 1980s, the area of interest that drew social scientists, as Ebaugh (2002, p. 380) maintains, was that of social movements, where, in addition to various secular social movements (e.g. civil rights, feminism, environmentalism), social scientists began to pay attention to the proliferation of NRMs. Therefore, NRMs provided 'a pragmatic attitude and holistic world views', and this shift from 'institutional religion has mirrored the development of society from a rigid structure in the modern era, where religion remained a private matter, to a more flexible option, better suited to the post modern subject' (Selinger, 2004, p. 532). However, it is important to recognize whether the proliferation of NRMs, as Beckford (2000) argues, has created any real and lasting innovation in theories, methods and conceptual frameworks studying religion. New religious movements which led to the emergence of new forms of 'community' made a space for believers to reaffirm and strengthen their belief and sense of belonging (Selinger, 2004, p. 532) which in turn strengthens social capital.[4] Therefore, a renewed focus on civil society has opened up opportunities for many sociology subdisciplines to focus on and analyse the importance of religion.

For Ebaugh (2002, p. 390), the fourth theoretical approach is rational choice theory[5] which brought religious scholarship into the mainstream debate. It became a 'new paradigm' (e.g. Bankston, 2001) in the sociology of religion, advancing the idea that 'people [are] actively choosing to take on religion as a central part of their individual and collective identity' (Selinger, 2004, p. 533). One of the main ideas in rational choice theory in religion (RCTR) is that religious choice is or should be a rational activity. This is due to the 'Compensator' concept which places an emphasis on a constant potential human demand for religious goods over time and between societies. The application of rational choice theory in religion, as Davie (2007, p. 70) maintains, 'assumes on the one hand a purposive rational actor who is looking, amongst many other things, for religious satisfaction and on the other, the existence of a religious market from which the actor makes his or her selections'. Nancy Ammerman (2007a, p. 8) is sceptical, as are many other scholars of religion, regarding the extent of costs and rewards and market structures as the prime factor in explaining religious (and other) actions. Ammerman mentions that like rational choice theorists, many scholars in the sociology of religion agree that 'religious actors make decisions in much the same way as they make decisions about other aspects of their lives, and in many cases that means choosing the best market has to offer, given what one is willing to invest'. However, rational choice theory in religion is contentious (Ebaugh, 2002, p. 390), and thus Bruce (1999) argues that the idea of 'compensators' in RCT is 'redundant and misleading', while the whole idea of RCT in religion is less persuasive, especially when it goes beyond North American markets. Besides these theoretical intersections, there were a number of institutional shifts (e.g. tenure and promotion requirements), and an increase in funding for religious research in the 1990s created many opportunities for scholars of religion to be involved in mainstream academic activities (Ebaugh, 2002, p. 391).

Another important component in the recent rise of religious actors in development and related to globalization is the rise in migration, not only in the Middle East but also in Europe and the Americas. Migration and social mobility were important in the reconstruction of religious identity among the first generation and subsequent second or third generation migrants in the West. For instance, some of the biggest faith-based organizations (e.g. Islamic Relief and Muslim Hands) have not been exported to Europe but rather originated in the UK. Behind the origin of these organizations is the active role played by immigrant Muslims in the UK from Bangladesh and Pakistan (De Cordier, 2009, p. 611). Moreover, once these faith-based organizations were established in the 1980s and 1990s, many second generation Muslim immigrants with loose ties to their country of origin (e.g. Bangladesh) and educated in the West reached adulthood and became socially active, they contributed to the bringing of religion to development and social issues. These immigrants, who identify less with their country of origin, culture and tradition, have been compensating for this loss with increasingly deeper ties with the Islamic religion in the West. Moreover, a growing Muslim middle class in the UK has also been an important factor in this process of the growth of Islamic charitable activities and social and religious obligation to serve humanity (De Cordier, 2009, p. 612). Yet, the recent return of religion within academic disciplines and development practices needs to be understood as problematic. In the section that follows, I discuss how religion is being instrumentalized as well as discussing other problems related to the return and subsequent prominence of religion in development discourse and practice.

### *Is the return and prominence of religion in development discourse problematic?*

Due to the recent proliferation of academic, policy and institutional engagement with religion, it is important to keep a critical eye on the engagement of religion in development. In development literature, those who believe, as Cassandra Balchin (2011, p. 17) argues, that religion is the primary solution to development problems tend to think that 'development, which can be a bitter pill, will be "swallowed" as long as it is wrapped in the sugar coating of religion'. In order to explore the role of religion in development, Ter Haar and Ellis (2006, p. 353) ask 'whether religious and spiritual resources produce a type of knowledge that is, or could be relevant to development', and the answer is definitely in the affirmative. In the same vein, Harper and colleagues (2008, p. 2) raise the question as to whether religious organizations or religious knowledge have the potential to bring the poor out of poverty. Therefore, in most cases, scholars dealing with the role of religion in development emphasize the positive aspects of development informed by religious belief and practised by faith-based organizations.

With the focus on the affirmative action of religiously informed knowledge and organizations, research on the role of religion in development also tends to focus on the comparative advantages of religious or faith-based organizations over secular organizations. Religious organizations or FBOs in comparison with government and secular organizations are more sensitive to people in times of disaster and conflict, and are more responsive to people's needs. At the same time, these organizations are flexible in their provision; they act honestly and sincerely whether it is in relief distribution or health care (Lunn, 2009, p. 944). These organizations, as Katherine Marshall, Director of the Development Dialogue on Values and Ethics at the World Bank (now defunct), argues, are effective because 'they are the ultimate community organizations' (The Pew Forum, 2006) reaching the poorest of the poor and gaining trust which ultimately makes them more effective (Clarke and Jennings, 2008). Thus 'they may even prove to be the most effective and lasting of the development agencies' (Mayotte, 1998, p. 66). FBOs, by acting through bifocal lenses (spiritual and material), reaching global faith-based donors and employing dedicated volunteers, are very successful in their development work for the poor. Some argue that a 'religious idiom of development' allows faith-based organizations to claim a 'higher purpose' for their work beyond material advances to achieve social justice and human dignity (Occhipinti, 2005). Therefore, the main thread in the research on the role of religion in development tends to view religion and religious or faith-based organizations as a relevant, important and useful tool (though for some not only a tool) for development practices.

There is also a tendency among donors and policy makers to see religion as 'the only developmental issue to the exclusion of the others' and rush to 'find the religious' which in most cases lack sophisticated knowledge of diversity among religious groups (Balchin, 2011, pp. 16–17). Due to the rush to 'find the religious', many mainstream development organizations' policies lack analytical tools for informed engagement with their subject, leading to 'misleading' and 'distorted' development outcomes. For example, the UK Department for International Development (DFID) funded projects considering how *shari'a* might be used to advance women's rights in northern Nigeria failed to match their recommendations with Nigerian constitutions; rather, its 'highly conservative content was far less progressive' (Balchin, 2011, p. 17). Therefore, the recent return of religion in development and in policy as 'religion is the solution' or 'Islam is the solution' is another instrumentalization of religion, as they focus solely on the positive role of religion and religious or faith-based organizations in the donor-led development efforts.

On the contrary, de Kadt (2009, p. 784), argues, 'the side-effect of the activities of FBOs in development are likely to be even more negative when the beliefs promoted are rigid, inflexible and self-assured' which will in turn pose limitations on individual freedom. Moreover, research (e.g. Ahmad, 2009) has also shown that religious or faith-based organizations are sometimes viewed with suspicion due to their alleged use of development activities to justify their proselytization in which the poor are the most vulnerable. Therefore, those who tend to see religion as the obstacle to development argue, 'If only these people get rid of their religion, then development will happen' (Balchin, 2011, p. 16). Both of the tendencies which confirm the affirmative action of FBOs as the 'solution to development' on the one hand and the negative aspect of FBOs activities and claiming 'religion as an obstacle' to development on the other hand instrumentalize religion.

Another problem in the recent rise of religion in the development field is the issue of inclusion and exclusion. One such issue is the preferential treatment of donors in funding FBOs with a particular faith orientation. Therefore, there is a tendency among Western donors to fund mainly Christian aid and development agencies while there are many agencies from other faith traditions working in development (Benthall and Bellion-Jourdan, 2003). Moreover, McDuie-Ra and Rees (2010) recently analysed the World Bank's engagement with religious actors and found that national and international development systems emphasize formalized religious actors (e.g. faith-based organizations). Thus these organizations and donors ignore the importance of the critical roles played by the informal religious actors in negotiating, setting and contesting the development agendas. Even academic research on the role of religion in development tends to focus on the organizational formal religion and thereby ignores the importance of activities that occur outside of organized religious events and institutions (e.g. church attendance or five prayer times for Muslims): what Ammerman (2007b, p. 5) calls 'everyday religion'. For example, while Gerard Clarke (2006, p. 840), one of the most prominent scholars in religion and development, is critical of DFID for having a singular focus on religious NGOs, his argument and classification of religious actors in development is more organizational and formal rather than informal.[6] Therefore, those studies in religion which focus on the practice of rituals, traditions and inner belief are not well represented in the discussion on 'religion in development' and hence overlook more complex aspects of the intersection between religion and development.

Both the practice and the literature of the role of religion in development tend to focus on faith-based organizations as an unproblematic and homogeneous category. It thereby misses the varied politics of religious actors. However, McDuie-Ra and Rees (2010, p. 3) argue that 'religious actors are deeply involved in both top down development *and* in contesting development; thus a singular form of agency cannot be generalized to all religious actors involved in development'. Therefore, lumping together a wide variety of organizations – large or small, volunteer and professional, grassroots or global – under the banner of 'faith-based organizations' runs the risk of over-generalization and overlooks the heterogeneity of religious organizations. It is significant that the literature on the role of religious actors in development tends to lack a 'consideration for the mutually constitutive relationship between secular and the sacral elements at the local level and increasingly at the international level' (McDuie-Ra and Rees, 2010, p. 21). Yet the distinction between the secular and faith-based organizations, which is often presented as a simplistic dichotomy, needs to be more critically and openly addressed by researchers.

## A way forward to understanding religion and development

The recent resurgence of religion in the development space and its related critics has led me to adopt multiple perspectives to explain the interplay between religion and development in the developing country context. For this book I based my conceptual framework on the governmentality approach advanced by Foucault and the social scientists who follow him. Thus Foucauldian ideas on governmentality in relation to neoliberalism provide the framework of understanding in my research to see how non-state actors, as the champions of neoliberalism, approach development through intervention (e.g. microfinance). I included neoliberal governmentality as a technique, a mechanism and a process to induce self-help approaches, economic rationality, accountability, transparency and professionalism along with disciplinary mechanisms that are designed to direct the behaviour of the subject be it as a beneficiary or as a NGO worker, in 'the way which one conducts people's conduct' which for Foucault is governmentality (Senellart, 2007, p. 388). My research conjoins a neoliberal governmentality approach with the moral economy and everyday religion to explain the emerging hybrid form of governmentality. Therefore, I use a number of theories and perspectives to construct a clear understanding and explanation of the intricate interplay between religion and development in the South, and particularly in Bangladesh.

### *Everyday/lived religion*

I opt for an 'everyday religion' approach which raises the critical question as to how we understand the role of religion in society. We do this by privileging 'the experience of the nonexperts, the people who do not make a living being religious or thinking and writing about religious ideas … [where] everyday implies the activity that happens outside organized religious life' (Ammerman, 2007a, p. 5). This approach echoes the concept of lived religion which, as McGuire (2008, p. 12) argues, helps us to explain 'how religion and spirituality are practiced, experienced and expressed by ordinary people (rather than by official spokespersons) in the context of their everyday lives'. Therefore, this approach looks at the many ways in which religion may be interwoven and lived within the lives of the people under any observation. Although, in the sociology of religion, much research has been conducted about the role of formal religious institutions and surveys undertaken about religious belief, the behaviours of large populations are problematic due to their 'remoteness from what constitutes the reality of religion in the lives of many people' (Berger, 2007, p. v).

Adopting 'everyday/lived religion' as an analytical approach in this book will allow me to define which practices constitute religion and piety for the rural women who are outside of any academic discourse. At the same time, this approach will help me to understand the activities and practice, meaning and purpose of religion among the faith-based service provider, because observing everyday religion does not 'discount the influence of the "formal" organized religious events and institutions' (Ammerman, 2007a, p. 5). Therefore, using everyday/lived religion as an analytical approach also acknowledges the importance of official religion and what religious organizations promote as religious (McGuire, 2008, p. 15). 'Everyday religion' will help me to understand the characteristics and dynamics of religion in the social world as well as to ask how religion operates in the modern world to help me understand my participants and to see when, and where, their experiences are defined as religious/spiritual. Therefore, I will ground my analysis in such a way that it will entail the everyday ways and practices people use to relate to the things they experience as religious. It will also show what makes some social events and practices (women in religious gatherings) or individual or organizational actions (e.g. Islamic microfinance) religious in the minds of the actors and the acted as well as how these experiences are figured in the social and cultural context of neoliberal development (Ammerman, 2007a, p. 5).

Neoliberal capitalism and market conditions, as Tugrul Keskin (2012, p. 17) argues, 'are powerful forces that shape and influence the daily life of individuals and have far-reaching impacts, both in our work lives and our belief systems'. Thus, it is imperative to understand how secular organizations as well as FBOs (re)shape individuals through governing the behaviour or practice (economic and spiritual/religious) of their rural subjects (e.g. microfinance beneficiaries). Therefore, everyday religion is the framework that helps me to uncover everyday practice and it is this practice that allows me to understand the ways in which people construct what is religious and in particular Islamic practice. Understanding such practices of everyday religion helps me to explore how neoliberal practice (of Islamic NGOs in particular) interacts with local men's and women's lives.

### *Neoliberalism, development and religion*

In the 1980s, neoliberalism replaced modernization as the dominant theory of development to achieve economic growth. These two dominant development paradigms were adopted and advocated by the world's major financial institutions; for example, the World Bank and the IMF have advocated secular development in order to achieve and sustain growth in the Global South, but have ignored the importance of religion in their approaches to development. Since the 1980s a shift in the global political economy and the associated ideology of neoliberalism needed to be addressed with the issue of religion. Neoliberalism through the expansion of commodification and marketization has penetrated life beyond the 'economic sphere'. Thus sociologists (e.g. Beyer, 1994) seek to understand the interplay of neoliberalism and globalization with religion. However, international relations scholars have emphasized the study of religion as 'a global force founding political–religious transnational movement', whereas anthropologists consider religion 'not as exceptional phenomena but one deeply embedded in the lives of the people they study' (Bradley, 2009, p. 266). In spite of different academic traditions, scholars agree that religion has returned to both a national and a transnational development process. However, it is important, as I would argue, to explore the recent shift where traditional moral understandings have converged with the rise of a neoliberal, free market ideology and the concomitant withdrawal of state-sponsored social welfare programmes.

A precise definition of neoliberalism is hard to find, and different scholars tend to argue for or against the idea of neoliberalism. However, the common assumption is that neoliberalism is about the supremacy of the market. Neoliberalism, in general, is the ideology and theoretical premise for the market-driven reforms which lead to the withdrawal of the state from many social welfare provisions through deregulation, privatization and marketization. Neoliberalism, as defined by David Harvey (2005, p. 2), is 'a theory of political economic practices that proposes that human well-being can best be advanced by liberating individual entrepreneurial freedoms and skills within an institutional framework characterized by strong private property rights, free markets and free trade'. Pierre Bourdieu (1998, p. 35) understands neoliberalism as:

> A new kind of conservative revolution [that] appeals to progress, reason and science (economics in this case) to justify the restoration and so tries to write off progressive thought and action as archaic. It sets up as the norm of all practices, and therefore as ideal rules, the real regularities of the economic world abandoned to its own logic, the so-called laws of the market. It reifies and glorifies the reign of what are called the financial markets, in other words the return to a kind of radical capitalism, with no other law than that of maximum profit, an unfettered capitalism without any disguise, but rationalized, pushed to the limit of its economic efficacy by the introduction of modern forms of domination, such as 'business administration', and techniques of manipulation, such as market research and advertising.

Neoliberalism has been pervasively advocated by the World Bank and the IMF; developing countries in Africa and Asia had no alternative but to adopt neoliberal policies, which in turn weakened an already fragile or vulnerable state. Although neoliberalism has posed varied consequences in different societies, it has been far-reaching; as Harvey (2005, p. 3) argues, 'almost all states ... have embraced, sometimes voluntarily and in other instances in response to coercive pressures, some version of neoliberal theory and adjusted at least some policies and practices accordingly'. As a result, neoliberalism has exposed large segments of the world population to impoverishment (Harvey, 2005, p. 76) through the withdrawal and reduction of the state's role in many areas of human welfare. Therefore, the process of neoliberalization, as Harvey (2005, p. 3) argues, has

> entailed much 'creative destruction', not only of prior institutional frameworks and powers (even challenging traditional forms of state sovereignty) but also divisions of labour, social relations, welfare provisions, technological mixes, ways of life and thought, reproductive activities, attachments to the land and habits of the heart.

Thus a new form of power relations and a new upward distribution of capital and wealth has emerged, while civic virtue has been undermined and political culture has been depoliticized, since 'collective life is organized around the modalities of privatization, deregulation, and commercialization' through a 'slavish celebration of the free market as the model for organizing all facets of everyday life' (Giroux, 2005, p. 4). Therefore, Karl Polanyi's argument is very important, as he suggests that 'to allow the market mechanism to be the sole director of the fate of human beings and their natural environment ... would result in the demolition of the whole society' (Polanyi, 1946, pp. 78–79).

The initial rise of neoliberalism as an economic and political strategy was associated with the neoliberal regime shift in Britain and the USA in the late 1970s, and hence did not gain prominence among policy makers until that period (Cahill, 2009, p. 302; Jessop, 2002, p. 452). Therefore, the period of 1978 to 1980 with the election of Margaret Thatcher as Prime Minister in the UK, Ronald Regan[7] as President of the USA, along with Deng Xiaoping's steps towards the liberalization of a communist-ruled economy (China) and Paul Volcker's takeover of the US Federal Reserve, has led social and economic history in a new direction – to a neoliberal age (Harvey, 2005, p. 1). However, the ideology and theories of neoliberalism may be traced to that of liberalism. The resurgence of liberalism in the form of neoliberalism has often been attributed 'to a successful hegemonic project voicing the interests of financial and/or transnational capita' (Jessop, 2002, p. 455) which has become 'the dominant political and ideological form of capitalist globalization' (Brenner and Theodore, 2002, p. 350). Although neoliberalism gained prominence in the 1970s, and became hegemonic throughout the 1980s and 1990s, the intellectual tradition of neoliberalism is rooted in the post-war writings and ideas of economist Friedrich von Hayek and his students, such as Milton Friedman (Brenner and Theodore, 2002, p. 350; George, 1999). However, debate over the extent of the impact of neoliberalism on economic development still captures a significant part of the development debate and theory, though many have declared the 'end of neoliberalism' since it has reached its 'ultimate limits' (Comaroff, 2011, p. 142). For my research it is imperative to consider how neoliberalism affects/interacts with religion and development. Some authors have talked about 'Islam's marriage with neoliberalism', while others have shown how economic reforms and neoliberal restructuring are 'conceived of and acted on as matters of religious piety and spiritual virtue', which Rudnyckyj (2009, p. 132) maintains is 'spiritual economy'. Others emphasize the role of religion and faith-based organizations in development practices as a response, as well, in relation to the failure of the dominant development discourses.

### *Neoliberal governmnetality*

Michel Foucault (1997, p. 81) defines governmentality 'in the broad sense of techniques and procedures for directing human behaviour. Government of children, government of souls and consciences, government of a household, of a state, or of oneself.' Thus, Foucault argues, governmentality is 'the conduct of conduct [conduit de conduit]' (Foucault, 2008), and ranges from 'governing the self' (subjectivation) to 'governing others' (subjectification) (Dean, 1999; Foucault, 1983; Gordon, 1991; Lemke, 2002, p. 51). This definition is not as simple as it looks. Foucault uses conduct here both as a noun and a verb. As a noun, conduct may be viewed as 'roughly equivalent to behaviour, action, comportment, or the embodied repertoire of what sociologists call *habitus*' (Dean, 2002, p. 119). As a verb, to conduct means to lead, to guide and to direct. Therefore, governmentality as 'the conduct of the conduct' (Foucault, 1983) means the 'array of techniques and practices that political agencies and authorities have deployed to govern and shape the activities of their subject population' (MacKinnon, 2002, p. 308). Governmentality, therefore, as defined by Foucault (1991, p. 84), is:

> The ensemble formed by the institutions, procedures, analyses and reflections, the calculations and tactics that allow the exercise of this very specific albeit complex form of power, which has as its target the population, as its principle form of knowledge political economy, and as its essential technical means of apparatuses of security.

Foucault's concept of governmentality has been extended to neoliberalism as many scholars (e.g. Larner, 2000; Lemke, 2001, 2002; Rose, 1996) explore how techniques and practices of governance change under neoliberalism. These scholars have argued that under neoliberalism, state responsibility for welfare is replaced with that of 'personal responsibility' and 'self-care' by the entrepreneurial, competitive and rational economic individual (Lemke, 2001, pp. 202–203), and that this is an attempt to 'shape human conduct by calculated means' (Tania Murray, 2007, p. 275). At the core of neoliberal governmentality lies the strategic production of the 'social conditions that encourage and necessitate the production of *Homo economicus*' (Hamann, 2009, p. 37). *Homo economicus* or 'economic man' is a specific form of subjectivity rooted in traditional liberalism that regards *Homo economicus* as a 'man of exchange', whereas in neoliberalism it turns into a 'rational economic man'. In neoliberalism, as Michel Foucault (2008, p. 226) argues, '*Homo economicus* is an entrepreneur, an entrepreneur of himself'. Neoliberalism 'strives to ensure that individuals are compelled to assume market-based values in *all* of their judgments and practices to amass sufficient quantities of "human capital" and thereby become "entrepreneurs of themselves"' (Hamann, 2009, p. 38). Therefore, I borrow one specific idea from Foucauldian scholarship and that is to see the style of governmental control foreseen by the ordo- and neoliberal to examine the reorganization of social relations around the notion of enterprise. In this enterprise model, individuals are encouraged to view their lives and identities as a type of enterprise based on economic interest (McNay, 2009, p. 56) and hence remodel the subjective experience of the self around the economized notion of enterprise (McNay, 2009, p. 62).

### *Faith-based/spiritual economies and pious neoliberalism*

Spiritual economies and pious neoliberalism point to a set of ascetic practices that involve individual ethical transformation to instil neoliberal values, such as transparency and accountability, for organizational analysis. Spiritual economy, Rudnyckyj (2009, p. 132) maintains, 'conceptualizes how economic reform and neoliberal restructuring are conceived of and acted on as matters of religious piety and spiritual virtue'. This, in turn, elucidates how two different domains of modern society, capitalism and religion, are brought together to create a 'new ethical orientation towards oneself, one's work and one's collectivity'. This approach to analysing the 'developing faith' instead of 'faith in development' reminds us of Weber's (1976) ideas on protestant ethics and the rise of capitalism in the West. Instead, Rudnyckyj's approach elaborates upon how producing spirituality as an object of intervention reconfigures work as a form of religious worship, which emphasizes individual accountability (to God) and entrepreneurial responsibility as a strong moral or ethical responsibility. Therefore, this spiritual or religious intervention involving efforts to connect individual religious piety to broader projects of economic transformation and development (Rudnyckyj, 2010, p. 135) creates a spiritual economy which consists of three primary components:

1 Reconfiguring work as a form of worship and religious duty.
2 Objectifying spirituality as a site of management and intervention.
3 Inculcating ethics of individual accountability that are deemed commensurable with norms of transparency, productivity and rationalization for the purpose of profit (Rudnyckyj, 2010, p. 131).

Thus Rudnyckyj's attempt to blend religion with neoliberal globalization looks at globalization as practice, where religious (Islamic) practices are reconfigured to optimize the efficiency and productivity of workers in an increasingly global economy where religious practices are not necessarily opposed to but rather are conducive to globalization (Rudnyckyj, 2010, p. 19). In the same vein of spiritual economy, Mona Atia (2012) blends Islamic practice with neoliberalism to call it 'pious neoliberalism'. Pious neoliberalism, as Atia (2012, p. 809) defines it, is 'the discursive combination of religion and economic rationale in a manner that encourages individuals to be proactive and entrepreneurial in the interest of furthering their relationship with God'. The idea of pious neoliberalism entails the cultivation of a neoliberal subject who works towards individualism, self-improvement, productivity and entrepreneurship, and who values science, efficiency, wealth and accountability as well as considering religiosity as a necessary component of self-actualization (Atia, 2012, p. 811).

If spiritual economies and pious neoliberalism are about the reconfiguration of religious piety in line with economic and neoliberal restructuring, my intention would be to use this approach to see whether and how the transnational NGOs, as well as local NGOs with transnational links, use neoliberal ideology and economic development models to see development activities as a form of piety and in line with success in the life hereafter.

We still live in an era which can be easily characterized as neoliberal capitalism that has been shaping every aspect of an individual's daily life, from eating habits to the practice of religion (e.g. prayer). It is therefore important to understand why it is that neoliberalism in Muslim countries has often resulted in an increase rather than a decrease in religious social and political activity and organization (Keskin, 2012). This book contributes to our understanding of the compatibility between religious and neoliberal values through an exploration of activities of religious, particularly Islamic, NGOs in Bangladesh. It outlines how we can address this issue from a more nuanced theoretical framework. I adopt and discuss different theoretical approaches to deal with the concept of a NGO-led 'development' and the crisis in the existing theories of development. I follow this with a discussion of suitable theoretical frameworks; for example, ideas of everyday religion, neoliberalism and spiritual economies and pious neoliberalism, and neoliberal governmentality that I use in this book. Throughout the book I particularly used the idea of neoliberal governmentality, and introduce the idea of 'pious governmentality' (in Chapter 4) to link the technology of economic rationality with the Islamic practice of Islam to explain how Islamic NGOs work through the neoliberal framework of development practice in Bangladesh.

## Notes

1 For an in-depth analysis on the issue of religion and development, see *World Development*'s entire issue 7–8 of volume 8.
2 See e.g. Clarke (2006, 2009, 2010); Clarke (2011); Marshall (2001); Rakodi (2012); Ter Haar and Ellis (2006); Tomalin (2006).
3 See the project details at www.religionandsociety.org.uk/.
4 Robert Putnam's idea of social capital and arguments that American prefers 'bowling alone' engendered a robust debate which led many social scientists to engage with civil society and social capital and the role of religion in such a context. For an enriched debate on Putnam's arguments see *American Behavioral Scientist*'s Special Issue of September 1998.
5 The theory took form in the 1980s through the work of Rodney Stark and collaborators such as Roger Finke, Laurence Iannaccone and William Bainbridge.

6 For example, Gerard Clarke (2006, p. 840) classifies FBOs into faith-based representative organizations or apex bodies, faith-based charitable or development organizations, faith-based missionary organizations and faith-based radical, illegal or terrorist organizations.

7 In general, Thatcherism and Reaganism represented aggressive programmes of neoliberal restructuring during the 1980s. However, a moderate version of neoliberal politics and programmes was represented in countries such as Canada, Germany, the Netherlands, New Zealand, and even in Scandinavian countries like Sweden (Brenner and Theodore, 2002, p. 350).

## References


Ahmad, M. M. (2009). For God's Sake: The Religious Non-governmental Organizations in Bangladesh. In F. C. Khan, A. Ahmad and M. Quddus (eds), *Recreating the Commons? NGOs in Bangladesh* (pp. 183–206). Dhaka: The University Press.

Ammerman, N.T. (2007a). *Everyday Religion: Observing Modern Religious Lives*. New York: Oxford University Press.

Ammerman, N.T. (2007b). Introduction: Observing Modern Religious Lives In N. T. Ammerman (ed.), *Everyday Religion: Observing Modern Religious Lives* (pp. 3–18). New York: Oxford University Press.

Atia, M. (2012). 'A Way to Paradise': Pious Neoliberalism, Islam, and Faith-based Development. *Annals of the Association of American Geographers, 102*(4), 808–827.

Balchin, C. (2011). Religion and Development: A Practitioner's Perspective on Instrumentalisation. *IDS Bulletin, 42*(1), 15–20.

Bankston, C. L. (2001). Book Review of Acts of Faith: Explaining the Human Side of Religion. *Review of Religious Research, 42*(3), 332–334.

Basch, L., Schiller, N. G. and Blanc, C. S. (1994). *Nations Unbound: Transnational Projects, Postcolonial Predicaments and Deterritorialized Nation-states*. London: Gordon and Breach.

Beckford, J. (1989). *Religion and Advanced Industrial Society*. London: Routledge.

Beckford, J. (2003). *Social Theory and Religion*. Cambridge: Cambridge University Press.

Beckford, J. (2000). 'Start Together and Finish Together': Shifts in the Premises and Paradigms Underlying the Scientific Study of Religion. *Journal for the Scientific Study of Religion, 39*(4), 481–496.

Benthall, J. and Bellion-Jourdan, J. (2003). *The Charitable Crescent: Politics of Aid in the Muslim World*. London: I. B. Tauris.

Berger, J. (2003). Religious Nongovernmental Organizations: An Exploratory Analysis. *Voluntas: International Journal of Voluntary and Nonprofit Organizations, 14*(1), 15–39.

Berger, P. L. (1999). *The Desecularization of the World: Resurgent Religion and World Politics*. Washington, DC: Ethics and Public Policy Center.

Berger, P. L. (2007). Foreword. In N. T. Ammerman (ed.), *Everyday Religion: Observing Modern Religious Lives*. New York: Oxford University Press.

Berger, P. L. (2009). Faith and Development. *Society, 46*(1), 69–75.

Beyer, P. F. (1994). *Religion and Globalization* (Vol. 27). London: Sage.

Bhatt, C. (1997). *Liberation and Purity: Race, New Religious Movements and the Ethics of Postmodernity*. London: UCL Press.

Bourdieu, P. (1998). *Acts of Resistance: Against the Tyranny of the Market*. New York: Free Press.

Bradley, T. (2009). Religion and Globalisation: Bringing Anthropology and International Relations Together in the Study of Religious-political Transnational Movements. *Globalizations, 6*(2), 265–279.

Brenner, N. and Theodore, N. (2002). Cities and the Geographies of 'Actually Existing Neoliberalism'. *Antipode, 34*(3), 349–379.

Brouwer, S., Gifford, P. and Rose, S. D. (1996). *Exporting the American Gospel: Global Christian Fundamentalism*. New York: Routledge.

Bruce, S. (2002). *God is Dead: Secularization in the West*. Oxford: Blackwell.

Cahill, D. (2009). 'Actually Existing Neoliberalism' and the Global Economic Crisis. *Labour and Industry, 3*(3), 298–316.

Calhoun, C. (1999). Symposium on Religion. *Sociological Theory, 17*(3), 237–239.

Castles, S. (2001). Studying Social Transformation. *International Political Science Review, 22*(1), 13–32.

Clarke, G. (2006). Faith Matters: Faith-based Organisations, Civil Society and International Development. *Journal of International Development, 18*(6), 835–848. doi: 10.1002/jid.1317.

Clarke, G. (2007). Agents of Transformation? Donors, Faith-based Organisations and International Development. *Third World Quarterly, 28*(1), 77–96.

Clarke, G. (2009). Religion and International Development. In J. Haynes (ed.), *Routledge Handbook of Religion and Politics* (pp. 385–402). New York: Routledge.

Clarke, G. (2010). Trans-faith Humanitarian Partnerships: The Case of Muslim Aid and the United Methodist Committee on Relief. *The European Journal of Development Research, 22*(4), 510–528. doi: 10.1057/ejdr.2010.22.

Clarke, G. and Jennings, M. (2008). Introduction. In G. Clarke and M. Jennings (eds), *Development, Civil Society and Faith-based Organizations: Bridging the Sacred and the Secular*. New York: Palgrave Macmillan.

Clarke, M. (2011). *Development and Religion: Theology and Practice*. Cheltenham: Edward Elgar.

Comaroff, J. (2011). The End of Neoliberalism? What Is Left of the Left. *The ANNALS of the American Academy of Political and Social Science, 637*(1), 141–147.

Davie, G. (2007). *The Sociology of Religion*. London: Sage.

De Cordier, B. (2009). Faith-based Aid, Globalisation and the Humanitarian Frontline: An Analysis of Western-based Muslim Aid Organisations. *Disasters, 33*(4), 608–628.

De Kadt, E. (2009). Should God Play a Role in Development? *Journal of International Development, 21*(6), 781–786. doi: 10.1002/jid.1617.

Dean, M. (1999). *Governmentality: Power and Rule in Modern Society*. London: Sage.

Dean, M. (2002). Powers of Life and Death beyond Governmentality. *Cultural Values, 6*(1–2), 119–138.

Deneulin, S. and Rakodi, C. (2011). Revisiting Religion: Development Studies Thirty Years On. *World Development, 39*(1), 45–54.

Ebaugh, H. R. (2002). Presidential Address 2001: Return of the Sacred: Reintegrating Religion in the Social Sciences. *Journal for the Scientific Study of Religion, 41*(3), 385–395.

Edelman, M. and Haugerud, A. (2005). Introduction: The Anthropology of Development and Globalization. In M. Edelman and A. Haugerud (eds), *The Anthropology of Development and Globalization: From Classical Political Economy to Contemporary Neoliberalism* (pp. 1–74). Oxford: Blackwell.

Eisenstadt, S. N. (1974). Studies of Modernization and Sociological Theory. *History and Theory, 13*(3), 225–252. doi: 10.2307/2504778.

Escobar, A. (2012). *Encountering Development: The Making and Unmaking of the Third World*, with a new Preface by the author/Arturo Escobar. Princeton, NJ: Princeton University Press.

Featherstone, M. (ed.). (1990). *Global Culture*. London: Sage.

Ferguson, J. (1990). *The Anti-politics Machine: 'Development', Depoliticization and Bureaucratic Power in Lesotho*. New York: Cambridge University Press.

Foucault, M. (1983). The Subject and Power. In H. D. Reyfus and P. R. Abinow (eds), *Michel Foucault: Beyond Structuralism and Hermeneutics* (pp. 208–226). Brighton: Harvester.

Foucault, M. (1991). The Foucault Effect: Studies in Governmentality: With Two Lectures by and an Interview with Michel Foucault. In G. Burchell, C. Gordon and P. Miller (eds), *The Foucault Effect: Studies in Governmentality: With Two Lectures by and an Interview with Michel Foucault* (pp. 87–104). Chicago, IL: University of Chicago Press.

Foucault, M. (1997). *The Essential Works of Michel Foucault* (Vol. 1, *Ethics: Subjectivity and Truth*). London: Allen Lane.

Foucault, M. (2008). *The Birth of Biopolitics: Lectures at the College de France, 1978–1979*, trans. G. Burchell, ed. A. I. Davidson. New York: Palgrave Macmillan.

Frank, A. G. (1969). *Capitalism and Underdevelopment in Latin America*. New York: Monthly Review Press.

George, S. (1999). *A Short History of Neoliberalism*. Paper presented at the Conference on Economic Sovereignty in a Globalising World, Bangkok, 24–26 March.

Giroux, H. A. (2005). The Terror of Neoliberalism: Rethinking the Significance of Cultural Politics. *College Literature, 32*(1), 1–19.

Gordon, C. (1991). Governmental Rationality: An Introduction. In G. Burchell, C. Gordon and P. Miller (eds), *Foucault Effect: Studies in Governmentality* (pp. 1–51). Hemel Hempstead: Harvester Wheatsheaf.

Goulet, D. (1980). Development Experts: The One-eyed Giants. *World Development, 8*(7), 481–489.

Hamann, T. H. (2009). Neoliberalism, Governmentality, and Ethics. *Foucault Studies*, 37–59.

Harper, M., Rao, D. S. K. and Sahu, A. K. (2008). *Development, Divinity and Dharma: The Role of Religion in Development and Microfinance Institutions*. Rugby: Practical Action Publishing.

Harvey, D. (2005). *A Brief History of Neoliberalism*. Oxford and New York: Oxford University Press.

Hefferan, T. (2007). Finding Faith in Development: Religious Non-governmental Organizations (NGOs) in Argentina and Zimbabwe. *Anthropological Quarterly, 80*(3), 887–896.

Jessop, B. (2002). Liberalism, Neoliberalism, and Urban Governance: A State-theoretical Perspective. *Antipode, 34*(3), 452–472.

Keskin, T. (2012). Sociology of Islam. In T. Keskin (ed.), *Sociology of Islam: Secularism, Economy and Politics* (pp. 1–18). Reading, UK: Ithaca Press.

Kurti, N. (1997). Globalization in the Discourse of Otherness in the 'New' Eastern and Central Europe. In T. Modood and P. Werbner (eds), *The Politics of Multiculturalism in the New Europe* (pp. 29–53). London: Zed Books.

Larner, W. (2000). Neo-liberalism: Policy, Ideology, Governmentality. *Studies in Political Economy, 63*(autumn), 5–25.

Latouche, S. (1993). *In the Wake of the Affluent Society: An Exploration of Post-development*. London: Zed Books.

Lemke, T. (2001). 'The Birth of Bio-politics': Michel Foucault's Lecture at the Collège de France on Neo-liberal Governmentality. *Economy and Society, 30*(2), 190–207.

Lemke, T. (2002). Foucault, Governmentality, and Critique. *Rethinking Marxism, 14*(3), 49–64.

Lunn, J. (2009). The Role of Religion, Spirituality and Faith in Development: A Critical Theory Approach. *Third World Quarterly, 30*(5), 937–951.

MacKinnon, D. (2002). Rural Governance and Local Involvement: Assessing State–Community Relations in the Scottish Highlands. *Journal of Rural Studies, 18*(3), 307–324. doi: 10.1016/s0743–0167(01)00048–1.

Marshall, K. (2001). Development and Religion: A Different Lens on Development Debates. *Peabody Journal of Education, 76*(3–4), 339–375.

Mayotte, J. A. (1998). Religion and Global Affairs: The Role of Religion in Development. *SAIS Review, 18*(2), 65–69.

McDuie-Ra, D. and Rees, J. A. (2010). Religious Actors, Civil Society and the Development Agenda: The Dynamics of Inclusion and Exclusion. *Journal of International Development, 22*(1), 20–36.

McGuire, M.B. (2008). *Lived Religion: Faith and Practice in Everyday Life*. Oxford: Oxford University Press.

McNay, L. (2009). Self as Enterprise Dilemmas of Control and Resistance in Foucault's The Birth of Biopolitics. *Theory, Culture and Society, 26*(6), 55–77.

Occhipinti, L. A. (2005). *Acting on Faith: Religious Development Organizations in Northwestern Argentina*. Oxford: Lexington Books.

Pieterse, J. N. (1988). A Critique of World System Theory. *International Sociology, 3*(3), 251–266.

Pieterse, J. N. (2010). *Development Theory* (2nd edn). London: Sage.

Polanyi, K. (1946). *Origins of Our Time: The Great Transformation*. London: Victor Gollancz.

Portes, A. (1997). Neoliberalism and the Sociology of Development: Emerging Trends and Unanticipated Facts. *Population and Development Review, 23*(2), 229–259. doi: 10.2307/2137545.

Rakodi, C. (2007). Understanding the Role of Religions in Development: The Approach of the RAD Programme. *RaD Working Papers Series*. International Development Department, School of Public Policy, University of Birmingham.

Rakodi, C. (2012). A Framework for Analysing the Links between Religion and Development. *Development in Practice, 22*(5–6), 634–650. doi: 10.1080/09614524.2012.685873.

Rose, N. (1996). Governing 'Advanced' Liberal Democracies. In A. Barry, T. Osborne and N. Rose (eds), *Foucault and Political Reason: Liberalism, Neo-liberalism and Rationalities of Government* (pp. 37–64). Chicago, IL: University of Chicago Press.

Rostow, W. (1960). *The Stages of Economic Growth: A Non-communist Manifesto*. Cambridge, MA: Harvard University Press.

Rudnyckyj, D. (2009). Spiritual Economies: Islam and Neoliberalism in Contemporary Indonesia. *Cultural Anthropology, 24*(1), 104–141.

Rudnyckyj, D. (2010). *Spiritual Economies: Islam, Globalization, and the Afterlife of Development*. Ithaca, NY: Cornell University Press.

Selinger, L. (2004). The Forgotten Factor: The Uneasy Relationship between Religion and Development. *Social Compass, 51*(4), 523–543.

Sen, A. K. (1999). *Development as Freedom*. New York: Oxford University Press.

Senellart, M. (2007). Course Context. In M. Senellart (ed.), *Security, Territory, Population.*

*Lectures at the Collège de France (1977–1978) Michel Foucault* (pp. 377-378). New York: Palgrave Macmillan.

Tania Murray, L. (2007). Governmentality. *Anthropologica, 49*(2), 275–281.

Ter Haar, G. and Ellis, S. (2006). The Role of Religion in Development: Towards a New Relationship between the European Union and Africa. *The European Journal of Development Research, 18*(3), 351–367.

The Pew Forum. (2006). Religion and International Development: Interview with Katherine Marshall. Retrieved 29 June 2009 from www.pewforum.org/Government/Religion-and-International-Development.aspx.

Tomalin, E. (2006). Religion and a Rights-based Approach to Development. *Progress in Development Studies, 6*(2), 93–108.

Tomalin, E. (2007). Sociology, Religion and Development: Literature Review. *RaD Working Papers Series* (Vol. 4). Birmingham: University of Birmingham.

UNDP. (1990). *Human Development Report 1990*. New York: United Nations Development Programme.

Ver Beek, K. A. (2000). Spirituality: A Development Taboo. *Development in Practice, 10*(1), 31–43.

Wallerstein, I. (1974). The Rise and Future Demise of the World Capitalist System: Concepts for Comparative Analysis. *Comparative Studies in Society and History, 16*(4), 387–415.

Wallerstein, I. (1983). Crisis. In A. Bergesen (ed.), *Crisis in the World System* (pp. 21–36). Beverly Hills, CA: Sage.

Wallerstein, I. (1984). *The Politics of the World Economy: The States, the Movements, and the Civilisations*. Cambridge: Cambridge University Press.

Weber, M. (1976). *The Protestant Ethic and the Spirit of Capitalism*, trans. T. Parsons (2nd edn). London: Allen & Unwin.

Wolfensohn, J. D. (2004). Millennium Challenges for Faith and Development. *Speech at The Third Annual Richard W. Snowdon Lecture in the Interfaith Conference of Metropolitan Washington*. Washington, DC.

# 2 Dynamics of development

## Demystifying NGO-led development practice

This chapter examines key discourses on development in Bangladesh. Since the creation of the state of Bangladesh in 1971, NGOs have become a very active part of reconstruction and economic development. However, the discourses and models used by secular NGOs in Bangladesh have been dominated by modernization and neoliberal ideologies since their inception. On the other hand, religion has played and still plays one of the most significant roles in the development and politics of Bangladesh. On many occasions Bangladesh has witnessed a conflict between 'secular' NGOs and religious authorities, particularly in the 1990s. During the same period, Islamic NGOs emerged on the development scene and increasingly became agents of transformation with no resistance from religious authorities or the public. Those who criticize secular NGOs have emphasized the issue of religion, the disempowerment of women and the orientating of women to the global capital market, the disintegration of family norms and a disregard for the traditions and norms of Bangladeshi society.

In this context, the emergence of religious NGOs or particularly Islamic NGOs in Bangladesh represents a movement in development from state weakness and the evacuation of service delivery and the emergence of secular NGOs, which resulted in shortcomings in their secular development model, leading to the rise of Islamic NGOs. Although this process of development may look like a linear process, it is instead complex in nature. This process also, as I argue, links with the global resurgence of 'religious alternatives' in development in the milieu of the neoliberal restructuring of the economy and society in the global periphery.

In Bangladesh, to understand the emergence of Islamic NGOs as agents of transformation, this book focuses on problems of development led in particular by secular NGOs. Therefore, the main aim of this chapter is to present a critical understanding of NGO-led development and neoliberal agendas adopted by NGOs, and the 'religious alternatives' to this understanding in the context of Bangladesh. In doing so, this chapter begins by explaining the social transformation of Bangladeshi society since the 1990s, followed by a discussion on Islam, politics and NGOs in Bangladesh. Next, this chapter looks at the context of the emergence of NGOs and their prominence in the nation-building project. It also focuses on what went wrong with this emergence of secular NGOs in conjunction with modernization, neoliberalism and globalization projects at grassroots level in Bangladesh.

## Social transformation of Bangladeshi society

Over the past few decades, particularly since the 1990s, Bangladeshi society has undergone a huge transformation in its political structure, and the social relations in the everyday life of its people. The independence of Bangladesh in 1971 promised socialist reform that came to an end with the military coup d'état in August, 1975. The period between 1975 and 1990 represents the period of the rule of military and economic stagnation. With the return of democracy in 1991 and in the subsequent decade, Bangladesh reached one of the most important stages of development and a huge social change which, following Stephen Castles (2001), I call the period of social transformation in Bangladesh. Adopting a social transformation perspective entails complexity in the area of development, globalization and the prominence of NGOs in development in Bangladesh. Social transformation, as Castles (2001, p. 15) maintains, may be seen as the antithesis of globalization in a dialectical sense where it is a part of globalization as well as opposing its central ideologies. A social transformative perspective provides a critical assessment of the dominant neoliberal theories of globalization and neoliberalism. It provides a critical assessment of the social consequences of the unregulated market which is the central idea of neoliberalism. To understand the contemporary society of Bangladesh requires a form of inquiry that starts from a situation of rapid and generalized changes called social transformation. This leads us to explore 'the complexity, interconnectedness, variability, contextuality and multi-level mediations of global changes' (Castles, 2010, p. 2) in order to understand the recent rise of religion in global development discourse and its local implications. I will first outline the characteristics of this social transformation, and then focus on the implications for Bangladeshi society in general.

Bangladesh adopted market-oriented liberalizing policy reforms, known as structural adjustment, towards the mid-1980s during the military regime, and continued throughout the democratic regime in the 1990s and onward (Nuruzzaman, 2004). The reform policies adopted in Bangladesh include demand management policies (cuts in government expenditure, currency devaluation), Structural Adjustment Programmes (trade liberalization, withdrawal of subsidies, etc.) and institutional policies (denationalization, privatization of economic activities, etc.) (Nuruzzaman, 2004, p. 34). Therefore, the privatization of state-owned industries, downsizing of industrial units, closing down of 'loss-making' enterprises and retrenchment of workers have been a high priority of successive governments in Bangladesh (Muhammad, 2012). The origin and growth of the export-oriented ready-made garments (RMG) industry in Bangladesh coincided with these reforms, particularly the new import policy which was adopted in 1982 and subsequent incentives for stimulating investment in RMGs in the early 1990s (Kabeer and Mahmud, 2004, p. 137). Since these RMGs are produced mostly in a single city (i.e. Dhaka and its surroundings), and employ around 5.5 million workers of whom 80 per cent are women, this has huge implications for development and gender issues. During the same period, Bangladesh also encouraged the exponential growth of NGOs to provide various services, including credit, health and education. This neoliberal turn in Bangladeshi state policies has had major implications for the social and economic well-being of its people.

The World Bank (1995, pp. 105–106) indicated three significant benefits of privatization in Bangladesh, including 'arresting the losses incurred by the nationalized industries, public sector efficiency improvement and encouragement of private entrepreneurs through a firm commitment to private sector'. The positive implications of such changes include the fact that Bangladesh's per capita GDP has more than doubled since 1975, indicating macroeconomic growth. Life expectancy rose from 55.2 years in 1980 to 69.2 in 2013, population growth rates of 3 per cent a year have been halved, and there has been reduced child mortality, reduced fertility rates from 7.3 (1974) to 2.7 (2007) and increased labour force participation, as well as increased participation in decision-making processes at the household level by women (Hossain, 2012).

However, in spite of many positive aspects of transformation, there are important negative consequences. For example, at the economic level, this neoliberal turn of the Bangladeshi state has produced more inequality; there are now only 40 to 50 families who effectively control the total industrial and financial assets, whereas the vast majority (e.g. industrial and agricultural labour, small businesses, marginal and small farmers, the rural and urban poor) are victims of such policy change (Nuruzzaman, 2004, p. 33). At the societal level, increased 'feminization of the labour force' without protective measures in place produced, particularly among the RMG workers, a high level of work-related stress, sexual harassment causing embarrassment, an inability to concentrate on work, a decline in productivity, fear, anxiety as well as depression and shame (Khosla, 2009, p. 294). The rise of RMGs and decreased employment opportunities in the rural areas has increased the internal migration of female labour to the city (e.g. Dhaka) and international migration (e.g. in Southeast Asia and the Middle East) with the help of microcredit. In spite of many positive consequences this has also resulted in family disintegration, particularly in joint or extended families, and separation and divorce. A newspaper report shows that 'the incidence of divorce (dissolution of marriage) is increasing significantly in the city [Dhaka] as 50,000 divorce-seeking petitions were recorded at the Dhaka City Corporation's (DCC) marriage and divorce section in last three months', as 'now many women have decent jobs, they are self-reliant and aware of their rights. So, if they sense that the partnership is a mismatch, they immediately seek relief from it' (Arzu, 2010).

During the same period of the neoliberalization of state policies, there occurred a growth of NGOs that coincided with and became a potential source of service delivery due to the withdrawal of the state and the privatization of the economy. Although it is not easy to identify the causal mechanisms of the social transformation that has been taking place in Bangladesh, NGOs and their microcredit as a neoliberal product (as discussed later in this book) was one of the main aspects that needed to be investigated. For example, NGOs and their microcredit programmes may have been a contributing factor in the social transformation by promoting human and social capital and mobility for rural women, and their enhanced agency and empowerment in a traditional Muslim society (e.g. Hashemi *et al.*, 1996; Pitt *et al.*, 2003). Yet, research (conducted by Goetz and Gupta, 1996; Karim, 2008, 2011; Montgomery *et al.*, 1996; Parmar, 2003; Rahman, 1999) shows many negative consequences of NGO intervention, and microcredit in particular. Yet, in the 1990s there are several incidences of clashes between the rural religious leader and activists with NGO workers and beneficiaries.

There are many explanations for such a conflict between secular NGOs and religious elites over gender issues. In interpreting the backlash, NGOs were accused by the Mullah of doing anti-Islamic work by charging interest (which is strictly prohibited in Islam) on microcredit, by bringing women out of their homes and making them shameless, which violates the norms of *purdha* (veil/seclusion), and by breaking up the traditional family system of the village (Naher, 2005, p. 147). On the other hand, pro-secular, pro-modernist or the liberal intelligentsia and the NGOs have treated the religious rights which comprise the Islamists and their allies as 'backward', 'traditional' and 'reactionary', and the main impediment to development (Shehabuddin, 1999, p. 1026; G. D. Wood, 2009) and, hence, produced the backlash. To gain a deeper insight into this issue, I need to frame it in the wider context of Islam, politics and the NGOs' discourse in Bangladesh.

## Islam, politics, NGOs and Bangladeshi state: implications for development

British colonial rule in India ended in 1947, giving birth to the two independent states of India and Pakistan. However, the emergence of these new states was based on the idea of a 'two-nation theory'[1] which emphasizes the primacy of religion in establishing two successor states: the predominantly Hindu India and the predominantly Muslim Pakistan. Bengali Muslims joined Pakistan, emphasizing their Muslim identity (Jahan, 2005, p. 217), and the area was named East Pakistan.[2] Since the partition of India, Pakistan emerged as a tyrant to the Bengali Muslim population in terms of the economy, culture and language. Postcolonial Pakistan, as a 'military-bureaucratic oligarchy' (Alavi, 1972, p. 64), produced uneven economic development and hence unequal regional development, and 'fomented the movement for regional autonomy in East Pakistan, paving the way for the independence of Bangladesh in 1971' (Khondker, 2004, p. 23).

The emergence of Bangladesh has seen opposition from supporters of Pakistan[3] in Bangladesh who dreamed of a united Pakistan based on Muslim identity. Following the emergence of Bangladesh in 1971 based on 'Bangalee nationalism', the government opted for a secular nationalist ideology as embodied in its

Constitution (Hashmi, 2003, p. 102). But the principle of secularism was subsequently replaced by a commitment to an Islamic way of life through a series of constitutional amendments and government proclamations between 1977 and 1988 (Karlekar, 2005, p. 53).[4] The problem with identity formation (whether Bangalee, Bangladeshi or Muslim) is linked with this because the 'Bangladeshi state has solidified neither from its earlier secular character, nor from its later Islamic character' (Karim, 2004, p. 311). Hence, Karim (2004, p. 293) argues that the state promotes two contending ideologies in Bangladesh. One of these is women's full citizenship rights; the other is Islamic politics and education which impede women's rights. In this context it is identifiable that the government patronizes *Madrassahs* (religious education schools) alongside secular education. In 1977/1978 there were 1,976 *Madrasahs* but that number reached 15,661 in 2002 (Karim, 2004, p. 297).[5] Many authors have claimed that the exponential growth of *Madrasah* education and especially *Kawmi Madrasah* played a pivotal role in the 'Islamization Project' and rise of Islamist militants in the country (Datta, 2007; Kumar, 2009a).

Moreover, Bangladesh has a two-tiered social structure where at one level an urban educated (Western-type) elite advocates secularism, women rights, etc. and on another level a majority of people who are poor, rural and illiterate are not considered in the nation-making project (Karim, 2004, p. 301). Thus the attempt of the minority (the urban elite and NGOs) to 'stigmatize the majority as primordially oriented' is 'moral arrogance and worse ... political folly' (Madan, 1998, p. 299). Moreover, the 'secularization project' of the state, as elsewhere in the world, does not correspond to and reflect the desires of the majority of its people. The politics of the two main parties – the BNP (Bangladesh Nationalist Party), a pro-religious party, and the Awami League, a pro-secular party – made concessions for the Islamist groups and parties in the hope of maintaining power or of destabilizing the ruling party (Riaz, 2003, p. 313). Moreover, it is also imperative to look at the use of 'state religion' in the Constitution of Bangladesh and its subsequent amendments.

After independence in 1971, though the state of Bangladesh started its journey with the leadership of Sheikh Mujibur Rahman on a secular basis of nationhood, religion soon became an important component. The Constitution of Bangladesh, adopted by the Bangladesh Parliament on 4 November 1972, in paragraph 2 of its preamble, accepted 'nationalism', 'socialism', 'democracy' and 'secularism' as fundamental principles of the state (Maniruzzaman, 2001). The Mujib regime was brought to an abrupt end through his gruesome murder by a group of disgruntled officers of the Bangladesh Army on the night of 15 August 1975 (Khan, 2001) With the change of regime, nationalism in Bangladesh took an explicit turn towards religion. Islam and other religious beliefs (e.g. Hinduism in Bangladesh) represent the 'inner core' of rural villagers and inform their daily practices. It was clear that the coup leaders wanted to capitalize on the prevailing public mood, which was increasingly enthusiastic about the adoption of Islamic values. They therefore used Islam to secure and to a certain extent legitimize their position (Banu, 1992; Riaz, 2003). From that moment on, Bangladesh shook off its garb of secularism and began to move towards Islamization. Ziaur Rahman was the first military ruler to come to power through illegitimate means and to begin the steady Islamization of the polity (Karim, 2004).

Through the proclamation of Order no. 1 of 1977, the ideal 'Bismillah-ar-Rahman-ar-Rahim' (In the name of Allah, the most Gracious, and the most Merciful) was inserted at the beginning of the Constitution above the preamble. Through the same proclamation, Article 8, clause 1 was substituted by 'the principles of absolute trust and faith in the Almighty Allah, nationalism, democracy and socialism meaning economic and social justice, together with the principles derived from them … shall constitute the fundamental principles of state policy' (Government of Bangladesh, 1991; Islam, 2001).

The military ruler Lt. General H. M. Ershad, through the Eighth Amendment to the Constitution of Bangladesh on 7 June 1988, declared Islam as the state religion of Bangladesh (Article 2, clause A) with the provision that other religions may be practised in peace and harmony in the Republic (Government of Bangladesh, 1991; Islam, 2001; Mohsin and Guhathakurata, 2007). The most recent amendments (fifteenth amendment) by the current ruling party, the Bangladesh Awami League, have opted to return to the original (1972) Constitution, which, however, ended up as a blend of religion and secularism. This amendment re-established the four basic principles of the state (of the 1972 Constitution) to include secularism. At the same time, in this amendment Islam is still the 'state religion', which contradicts the ideal of secularism.

While the Bangladeshi state has gone through severe political turmoil since its independence in 1971, it remains virtually absent from the economy and has failed to restructure the already fragile economy of the country. In such a context, the Bangladeshi state turned to neoliberal policies, furthering privatization of the economy and shifting its responsibilities of services delivery to many non-state actors (e.g. NGOs). Thus it is important to look at the emergence of NGOs, both secular and religious, and their prominence in the nation-building project.

## The emergence of NGOs and their prominence in the nation-building project

Bangladesh has a long history of voluntary and non-profit activism. Hence the tradition of charity and voluntary activism was part of the everyday lives of its people. Economically well-off people from both Hindu and Muslim societies have endowed *vihars* and *madrashas*[6] as well as helped the poor due to their sense of belonging to a certain faith or religion. The establishment of *khanqahs* and *longerkahna*,[7] especially during the time of famine and crisis, provides free food to the needy. The first formal non-profit organization in this region was the Baptist Missionary Society established in 1793. The spread of education among the privileged class and the formation of a middle class has contributed to the rise of a large number of formal non-profit organizations in the form of *shava, samity, mojlish, anjuman*, etc.[8] during late nineteenth- and early twentieth-century Bengal.

The Kumudini Welfare Trust pioneered the native NGOs in Bangladesh, which were established in 1944. In 1943, Rai Bahadur Ranada Prasad Shaha established a dispensary and outdoor facility in his native village Mirzapur to serve the common people. The then Governor of Bengal, Lord Casey, inaugurated this 20-bed hospital on 27 July 1944, which led to the foundation of the Kumudini Trust.[9] This and other trusts and organizations were in the forefront of the emergence of non-state service provision, which achieved momentum in the 1960s with the establishment of BARD (Bangladesh Academy for Rural Development)[10] at Comilla. BARD introduced the 'Comilla Model' of cooperatives for rural peasants which devised integrated community development with a strong emphasis on agriculture (White, 1990). The success of BARD and its charismatic founder, Akhter Hamid Khan, provided, as Quddus and colleagues (2009, p. 8) argue, 'much inspirations to founders and leaders of the current generation of NGOs in Bangladesh'. In the course of the pre-independent Bangladesh period, activities of some international NGOs (e.g. CARE, CARITAS), though on a small scale, may be traced in this region.

In 1971, Bangladesh emerged as an independent nation following a nine-month war of liberation with Pakistan. Since its inception as a nation, NGOs have been strong agents of national development alongside the government in the context of a war-ravaged economy, famine, widespread poverty and political turmoil. Thus the post-war reconstruction period of Bangladesh in the 1970s has seen the emergence of today's largest domestic NGOs. The origin of the Grameen[11] Bank may be traced back to 1976 when Professor Muhammad Yunus, a Nobel Peace Prize Laureate, launched an action research project to examine the possibility of designing a credit delivery system to provide banking services targeted at the rural poor at Jobra and some of the neighbouring villages. In 1972, BRAC, a development organization dedicated to alleviating poverty by empowering the poor to bring about change in their own lives, was founded by F. H. Abed. During the same period, another pioneering NGO in rural health care services, Gonoshasthaya Kendra (G K),[12] started its post-war activities with the assistance of 22 volunteers and doctors at Bishmail, Savar in the Dhaka District. Another NGO, PROSHIKA,[13] began its activities in a few villages in Dhaka and Comilla districts in 1975 and emerged formally as an NGO in October 1976. In 1978, another large NGO, ASA (the Association for Social Advancement) was established, which, according to *Forbes Magazine*, became the World's top NGO in 2007 in providing microfinance (Quddus *et al*., 2009, p. 9).

During the later decades, several other prominent domestic NGOs emerged as actors in development practices in Bangladesh. During the 1990s, NGOs proliferated more than ever before, and there were around 22,000 local and national NGOs working in the country. This was a result of increased privatization and decreased political participation in the Western countries during the 1980s along with the local Bangladeshi factor; for instance, the absence of a strong state in the 1980s. These NGOs play a pivotal role in the nation-building process both in the provision of service delivery and as a vehicle of progressive organization in the local and global context (Chowdhury, 2009, p. 221).

The growth of NGOs in the 1980s in Bangladesh reflects the shift from their role of 'conscientization' to service provision, thereby reflecting 'donor preferences for a less radical model of civil society and for more emphasis on service provision' (World Bank, 2006a). One of the important features in the development of NGOs in the 1980s was reflected in their role as 'aid-dependent service delivery agents supportive to military regime' in Bangladesh (World Bank, 2006a, p. 3). In the late 1980s the funding of NGOs gained momentum. The return to democracy in Bangladesh at the beginning of the 1990s saw the development of NGO advocacy work. A significant growth in the number of NGOs in Bangladesh also became an indicator of involvement of Western donors in development practices in Bangladesh.

Up until May 2015, a total of 2,386 NGOs were registered with the NGO Affairs Bureau of Bangladesh (NGOAB).[14] During 1990/1991 there were 494 NGOs (local: 395; foreign: 99) registered with NGOAB which increased to 1997 (local: 1,807; foreign: 190) during 2005/2006. A local NGO must be registered with the NGOAB to receive funding from a foreign donor. However, not all NGOs are officially registered with the NGOAB. At present, a total of 45,000 NGOs are registered with the social welfare services department under the Ministry of Social Welfare (World Bank, 2006b, p. 2).

In the context of the exponential growth of domestic NGOs in Bangladesh, one important factor is the involvement of Western donors with domestic NGOs through funding methods that bypass the state. For example, during 1990/1991, the share of foreign aid to NGOs as a portion of total aid to Bangladesh was around 11 per cent. However, it reached approximately 28 per cent during 2002/2003. Although the overall flow of aid to Bangladesh, as a component of GDP, has decreased recently, it has not resulted in a fall in aid flows to the NGOs, indicating a sustained flow of foreign aid to them.[15] However, the main arguments for donor preference for NGOs over state machinery include the advantages of flexibility, dedication of staff to development work, and the small nature of operation and accountability. Due to these opportunities, NGOs are assumed to be better able to get the required job done (Quddus *et al.*, 2009, p. 17).

To turn to the nation-building project, it is evident that since the independence of Bangladesh, NGOs have positioned themselves in a continuum which ranges from service delivery to 'conscientization' (consciousness-raising) and empowerment (D. Lewis, 2004, p. 309). The 'NGO-ization' of nation-building projects as understood in Bangladesh emphasizes the service provision of NGOs as well as their ability to be a vehicle for progressive organization (Chowdhury, 2009, p. 221) and to create community identity during the period from post-war reconstruction to the expansion of democracy. Nation-building is a contested term, and hence there is no precise definition of the term (Talentino, 2004, p. 559). Since the post-cold war period, nation-building however has moved out of its traditional conceptualization (of creating nationhood) and emphasizes post-conflict state construction. Therefore, nation-building has state-building as its ultimate goal. The top-down approach to nation-building implemented by the outsider (e.g. the donor) focuses only on one aspect of nation-building, i.e. to rebuild the collapsed state through providing effective governance and democratization; extending principles of human rights thereby addresses only the short-term needs of the state. On the contrary, a bottom-up approach, which is considered to be an internal process initiated by the grassroots associations, plays a pivotal role in binding people together for a common cause within the state. It tries to bring individuals together by focusing on the benefits of intergroup relations, adding the element of citizens' agency which is important for state- and identity-building (Talentino, 2004, pp. 558, 561).

As mentioned earlier, NGOs, particularly indigenous NGOs, have had a huge effect on post-liberation state-building in Bangladesh. For example, *Gano Shasthya*, an NGO founded by the freedom fighter Dr Zafarullah, has its roots in a mobile medical unit that provided support to the freedom fighters of the 1971 war of liberation. RDRS (Rangpur Dinajpur Rural Services) began its activities in the northwest of Bangladesh to assist people with post-war rehabilitation services and infrastructure development. BRAC began by providing relief and rehabilitation support to the war-displaced people of northeast Bangladesh (Zohir, 2004, p. 4109). Subsequently, the activities of NGOs moved in a new direction to include a credit-based approach to policy advocacy. Although credit-based programmes are dominant on the NGO agenda, education and health are also an important part of their activities. Although the Government of Bangladesh has increased its budget allocation for education since the 1990s, it remains in the lowest ranks in South Asia and around 400 NGOs provide a primary education service. There are around 37,000 government schools for 12 million pupils (Quddus *et al.*, 2009, p. 13), while BRAC alone has 32,000 schools providing primary education in Bangladesh. According to BRAC's website:

> In sheer size, BRAC operates the largest private school system in the world: 1.2 million students (70 per cent of them are girls) are enrolled at present in 32,000 BRAC schools that provide four years of non-formal primary education. So far almost 5 million children have already graduated and got their basic education from these schools and close to 95 per cent enrol into secondary schools.[16]

In the case of health care, NGOs have played a vital role in providing the necessary health care services to the poor who are 'unreachable' and the ratio of government to NGO spending on health care is around 3 : 1 (Quddus *et al.*, 2009, p. 13). According to BRAC's health care programme database, under the Essential Healthcare Program, BRAC has 80,000 community health volunteers or *shasthya shebikas* and 7,900 community health workers or *shasthya karmis*, which provide a cost-effective bridge between the community they serve and the formal health systems.[17]

By the year 2000 NGOs had reached more than 90 per cent of rural communities in Bangladesh (World Bank, 2006a, p. 2). Grameen Bank[18] reached

7.95 million[19] people alone (of whom 97 per cent are women) with their micro-credit programme. BRAC has 8.5 million borrowers, Proshika one million, and ASA nearly one million. Therefore, NGOs have a very strong rural support base compared with the government. NGOs in Bangladesh provide two-thirds of institutional credit in rural areas (Sobhan, 1997, p. 133). In Bangladesh, neither the government banks nor the traditional money lenders loan to the very poor because they lack physical collateral. This financial dependency on the NGO has given them the power to act as patrons of the poor. They constitute, as Karim (2008, p. 12) notes, a 'modern landlord with a global vision'. NGOs are a major source of employment in a country with limited job opportunities open to its burgeoning young population. Young college graduates seek entry-level jobs with NGOs. NGOs are seen as the future – a promise of a better life and, for the better educated, an opportunity to go abroad for training (Karim, 2008).

However, the exponential growth of the NGO sector and subsequent emergence of NGOs as 'non-accountable' and parallel to the state in terms of service provision and power relations has prompted debate on the potential of NGOs in nation-building projects in Bangladesh. Therefore, the NGO-ization of the nation-building project is contested (Chowdhury, 2009, p. 217) and hence some scholars (e.g. Edwards and Hulme, 1996; Fisher, 1993; Salmon, 1994) criticize this NGO-ization process in Bangladesh. The development of the 'NGO-ization' of the nation-building project, critics argue, represents 'state failure' in service delivery (Fisher, 1993) and the accommodation of a neoliberal logic of market principles as well as a challenge to 'sovereignty and internal legitimacy of the state' (White, 1999, p. 312). Moreover, a web of dependency among the rural poor and the vulnerable through NGO credit financing and refinancing, and the changes in the household dynamics, resulting in changes in gender relations through the breeding of 'secular feminism'[20] (Khan *et al.*, 2009, p. xxv) has induced vulnerability rather than salvation. White (1999, p. 311) rightly argued that these NGOs are 'Bangladeshi but foreign funded; they claim to speak for the poor majority in a way that potentially threatens the scope and legitimacy of state aspirations to embody the nation'. Moreover, the development of the NGO sector has also been understood as the expansion of market forces and the domination of 'neoliberal ideology and imperialism' (Karim, 2008), and hence has produced, as some authors argue, a 'contested' relationship between the state, donors and NGOs (e.g. Edwards and Hulme, 1996; Haque, 2002; D. J. Lewis, 1997) in Bangladesh.

## Secular and religious NGOs in Bangladesh: a brief sketch of NGO activities in Bangladesh

This chapter has already explored the emergence and exponential growth of NGOs in Bangladesh and their prominence in the nation-building project. This section will mainly give a picture of some of the dominant secular as well as religious NGOs in Bangladesh to explain their different types of activities. I will discuss secular NGOs in the first section followed by a discussion of the religious NGOs, as religious NGOs came to development practice after the secular NGOs. This also implies that we need to explain the secular NGOs to understand the growth of religious NGOs.

### *Secular or mainstream conventional NGOs*

Bangladeshi NGOs started with advocacy, consciousness-raising and social mobilization, and moved to service provision during the 1980s and 1990s under donor imperatives (Quddus *et al*., 2009, p. 3). Whether small or large,[21] on average, an NGO in Bangladesh provide 4.4 different services such as credit, health and education (Gauri and Galef, 2005, p. 2050). The large majority of NGOs in Bangladesh provided microfinance (96 per cent of the large NGOs), followed by health care (48 per cent of the large NGOs and 60 per cent of the small NGOs) and sanitation (43 per cent of large NGOs and 56 per cent of small NGOs). The main reason for the high concentration on microcredit, as Gauri and Galef (2005) argue, is the fact that credit 'was an important source of revenue for NGOs' while the huge success of Grameen Bank in credit delivery was an example for NGOs to follow in order to be successful in NGO business.

I will now focus on the three major NGOs in Bangladesh, including Grameen Bank, BRAC and ASA (the Association for Social Advancement) to describe the types of programmes and activities in brief. The main programme of activities of Grameen Bank is microcredit. According to Grameen Bank (GB),[22] it has 2,565 branches and 22,124 staff through which the bank has reached a total number of 8.35 million people in 81,379 villages, of which 96 per cent are women. Its microcredit ranges from micro loans to education loans and micro enterprise loans. It also provides housing loans to its borrowers and scholarships for its borrowers' children. GB has set up a number of companies, though it claims that 'they are all independent companies, registered under the Companies Act of Bangladesh, with an obligation to pay all taxes and duties, just like any other company in the country',[23] one of which is the largest telecom company in Bangladesh: Grameen Phone[24] (Muhammad, 2009, p. 36).

BRAC is one of the largest NGOs in the world; it is based in Bangladesh with a global outreach. The *Global Journal* which is based in Switzerland published a list of the 100 Best NGOs in the world and put BRAC as the Number One NGO.[25] On its website BRAC claims that it works in 69,421 villages covering a total population of 110 million in Bangladesh. According to BRAC's website, it has 49,405 full-time employees and 6,532,649 BEP teachers.[26] Up until 2008, BRAC had created jobs for 8,523,882 people. The main programme of activities in Bangladesh includes Microfinance (5.54 million beneficiaries), Agriculture and Food Security, Education, Health, Human Rights and Legal Services, Disaster, Environment and Climate Change. In the case of its education programme BRAC claims that '1.14 million children currently enrolled in BRAC's 38,000 primary and pre-primary schools, with 9.51 million graduates and over 260,000 teens from disadvantaged backgrounds get life skills training in BRAC's youth empowerment clubs'.[27] BRAC Investment and related institutions include BRAC

University, BRAC Bank Ltd, bracNet, Documenta Ltd and Delta BRAC Housing Finance Corp Ltd. BRAC Social Enterprises include Aarong, BRAC Dairy & Food Project, BRAC Agriculture & Livestock Enterprises, BRAC Printers, BRAC Print Pack, BRAC Tea Estates, Ayesha Abed Foundation and BRAC Solar & Biogas.

ASA is one of the largest NGOs in Bangladesh and was established in 1978. The prime programme of activities of this NGO is microfinance. ASA claims that it has reached 4.7 million beneficiaries with microfinance.[28] The other programme of activities includes education and health. Its subsidiary institute includes ASA University, ASA International and Hope for the Poorest (HP).

## *Religious NGOs in Bangladesh: the emergence of a new stakeholder in development*

Development practices in Bangladesh are dominated by secular NGOs which represent Western, neoliberal, market-driven models of development (Karim, 2008, p. 5). However, during the 1990s, a different type of development model based on the teachings of Islam was introduced into Bangladesh by Islamic NGOs. In the beginning, almost all of the Islamic NGOs were involved in humanitarian and disaster relief and rehabilitation. Later they moved into other social services, including education, health and *shari'a*-based microfinance and other activities. This section will detail the growth of Islamic NGOs in Bangladesh and will explore how effectively they make space in dominant secular development trajectories. First I will outline the origin and growth of Islamic NGOs in Bangladesh and, in particular, I focus on three Islamic NGOs.

As has been mentioned elsewhere, the Bangladeshi state is best described as a 'fragmented polity' where the formation of national identity confronts a secular, religious and ethno-linguistic divide. This is also evident in the NGO-led development practices in Bangladesh which have polarized the polity between pro-NGO (mainly so-called secular liberal democrats who are also beneficiaries of NGOs) and anti-NGO groups (Hashmi, 2003, p. 116). Therefore, the emergence of religious or faith-based NGOs in a fragmented state has critical significance for future development directions and outcomes. Due to the nature of the Bangladeshi state, it is therefore imperative as well as very interesting to see how religious NGOs and particularly Islamic NGOs have emerged and expanded as development partners and welfare providers in Bangladesh.

However, in the context of Bangladesh, though religious charity, as discussed in the earlier section, has been there for a long time, religious non-governmental organizations, particularly Islamic NGOs, are a very recent phenomenon which date back to the early 1990s.[29] Religious NGOs in Bangladesh include a wide variety of NGOs based on a particular type of religious belief. There is no complete list of religious NGOs in Bangladesh, and hence it is difficult to trace the exact numbers and details of all the religious NGOs. Religious NGOs, corresponding to my definition, include Christian, Muslim, Hindu and Buddhist NGOs. Although the role and visibility of Christian and Islamic NGOs is very explicit, Hindu and particularly Buddhist NGOs are just the opposite. Many of the religious NGOs working in Bangladesh are transnational in nature and some are, of course, local with foreign funding. Other NGOs are solely local in terms of funding without any financial backing or connections with transnational organizations. The largest Christian NGOs working in Bangladesh are CARITAS, World Vision, Solidarities, etc., while Islamic Relief and Muslim Aid are the largest Islamic NGOs in Bangladesh. However, all these NGOs are transnational in character with their origins in Western countries.

The development of Islamic NGOs in Bangladesh is not well documented, and hence it is difficult to locate the origins of such organizations. My search for Islamic NGOs shows that Islam Prochar Samity (the Association for Preaching Islam) was among the pioneers of local Islamic NGOs in Bangladesh. It was established in 1968 with the aim 'to expand Islamic Dawa to the people especially to the non-Muslim brethren'[30] (Association for Preaching Islam, 2012) and to provide social services to bring about social reforms in Bangladeshi society. While this NGO began its activities during the pre-independence period of Bangladesh, it registered with the Government of Bangladesh in 1981 under the Societies Registration Act (Registration no. Dha (d) 01067, dated 1 September 1981).

Rabitat-al Alam al-Islami, a Saudi Arabian charity organization, was the pioneer among the international Islamic NGOs to start activities in Bangladesh after independence. It started its relief activities in 1977 among the *Ruhinga* refugees (a Muslim minority group migrated from Myanmar) and then extended its operations among the *Biharis* (stranded Pakistanis living in Bangladesh) in Dhaka and tribal people in Chittagong Hill Tracts and Rangpur (Islami Bank Bangladesh Ltd, n.d.). The World Assembly of Muslim Youth, a Saudi-based Islamic NGO established in 1972, began working in Bangladesh in the 1970s with the aim of preaching Islam.[31] Certain other Islamic NGOs (e.g. the Islamic Education Society) also started its activities in Bangladesh in the 1970s. Yet the activities of these NGOs were mainly limited to preaching or *da'wa* and relief and rehabilitation.

The intensification of the activities of Islamic NGOs in Bangladesh started in the early 1990s – a decade of massive social transformation marked by the return to democracy from military dictatorship, the opening up of the market economy and rural–urban migration. In the same decade, secular NGOs increasingly faced a religious backlash from the rural religious elite. In addition, in 1991, one of the most devastating cyclones in the history of Bangladesh contributed to the development of these Islamic NGOs as non-state actors who became increasingly integrated into service delivery activities, as did other secular NGOs. Although there are no separate official statistical data on the number and activities of Islamic NGOs in Bangladesh, according to AMWAB, there are about 320 NGOs working with them. However, my personal communication with an AMWAB official reveals different data. The official list for AMWAB shows 280 such NGOs. Yet, the programme manager claims that only about 100 or 120 of these organizations are currently active. However, Kumar (2009b, p. 904) shows that there are now around 575 Islamic NGOs working in Bangladesh. It is worth mentioning that most of the Islamic NGOs in Bangladesh, like their secular counterparts, are of indigenous origin. This growth of Islamic NGOs corresponds to the tradition of charity in Bangladeshi society as well as obligatory religious duties of Muslims (e.g. in the form of collecting *zakat*). These Islamic NGOs work in diverse areas, including disaster aid, education, health and sanitation, and microfinance. Figure 2.1 shows the types of activities Islamic NGOs are undertaking in Bangladesh and reveals their concentration on microfinance and disaster relief and management programmes.

Figure 2.1 shows that 60 per cent of Islamic NGOs are engaged in credit-plus programmes which include microcredit, non-formal education, health and sanitation along with micro investment. Around 17 per cent of these NGOs are involved in a microcredit-only programme.

Islamic NGOs, particularly Muslim Aid and Islamic Relief, have made a significant contribution to the relief and rehabilitation programme since their inception in the 1990s. For example, during the period from 1991 to 1993 Muslim Aid reached 28,540 families and 30,000 families in 2007 with their humanitarian assistance (Muslim Aid, n.d., pp. 26–27). In addition, the microfinance programme of Muslim Aid has reached 1,433 villages covering 30 districts of Bangladesh (Muslim Aid, 2010, p. 6). A local Islamic NGO, the Islamic Bank Foundation, has set up six hospitals in four divisional headquarters of Dhaka, Rajshahi, Khulana and Barisal. The microfinance programme under the *Fael Khair* programme of the Islamic Development Bank had a total number of 77,101 beneficiaries in June 2011, of which 98.8 per cent were women (Islami

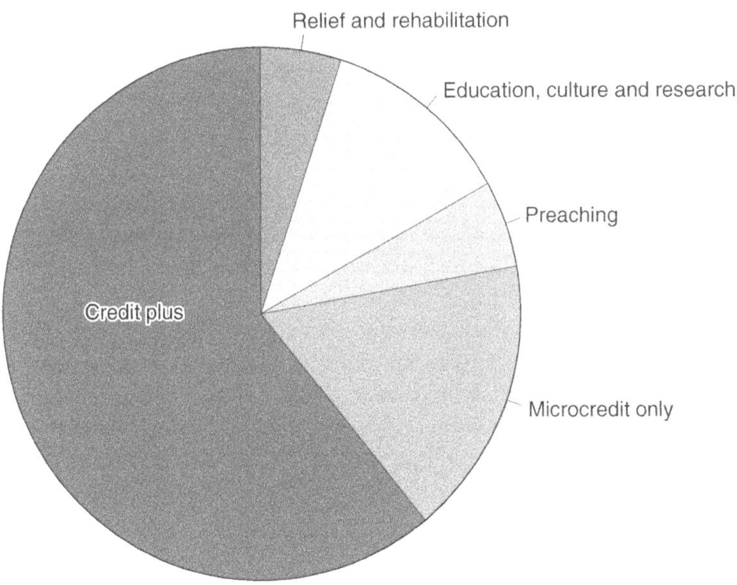


*Figure 2.1* Distribution of Islamic NGOs based on the types of programme (source: based on data provided in Akkas, n.d., p.17).

Bank Foundation, n.d.). Another Islamic NGO, MACCA, has adopted a comprehensive development programme based on *zakat* which is a very new kind of programme in the development discourse of Bangladesh. This organization provided Mosque-based education for 12,363 students up until 2007. In its comprehensive development programme called *Hasan* the organization served 1,561 households in 2007 (Masjid Council for Community Advancement, n.d.).

Recent studies have emphasized the potential of Islamic NGOs in areas of 'alternative' or a 'new kind of development', contrary to the conventional model of secular NGO-led development in Bangladesh. For instance, citing the example of the success of the *Hasana or 'Parshi'* model of development run by MACCA in Manikganj district, Mesbahuddin (2010) claims that 'an Islamic model of development' is emerging in Bangladesh. The humanitarian aid of Muslim Aid, especially its shelter project, under the 'Shajalal Model Village Program', as this research indicates, has become very efficient and transparent with the relief and rehabilitation programme, both during and post disaster management. Some research, focusing on the religious NGOs in Bangladesh, has found that religious NGOs are having problems gaining trust among the funding agencies as well as the mass of people (Ahmad, 2009).

No religious NGOs in Bangladesh, as Ahmad (2009, p. 183) has argued, are beyond suspicion. Christian NGOs, have long been suspected for their evangelical activities, particularly among the most vulnerable groups (including the indigenous population) of people. On the contrary, Islamic NGOs have been suspected by the people, secular intelligentsia, and even the state of promoting terrorism and obstructing secular development in Bangladesh.[32] Moreover, religious NGOs, as Ahmad (2009, p. 183) argues, mainly target people of their own belief system and are also corrupted (e.g. bribes to release funds from the government, plundering or misusing funds by NGO managers). However, a major shortcoming of his finding is that of his exploration of the local and very small religious NGOs which, in most cases, lack funding and managerial skills, and thus are corrupted.

Contrary to Ahmad's findings, D'Costa (2007, p. 231) mentioned that religious NGOs, particularly Christian NGOs (e.g. CARITAS, World Vision) have international partners and make space in the larger NGO community due to their effectiveness and innovations. However, her research lacks a detailed scrutiny of RNGOs and most importantly Islamic NGOs. Yet, these development efforts of Islamic NGOs need to be scrutinized critically to understand the potential of this 'new model of development' that I call the 'Islamic Model' of development in Bangladesh. Therefore, in the following section, I focus on how NGOs operate. I focus particularly on how the pertinent issues of globalization and the domination of neoliberal ideologies are working through NGOs that undermine state capacity and establish NGOs as parallel to the state or as a 'shadow state'.

## How do NGOs work?

Over time, the NGO sector has expanded and turned into a vehicle for progress and development, both ideologically and in practice, as detailed above. However,

NGOs, though they act initially as a social catalyst or social mobilizer, have become depoliticized over time. For example, in the beginning, BRAC in its ideological front represented a 'pseudo-radical rhetoric in its formulation of empowerment, which blends "conscientization theory" (of Paul Freire) with the Marxist rhetoric of class struggle' (Mannan, 2009, p. 89). This empowerment, as Chen (1986) argues, was the driving force behind 'a quiet revolution' in the lives of rural women in Bangladesh. However, the 'social mobilization' paradigm of development that might lead to the empowerment, collective actions and engagement with the broader political system has been replaced with the sole reliance on the 'service delivery' paradigm. This is either due to the pressure from the donor- and market-based neoliberal agendas or domestic pressure (socio-politico-religious factors). Hence, NGOs have become the most important source of 'service delivery' in the rural and isolated areas. Nevertheless, these NGOs are not only the most important providers of services for the rural people, but also the 'producer of social meanings and identities for actors associated with them' (Karim, 2004, p. 300). For example, starting one's own NGO and working with NGOs (e.g. as a female employee), he or she produces and reproduces his or her social status as well as identity (e.g. as elite and empowered woman where most of them lack power and authority).

## *Globalization, neoliberalism and the NGO as a shadow state*

A recent discussion[33] meeting under the banner of 'civil society' held on 8 June 2011 in Dhaka criticized the current government for its attempts to control the activities of NGOs in Bangladesh. This discussion was conducted by the 'most important figure in Bangladeshi Civil Society'.[34] One of the discussants emphasized:

> We, who are working for good governance, are being monitored. What is our fault … it is unjust not to acknowledge the work of NGOs and civil society and it means not acknowledge the truth. Now we see an implicit attack (from the Government) on the NGOs and the civil society. We have to stand against it.

Another discussant, a prominent journalist and writer, claimed that whenever the Awami League[35] comes to power, attacks are made on the NGOs. Therefore, a number of exponents of civil society in the country emphasized the role of NGOs, while at the same time many academics, especially those living abroad, have criticized the role of the NGOs as adherents of neoliberalism and Western globalization and financial capital. In such a context it is crucial to explore how secular NGOs may be understood as a representative and a vehicle of neoliberalism and globalization and to explore the problems of NGO-led development frameworks in Bangladesh.

It has already been revealed in the previous section that developmental NGOs were given free rein to grow and expand their rural outreach with Western aid.

The Western aid organizations also preferred the NGO sector as their aid partners. It enabled them to bypass the bureaucracy and corruption of the Bangladeshi state, and to directly reach targeted segments of the rural population. Over time, this developed into a lattice of dependent relationships among aid organizations, Western capital, NGOs and the Bangladeshi state. Therefore, some studies on NGOs see the rise of NGOs in Bangladesh as accompanied by a decline in state legitimacy (White, 1999) and the emergence of a new sovereignty, the rise of a 'shadow state' (Karim, 2008), and a 'virtual parallel state' (Clarke, 1998) or 'franchise state' (Wood, 1997) in Bangladesh. This is related to the triumph of NGOs as a vehicle of neoliberal governmentality.[36]

Although the literature on the critical perspectives of the role of NGOs is not profuse, some authors (e.g. Karim, 2008, p. 5), aptly depict how NGOs as agents of neoliberalism and globalization instrumentally appropriate rural women's honour and shame through the microcredit programme and their participation in it in Bangladesh. In the context of Nepal, Rankin (2001) has also depicted neoliberal development, by examining the microcredit strategy for poverty alleviation, which corresponds to the ideology of neoliberalism. Therefore, it is imperative to look at how neoliberal rhetoric and globalization translate into social action and into the production of its envisioned neoliberal subject through the intervention of NGOs in Bangladesh.

Globalization, as understood in the mainstream development literature, is related to economic globalization, meaning the removal of trade barriers and open markets, though the use of the term 'globalization' has been taken to mean different things to different people based on the purpose of explanation of the word.[37] Generally, as Castles (2001, p. 20) explains, 'Globalization refers to a process of change which affects all regions of the world in a variety of sectors including the economy, technology, politics, the media, culture and the environment'. Globalization, for Giddens (1990, p. 64), is understood in terms of a singular process or set of processes linked to modernity and articulated in 'time–space distanciation' which describes the process whereby remote interaction has become an increasingly significant feature of human life, and through which social systems that were previously distinctive have become connected and interdependent through the 'intensification of worldwide social relations'. For Robertson (1992, p. 8), globalization is 'the compression of the world and the intensification of consciousness of the world as whole'.

However, my intention in this book is not to enter into the theoretical debate on globalization; rather I will focus on how globalization and neoliberalism impacted upon the life of poor people in the South and how NGOs through their programmes and practices worked as a vehicle for 'neoliberal governmentality' in Bangladesh. My understanding of globalization engages with the understanding of the mobilization and transformation of the life of rural people in the Global South through what Arjun Appadurai (2001, p. 3) calls 'grassroots globalization' or 'globalization from below'.[38] However, Appadurai (2001, p. 31) understands grassroots globalization as 'new forms of social mobilization that proceed independently of the actions of corporate capital and the nation-state system'. My understanding of globalization is contrary to the conceptualization of globalization of Appadurai (2001); rather, I agree with the argument presented by Karim (2008) about grassroots globalization in the context of Bangladesh. With the example of the microcredit programme of Grameen Bank in Bangladesh she argues that grassroots globalization in Bangladesh works through and not against the corporate capital, donors, state, NGOs and members of the civil society, and hence creates a 'complex new map of social interdependencies' (Karim, 2008, 2011).

During the 1980s and mid-1990s, a number of academics (e.g. Appadurai, 1993, 1996; Kearney, 1995; Ong, 1999) have pointed out the radical weakening of the modern state in the wave of globalization where neoliberal ideology triumphs, which, as Harvey (2005, p. 64) argues, consider that human welfare is best served by the withdrawal of the state from welfarist policies. Therefore, the state as a source of regulation in diverse areas of social life and as the provider of education and health services as a set of citizenship entitlements was being substituted by private companies and institutions such as NGOs, aid organizations, the World Bank, IMF, etc. (Aretxaga, 2003, p. 394). Neoliberalism is seen as a rationality of governance or, in Ong's term, 'neoliberal governmentality', which 'results from the infiltration of market-driven truths and calculations into the domain of politics' (Ong, 2006, p. 4) and subjects citizens 'to market principles of discipline, efficiency and comparativeness'.

As has already been discussed, Bangladesh went through economic restructuring in the 1980s and 1990s with Structural Adjustment Programmes (SAPs) and other neoliberal policy agendas. It is also worth mentioning that since 1975 Bangladesh was under military rule until 1990 which, as Muhammad (2009) maintains, was conducive to the adoption of World Bank-IMF and Western donor prescriptions. G.D. Wood (2009, p. 50) explains how military rule was advantageous to adopting SAP:

> Military regimes, arising from coups, always have a problem of legitimation and constituency building, especially if they plan to become legitimate by metamorphosing into a political party. Since their oft stated initial mission was the 'clean up' of corrupt politicians, military leaders therefore have to find ways of by-passing the political elites they have just displaced.... There appear to be two classic options, often combined: decentralization; and alliance with NGOs, sometimes acting for the state under franchise.... Both options limit room for manoeuvre for potential opposition to government, either by keeping at arms length at local government level ... or by rewarding cooperating NGOs with more freedom of action and less bureaucracy in accessing foreign funds ... the outcome of this pragmatic equation was a substantial expansion of NGO activity and significant increase in direct donor support.

Since 1982, the government has become more interested in the privatization process and in transforming public enterprise into private enterprise. This period also experiences different targeted programmes for the poor in the name of a 'safety net' to rescue the victims of the economic 'reforms' or 'restructuring' through the adoption of Structural Adjustment Programmes (SAPs). During this period Bangladesh also experienced exponential growth in the microcredit programmes of NGOs as well as growth in the NGOs themselves. However, subsequent democratic governments since 1991 have also followed the same policies; for example, 'privatise, commercialise, hand over national resources to multinational corporations (MNCs)' formulated during military rule (Pegu, 2011). However, neoliberalism in Bangladesh, like many African countries, was problematic in the sense that 'the market-led alternative itself was equally problematic in a society only just emerging from its agrarian, pre-capitalist or at least mercantilist legacy' (Wood, 2009, p. 46). The meteoric rise of NGOs in the 1980s and 1990s in Bangladesh as elsewhere in the world was, as Devine (2009, p. 108) maintains, 'a direct response to the ideological shift taking place in the west, in particular the growing influence of a neoliberal analysis within the development industry'. With the increasing privatization of public services through NGOs, the World Bank and other international donor agencies helped the already weak state to withdraw from service delivery. This also reflects donors' preferences towards NGOs to disburse their loans and aid. For example, in Bangladesh donor preferences towards NGOs have increased and the total share of aid to NGOs was much higher than to the government (see Figure 2.1).

If we critically analyse the role of the World Bank in the expansion and changing nature of NGOs in Bangladesh, we see a shift in the programmes and agendas of NGOs which led to an increased commercialization of NGO programmes. For example, the World Bank report in 1996 recommended the following guidelines for NGOs in Bangladesh to integrate NGOs with the commercial finance market by:

> (a) developing an appropriate regulatory framework for financial operations of the NGO sectors; (b) encouraging large NGOs to establish themselves as banks: (c) encouraging 'wholesaling' of credit to established NGOs; and (d) using smaller NGOs as brokers to mobilize self-help savings groups.
>
> (World Bank, 1996, cited in Muhammad, 2009)

Therefore, an explicit shift in agendas and programmes of NGOs due to the adoption of neoliberal agendas reflects on how an NGO from a source of 'conscientization' and poverty alleviation became a corporate success. For example, Grameen Bank's subsidiary Grameen Phone (GP) started its operation with the declared aim of 'poverty alleviation' and 'helping the poor' by relying on its microcredit programme, offering its borrowers mobile phones as a commodity form of microcredit on the condition that borrowers would pay it back in instalments. At the outset, 348,733 borrowers of Grameen Bank received credit to buy mobile phones from Grameen Phone, which led to the foundation of the largest mobile phone company in Bangladesh with more than 35 million subscribers (as of October 2011).[39] The same corporate success is also true for BRAC and other large NGOs where NGOs turned to commercial ventures. Therefore, many microfinance institutions, as Muhammad (2009, p. 38) argues, have been 'transformed from charities to profitable companies through hugely successful initial public offerings'. These NGOs in Bangladesh, as Mannan (2009, p. 84) argues, 'open up the local markets for foreign products, transform money into capital'. In this process, NGOs transform 'millions of beneficiaries into market clients, petty commodity producers, and entrepreneurs'.

As providers of scarce resources, for example, credit and jobs for a large segment of the population, NGOs in Bangladesh have tremendous power in regulating people's behaviour and subjecting them to NGO mandates and priorities. These priorities are often prescribed by donors to the NGOs. Karim (2008, p. 7) argues that there are three different ways in which neoliberalism is operating through NGOs (for instance, microcredit policies of Grameen Bank in Bangladesh): (1) through microcredit loans, NGOs manipulate gendered notions of honour and shame to further capitalist goals, and instrumentally violate local norms of cohesion and community ('the economy of shame'); (2) the work of microcredit results in unanticipated neoliberal subjects, namely the female petty money lender who reproduces usury at multiple levels of society; and (3) since the NGO operates as a 'shadow state' with control over the lives of the poor recipients, NGOs may neutralize dissenting voices of the poor in public spaces.

Therefore, 'neoliberal governmentality' in Bangladesh as argued by Karim (2008, p. 6) is the subjection of a targeted population by non-state actors (e.g. NGOs) to a new form of governance through market-oriented mechanisms which replace the traditional sovereignty of the family with the economic sovereignty of the market and hence control and regulate people's lives. Although it is undeniable that neoliberalism and globalization have had a profound impact upon access to new routes of capital circulation and subsequent overseas labour migration for rural families in Bangladesh, it is also evident that through NGOs rural people have become 'consumers of products of multinational corporations such as financial capital' and 'remain dependent on multinational corporations for physical inputs' (Karim, 2008, pp. 8–9). In such a dependent relationship between the NGOs and rural people, the balance of power is always with the NGOs, and subsequently people refer to NGOs as *sarkar* or the state (Karim, 2008).

Many developing countries (e.g. Bangladesh) lack economic sovereignty; hence they are dependent on international corporations and IGOs such as IMF, the World Bank and Western capital, and must follow their prescriptions. Some of the recent publications from the World Bank regarding development in Bangladesh reveal the World Bank's intention and agendas with regard to development efforts. For example, a 1990 publication entitled 'Poverty and Public Expenditure in Bangladesh' repeatedly compared NGO activities with those of the state, and hence 'recommended the expansion of NGOs to supplement the government efforts and provide for improvement in delivery of services through competition' (White, 1999, p. 308). In this context, the role of the state in service delivery has been undermined by the World Bank's prescription to them to produce 'development with equity' through encouraging new frontiers of development: NGOs and the neoliberal market (World Bank, 1990). Making NGOs parallel to the state deteriorates the state's capacity and legitimacy. In 1996 another publication called 'Pursuing Common Goals: Strengthening Relations between Government and the Development NGOs in Bangladesh' states that its key purpose is 'to make a difference'. Its success 'can only be measured by the extent to which it can convince the Government and the NGOs to bring about the necessary changes in their policies and practices so that a more fruitful partnership can be fostered' (World Bank, 1990, p. 45).

Yet it is crucial to identify how this neoliberal prescription has really changed the rural subject or rural people. The main argument for the expansion of NGOs is to reduce poverty by allowing the poor to be independent of exploitative patrons, whether they be the state, money lenders or traditional banking systems (Yunus and Jolis, 2003). Therefore, it is inevitable that the poor will see NGOs as their salvation. Yet a critical understanding is required to evaluate the development outcome of what I call NGO-ization of these NGOs in terms of de-clientelization and disempowerment.

## *NGO-ization of rural life: welfare, de-clientelization and disempowerment*

Wood and Gough define de-clientelization as 'the process of de-linking client dependents from their personalized, arbitrary and discretionary entrapment to persons with intimate power over them' (Wood and Gough, 2006, p. 1708). To comprehend the de-clientelization process, it is important to understand the concept of the patron–client relationship in the context of Bangladesh. Patron–clientism is a complex, hierarchical and vertical pattern of relationships between the patron and the client. Patrons are usually landlords, money lenders or employers, especially in traditional and developing societies. Clients are usually poor landowners, tenants and sharecroppers with the vast majority of people landless, poor and unemployed (Davis, 2001, p. 86). Since this relationship is vertical, patrons are always exploitative, and poor people, finding no other alternatives, express loyalty to their patron in return for welfare or security provision. This causes significant suffering and disadvantage to the client in the long term.

Large parts of the world, especially developing areas, are characterized by informal security or welfare and insecure regimes (Wood and Gough, 2006, p. 1707). As people are much more reliant upon informal relations under community arrangements typically characterized by the patron–client relationship or the provision of welfare services by civil society, so decommodification-based[40] welfare needed to be shifted towards de-clientelization. Hence the process of de-clientelization can be the basis for improving the quality of rights and correlative duties.

In developing countries like Bangladesh, patron–client relationships display a high degree of exploitation and produce structured inequality. In such societies, 'disadvantage through a host of exclusionary processes of closure, monopolization and opportunity hoarding practices' are also produced (Davis, 2001, p. 100), usually by the patron. Therefore, strategies in social policy that try to reduce dependency on the patron are part of a process of de-clientelization. One such example is found in the microcredit programmes of various NGOs in Bangladesh and elsewhere in the world (Davis, 2001, p. 1708; Wood and Gough, 2006). Theoretically, microcredit tends to reduce dependence on patrons; i.e. it reduces dependence on the rapacious and usurious money lenders for continuing poor people's livelihoods. Other components of the 'third sector'[41] (for instance, cooperatives, mutual assurance societies and civil society) all contribute to de-clientelization.

Esping-Andersen (2000) regards the 'third sector' or the NGO sector as peripheral and not a distinct entity in welfare provision due to its insignificance in welfare provision and semi-public nature of this sector. Although Esping-Andersen (2000, p. 9) points out a few potential advantages of the third sector (including reducing the government's financial burden and the decentralization of welfare service delivery), nevertheless he argues that the sector remains concentrated on the 'margins' of society. Yet the third sector has proved to encompass a range of beneficiaries (e.g. the 'microcredit programme' model in Bangladesh) and their public welfare provision is undeniable in the developing world. In sum, most of the NGO literature and the NGOs themselves emphasize breaking the cycle of patron–client networks through the provision of microcredit.[42]

However, contrary to the above argument, it now quite clear from the emerging literature that NGOs in rural Bangladesh throw people into a dependent network rather than pull them back (Muhammad, 2009, p. 39). Pearl and Phillips (2001) argue that microcredit loans are consumed and thus function as a 'consumption stabilizer' (Ghosh, 2006). Moreover, although the use of credit is supposed to be for income-generating activities, evidence is found that credit is used to meet dowry demand among poor families (Muhammad, 2009, p. 39; Rahman, 1999, p. 77). This, however, may be related to persistent poverty and inequality in the structure of society. Moreover, Lewis and Hossain (2008, p. 44) divulge that rich microcredit receivers can benefit from such loans and those who are poor cannot, which indicates that microcredit from NGOs does not necessarily provide a vehicle for poverty alleviation of the poor.

Therefore, Muhammad (2009, p. 39) argues that nearly 50 per cent of borrowers had to take out further loans from other sources to repay their original loan. This led the rural poor becoming poorer and entering into the 'trap of microcredit'. The trap is such that once you borrow a loan and cannot pay the weekly instalments, to avoid default and harsh treatment or harassment by NGO officials (Karim, 2008), the poor recipient is compelled to take out loans with other NGOs. Since the NGO field officials are always under pressure from Head Office or the supervisory authority to disburse their loan, they do not care about the beneficiary's other NGO loans. In such a context the recipient of microcredit enters into the vicious cycle of microcredit or NGO dependency. Therefore, in many cases women are involved in as many NGOs as possible simultaneously, at times participating in more than three NGOs at once (Lewis and Hossain, 2008, p. 44; Muhammad, 2009, p. 39). Hence, loan repayment is undertaken through refinancing from the same or other NGOs, which enables the poor to enter into a cycle of dependency and vulnerability. The same findings are evident in the research of Gehlich-Shillabeer (2008, p. 402) in Bangladesh.

As has been mentioned earlier in this book, NGOs are designed to reduce the dependency of the rural poor on traditional money lending. However, research indicates that there is a reproduction of usury at multiple levels of society due to the intervention of the microcredit programme (Karim, 2008, p. 20) and that traditional money lending has increased. Karim (2008, p. 20) found in her study area that out of 230 NGO beneficiary households, 100 were involved in money lending. Again, this intensive practice of money lending has a connection with the repayment of loan instalments for which credit receivers are forced to borrow to repay their loans. It is also interesting to see the emergence of a money-lending system for Muslim women which was previously monopolized by Hindu men and after 1971 by Muslim men along with Hindus. On the other hand, microcredit in the rural areas has enabled many rich people to enter the micro-credit market, where richer clients use poor women as proxy to obtain the loan from the NGOs, meaning that rich clients use the loans while poor women join the NGO in exchange for monetary gain (Karim, 2008, 2011). This leads to the question as to whether the women, by joining in the NGOs, really 'progress' and become empowered.

However, in the NGO-led development discourse, women were targeted as the subjects of the NGOs whether in the name of microcredit or empowerment. Hence, a debate is evolving among academics about how empowered these female borrowers are at the end of the day, or whether they have just become a neoliberal subject. A large number of studies show the empowerment of women through the activities and particularly through the provision of microcredit (Hashemi *et al.*, 1996; Mahmud, 2003; Pitt and Khandker, 1995). One of the main arguments advanced by these researchers is that material or economic gain leads to decision-making power for women at the household level. Contrary to the positive verdict for empowerment, a large number of (influential) studies argue that access to microcredit instead reinforces patriarchal norms of women's subordination and hence worsens gender relations, and is disempowering women in rural Bangladesh (Goetz and Gupta, 1996; Karim, 2008, 2011; Montgomery *et al.*, 1996; Parmar, 2003; Rahman, 1999).

One of the most important works on microcredit programmes is the ethnographic study on Grameen Bank beneficiaries by Rahman (1999), who looks critically at the narratives of NGO-led empowerment of women in rural villages in Bangladesh. Using 'hidden' and 'public' transcripts as articulated by Scott (1990, pp. 42–44), and used by Rahman (1999), shows ideological justifications[43] that hide the true basis for why NGOs almost exclusively provide loans to women. Therefore, women are accepted in the credit programme due to their 'positional vulnerability'[44] in rural society. Women are targeted by the NGOs (e.g. Grammeen Bank), since they are an easily manipulated population (Selinger, 2008, p. 33).

Yet, tying women to the development programmes of NGOs for empowerment has immense implications for society and needs to be understood in the complex interplay among gender, Islam, NGOs and the state of Bangladesh. As Tomalin (2006, p. 12) argues, development discourse marginalizes people in the Global South and a rights-based development approach does not take into consideration the ways in which religious values shape social ethics. Rather, it neglects the cultural and religious context of human rights. This development approach of NGOs along with the political use of religion and contested state policies needs to be examined closely.

This chapter reveals that Bangladesh went through a huge social transformation during the past 30 years as a result of many factors, including the adoption of neoliberal policy. In the context of the emergence of NGOs as a vehicle of neoliberal policies and the subsequent prominence of NGOs in nation-building projects, it is evident that the NGO–state–social structure is in an antagonistic relationship, particularly in rural areas. During the same period the Bangladeshi state has helped to grow religious NGOs in the context of shifting religious and economic policy orientation of the state. Therefore, the emergence of Islamic NGOs with a different promise, namely one of blending religious values with secular development practice, raises many questions regarding the problems of secular NGO-led development, and the potential alternative as well as the potential of the rise of the Islamist. Therefore, it is necessary to examine what sort of Islamic ideological construct informs the programmes and activities as well as the identity of these Islamic organizations, which is the main theme of Chapter 3.

## Notes

1 The two-nation theory, the ideology of Pakistan, led to the partition of the Indian subcontinent in 1947 into two nations: India and Pakistan. The main argument of the two-nation theory was that the identity of Muslims in British India was their religion, rather than their language or ethnicity. Hence Indian Hindus and Muslims are two distinct nationalities, regardless of ethnic or other commonalities. Bangladesh (the then East Pakistan) a Muslim majority, though physically located thousands of miles away from Pakistan, was tied to Pakistan as its part during the independence from the British Empire.

2 During 1947 to 1955, its official name was East Bengal; however, it was called East Pakistan after that (Van Schendel, 2009, p. 96).

3 In Bangladeshi narratives these Pakistani supporters were against the war of liberation and committed war crimes known as 'Rajakar'; many of them now belong to the largest Islamic Political Party – the Bangladesh Jamaat-e-Islam. After the Bangladesh Awami League assumed power in 2008, it started the war crimes tribunal to punish war criminals.

4 In the latest amendment of the Constitution of Bangladesh, it has returned to its original 1972 Constitution with the provision of secularism and Islam as the state religion.

5 These *madrasah* students who are mainly poor male orphans and unequipped to face the challenge of the twenty-first century will inevitably go against modern ideas, rights and women's rights. Thus it is important to understand the role of the Bangladeshi state in the religious backlash against NGOs in Bangladesh.

6 In Sanskrit and Pali, the term *Vihar* means a Buddhist monastery. However, *Vihar* is sometimes used to denote a place for non-Muslim worship. *Madrasha* means the Islamic religious school in Bangladesh.

7 *Khanqah* is a Persian word introduced in the Bengal in the thirteenth century by the sufis of Persia to mean a house or abode of sufis and dervishes. A Langarhhana is a place where free food, called Langar, is distributed to all, and where food is prepared to be given to the poor. In many cases, this is also related to the Sufi Dergah.

8 The terms *shava, samity (*Bengali words), *anjuman* (Persian word) and *mojlish* (Arabic word) in Bangladesh are used to mean meetings, associations or organizations of different kinds.

9 For details on the Kumudini Trust, see www.kumudinibd.org.

10 The Bangladesh Academy for Rural Development (BARD) is located in Kotbari, a rural area along the Mainamati–Lalmai hill range in Comilla District. The Academy was established in 1959 basically as a training institute to train government officials and representatives of the local government and village organizations in various subjects relating to rural development. The Academy is famous for its evolved model 'Comilla Approach to Rural Development'. For details visit www.bard.gov.bd/default.htm.

11 Grameen is a Bangla word which means 'rural' or 'village' in English. Therefore, Grameen Bank literally means Rural Bank or Village Bank, or Bank for the Rural or Village People.

12 In Bangla, *Gono* means People, *Shasthaya* means Health, and *Kendra* means Centre; therefore, it literally means people's health care centre.

13. PROSHIKA is the acronym of three Bangla words, including *proshikhhon*, *shikhya* and *kormo*, meaning training, education and action in English, respectively.

14 The NGO Affairs Bureau of Bangladesh regularly updates the list of NGOs working in Bangladesh. For a detailed list, see www.ngoab.gov.bd/.

15 Details may be found at www.worldbank.org.bd/WBSITE/EXTERNAL/COUNTRIES/SOUTHASIAEXT/BANGLADESHEXTN/0,,contentMDK:20937545~pagePK:141137~piPK:141127~theSitePK:295760,00.html (accessed 2 June 2011).

16 For details of BRAC's education services visit www.brac.net/content/where-we-work-bangladesh-education (accessed 26 March 2012).

17 See details on BRAC's health care at www.brac.net/content/bangladesh-health-general-healthcare.

18 It is controversial to define Grameen Bank as an NGO rather than as a microfinance Institution.

19 For details, see www.grameen-info.org/index.php?option=com_content&task=view&id=26&Itemid=175.

20 Secular feminism implies the feminist movements in the Muslim world which have drawn their inspiration usually from Western models which view religion as antithetical to progress and the development of women. Feminists in Bangladesh, like civil society, are largely drawn from urban elite families with political connections and a strong academic background. While their elite status and Western education give them access to transnational networks, they are out of touch with women's organic role in their communities. Hence, this imported brand of feminism is often tied in with 'progress' and 'modernism' and lacks the local norms.

21 Gauri and Galef (2005, p. 2046) define those NGOs that have over 1,000 branches across the country as large.

22 See details on Grameen Bank at www.grameen-info.org/. The current data were accessed 4 June 2013.

23 See www.grameen-info.org/index.php?option=com_content&task=view&id=26&Itemid=175 (accessed 4 June 2013).

24 The following are those companies set up by Grameen Bank: (1) Grameen Phone Ltd; (2) Grameen Telecom; (3) Grameen Communications; (4) Grameen Cybernet Ltd; (5)

Grameen Solutions Ltd; (6) Grameen Information Highways Ltd; (7) Grameen Bitek Ltd; (8) Grameen Krishi Foundation; (9) Grameen Motsho (Fisheries) Foundation; (10) Grameen Uddog (Enterprise); (11) Grameen Shamogree (Products); (12) Grameen Knitwear Ltd; (13) Grameen Shikkha (Education); (14) Grameen Capital Management Ltd; (15) Grameen Byabosa Bikash (Business Promotion); (16) Grameen Trust; (17) Grameen Health Care Trust; (18) Grameen Health Care Service Ltd; (19) Grameen Danone Food Ltd; (20) Grameen Veolia Water Ltd; (21) Grameen Shakti; (22) Grameen IT Park Ltd; (23) Grameen Star Education Ltd; (24) Grameen Employment Services Ltd; (25) Grameen Fabrics and Fashion Ltd; (26) Grameen Distribution Ltd; (27) Grameen Shamogree Purbanchal Ltd; (28) Grameen Shamogree Uttaranchal Ltd; (29) BASF Grameen Ltd; (30) Grameen Fund; (31) Grameen Kalyan. See www.grameen-info.org/index.php?option=com_content&task=view&id=26&Itemid=175 for details (accessed 4 March 2013).

25 See www.brac.net/node/1384#.Ua2_idi59k0 (accessed 4 June 2013).

26 See details on BRAC at www.brac.net/index.php?nid=16.

27 See www.brac.net/content/who-we-are#.Ua3DD9i59k0 (accessed 4 June 2013).

28 See http://asa.org.bd/?page_id=18 (accessed 4 June 2013).

29 Although Islamic NGOs, particularly Transnational Muslim NGOs, started their operations in the 1990s, Christian NGOs and Hindu NGOs are, in some cases, older than the independent Bangladesh NGOs. Caritas, one of the leading Christian NGOs in Bangladesh, was founded in 1967 as the eastern branch of Caritas Pakistan. Following the cyclone of November 1970 it was reorganized and became known as CORR (Christian Organisation for Relief and Rehabilitation) and took on the character of a national organization on 13 January 1971. The name 'Caritas' was reintroduced in 1976 (CARITAS, 2011, www.caritasbd.org/). World Vision became involved in Bangladesh in response to the tidal surge that occurred in the coastal areas of the country in 1970, providing relief supplies to the disaster victims. During Bangladesh's liberation war (1971), World Vision carried out relief operations in Bangladeshi refugee camps in India (World Vision, 2011, http://bangladesh.wvasiapacific.org/about-us-mainmenu-84). The Hindu NGO Ramkrishna Mission was named after the great Hindu preacher Sri Ramkrishna. In 1899, it began its work in Bangladesh (Ramkrishna Mission, 2011, www.rkmdhaka.org/index.php?option=com_content&view=article&id=83:the-seed&catid=25:dhaka-centre&Itemid=167).

30 For details on the activities of Islam Prochar Samity visit www.apibangladesh.org/about-api.

31 Bangladesh Field Office activities of the World Assembly of Muslim Youth may be seen at http://wamy.org.bd.

32 In 2009, the government had been scrutinizing Islamic NGO activities and alleged some of them to be involved in Islamist militant funding. Especially after the incidence of country-wide terror bombing and suicide bombing by the Islamist Militant group 'Jama'atul Mujahideen Bangladesh' (JMB), the activities of Islamic NGOs have fallen under more suspicion.

33 The discussion was held at CIRDEP Auditorium in Dhaka and was entitled 'Democracy, Development and Civil Society: Working Environment with Auotonomy'; in Bangla: 'Gonotontra, Unnyan and Nagorik Samj: Shokioteya neya Kajer Poribesh'. See Prothom-Alo (2011).

34 These 'urban elite intelligentsia' who represent urban civil society are considered 'important' in the sense of their 'contribution' to society and at the same time many of them have frequently appeared in the electronic media. Some prominent participants in the discussion include the ex-adviser of the caretaker Government of Bangladesh Wahiduddin Mahmud, M. Hafizuddin Khan, Akbar Ali Khan, Rasheda K. Chowdhury, journalist A.B.M. Musa, Syed Abul Maksud, ex-ambassador Farhuk Sobhan, CPD's Dbeyo Pryao Bhattchyra, DU Professor Asif Nazrul, and SUJON's Bodiul Alam Majumdar.

35 The Awami League, a centre-left political party, has led the government since 2008.
36 For a discussion on the negative aspects of development through NGOs see Rahman (1999), Goetz and Gupta (1996), Karim (2004, 2008, 2011).
37 Attempts to chart the globalization of capital, the decline of the nation state and the rise of a new global culture include the essays in Giddens (1990), Robertson (1992) and Stiglitz (2002).
38 Globalization from below is associated with the social mobilization of grassroots people against globalization from above (e.g. the 'environmentalist' movement in climate change and global warming). Some authors argue that globalization from below has the potential to change the power equation, whereas globalization from above has rendered ordinary people powerless (Brecher *et al.*, 2000, p. 3). For Appadurai (2001, p. 3), 'globalization from below' or 'grassroots globalization' are forms of

> social mobilisation that proceed independently of the actions of corporate capital and the nation-state system … these social forms rely on strategies, visions, and horizons for globalization on behalf of the poor … which strives for a democratic and autonomous standing in respect to the various forms by which global power further seeks to extend its dominion.

39 For details on Grameen Phone see www.grameenphone.com/.
40 Decommodification, as Bonoli (1997, p. 353) argues, is a complex dimension in welfare analysis. For Esping-Andersen (1990, p. 37), decommodification refers to "the degree to which individuals, or families, can uphold a socially acceptable standard of living independently of market participation'. Since the industrial revolution, workers became commodified, which made them entirely dependent upon the market for their continued livelihood and survival. Thus decommodification became, as Esping-Andersen (1990, p. 22) argues, a shield against ill-will and welfare state decommodified labour to reduce reliance upon the markets for survival.
41 Gough and Wood argue that to apply Esping-Andersen's welfare state regime to the nations and peoples of the developing context requires a radical re-conceptualization. Hence it is essential to extend the focus from 'welfare state regimes' to 'welfare regimes' (Gough, 2004, p. 6; Wood and Gough, 2006, p. 1698). Thus extending the focus from a state–market–family system of welfare to a community-based relationship may possibly produce a better outcome in understanding welfare in the developing countries. Thus it is essential to include a wider range of actors to understand welfare in developing countries. These community-based relationships not only include the indigenous community practices, but also different clientelist networks (Wood and Gough, 2006, p. 1702) and different non-state and non-governmental organizations or, more broadly, the 'third sector' in welfare provision. At the same time, different international actors (e.g. international governmental organizations (IGOs), international non-governmental organizations (INGOs) and international financial institution (IFIs) and their aid, loans and also their conditionality, need to be taken into consideration to analyse the welfare outcomes in developing countries throughout Asia, Africa and Latin America. Moreover, the reorganization of international labour migration and remittances also needs to be included in welfare analysis as it plays a potential role in the insecurity and ill-will prevalent in many counties such as Bangladesh.
42 For example, BRAC, in one of its leading publications *The Net*, identified a patron–client dependency network in rural Bangladesh as one of the significant evils in development.
43 In his ethnographic work entitled *Women and Microcredit in Rural Bangladesh* (Rahman, 1999b) he provides both the NGO workers' and the borrowers' testimony in this regard.

44 Positional vulnerability is understood in relation to culturally and religiously patterned behaviours of women which are associated with limited physical mobility, 'submissiveness', 'modesty', 'purity', 'respectability', 'shyness' and *purdha* (Rahman, 1999a, pp. 73–75).

## References


Ahmad, M. M. (2009). For God's Sake: The Religious Non-governmental Organizations in Bangladesh. In F. C. Khan, A. Ahmad and M. Quddus (eds), *Recreating the Commons? NGOs in Bangladesh* (pp. 183–206). Dhaka: The University Press.

Akkas, S. M. A. (n.d.). Poverty Alleviation from Islamic Perspective: Lessons from Grassroot Experiments 26. Retrieved from: www.scribd.com/doc/12878903/Poverty-Alleviation-From-Islamic-Perspective (accessed 14 February 2010).

Alavi, H. (1972). The State in Post-colonial Societies: Pakistan and Bangladesh. *New Left Review, 74*(1), 59–81.

Appadurai, A. (1993). Patriotism and its Futures. *Public Culture, 5*(3), 411–429.

Appadurai, A. (1996). *Modernity at Large: Cultural Dimensions of Globalization* (Vol. 1). Minneapolis: University of Minnesota Press.

Appadurai, A. (2001). Grassroots Globalization and the Research Imagination. In A. Appadurai (ed.), *Globalization* (pp. 1–21). Durham, NC: Duke University Press.

Aretxaga, B. (2003). Maddening States. *Annual Review of Anthropology*, 393–410.

Arzu, A. (2010). Women Seek Divorce More Than Men, Say DCC Records: 50,000 Divorce-seeking Petitions in Last 3 Months; Extra Marital Affairs, Torture Main Reasons. *The Daily Star*. Retrieved from http://archive.thedailystar.net/newDesign/news-details.php?nid=162427 (accessed 13 November 2010).

Association for Preaching Islam. (2012). About Association for Preaching Islam. Retrieved from www.apibangladesh.org/about-api (accessed 3 January 2012).

Banu, U. A. B. R. A. (1992). *Islam in Bangladesh*. Leiden, The Netherlands: E. J. Brill.

Bonoli, G. (1997). Classifying Welfare States: A Two-dimension Approach. *Journal of Social Policy, 26*(3), 351–372.

Brecher, J., Costello, T. and Smith, B. (2000). *Globalization from Below*. Boston, MA: South End Press.

Castles, S. (2001). Studying Social Transformation. *International Political Science Review, 22*(1), 13–32.

Castles, S. (2010). Understanding Global Migration: A Social Transformation Perspective. *Journal of Ethnic and Migration Studies, 36*(10), 1565–1586.

Chen, M. A. (1986). *A Quiet Revolution: Women in Transition in Rural Bangladesh*. Dhaka: BRAC.

Chowdhury, E. H. (2009). Challenges for the Women's Movement in Bangladesh: Engaging Religion, Development and NGO Politics. In F. C. Khan, A. Ahmad and M. Quddus (eds), *Recreating the Commons? NGOs in Bangladesh* (pp. 207–248). Dhaka: The University Press.

Clarke, G. (1998). Non-governmental Organizations (NGOs) and Politics in the Developing World. *Political Studies, 46*(1), 36–52.

D'Costa, B. (2007). Faith, NGOs and the Politics of Development in Bangladesh. In H. James (ed.), *Civil Society, Religion and Global Governance: Paradigms of Power and Persuasion* (pp. 219–238). London: Routledge.

Datta, S. (2007). Islamic Militancy in Bangladesh: The Threat from Within. *South Asia: Journal of South Asian Studies, XXX*(1), 145–170.

Davis, P. (2001). Rethinking Welfare Regime: The Case of Bangladesh. *Global Social Policy, 1*(1), 79–107.

Devine, J. (2009). Organizational Success and the Informal Politics of Social Change. In F. C. Khan, A. Ahmad and M. Quddus (eds), *Recreating the Commons? NGOs in Bangladesh* (pp. 107–128). Dhaka: The University Press.

Edwards, M. and Hulme, D. (1996). Too Close for Comfort? The Impact of Official Aid on Nongovernmental Organizations. *World Development, 24*(6), 961–973.

Esping-Andersen, G. (1990). *The Three Worlds of Welfare Capitalism*. Cambridge and Oxford: Polity Press.

Esping-Andersen, G. (2000). The Sustainability of Welfare States into the Twenty-first Century. *International Journal of Health Services, 30*(1), 1–12.

Fisher, J. (1993). *The Road from Rio: Sustainable Development and the Nongovernmental Movement in the Third World*. Westport, CT: Praeger.

Gauri, V. and Galef, J. (2005). NGOs in Bangladesh: Activities, Resources, and Governance. *World Development, 33*(12), 2045–2065.

Gehlich-Shillabeer, M. (2008). Poverty Alleviation or Poverty Traps? Microcredits and Vulnerability in Bangladesh. *Disaster Prevention and Management, 17*(3), 396–409.

Ghosh, J. (2006). Development as a Nobel Cause. *Frontline*, 94–97.

Giddens, A. (1990). *The Consequences of Modernity: The Raymond Fred West Memorial Lectures*. Stanford, CA: Stanford University Press.

Goetz, A. M. and Gupta, R. S. (1996). Who Takes the Credit? Gender, Power, and Control over Loan Use in Rural Credit Programs in Bangladesh. *World Development, 24*(1), 45–63.

Gough, I. (2004). Welfare Regimes in Development Contexts: A Global and Regional Analysis. In I. Gough and G. Wood (eds), *Insecurity and Welfare Regimes in Asia Africa and Latin America: Social Policy in Development Contexts* (pp. 15–48). Cambridge: Cambridge University Press.

Government of Bangladesh. (1991). *The Constitution of the People's Republic of Bangladesh*. Dhaka: Government of Bangladesh.

Haque, M. S. (2002). The Changing Balance of Power between the Government and NGOs in Bangladesh. *International Political Science Review, 23*(4), 411–435.

Harvey, D. (2005). *A Brief History of Neoliberalism*. Oxford and New York: Oxford University Press.

Hashemi, S. M., Schuler, S. R. and Riley, A. P. (1996). Rural Credit Programs and Women's Empowerment in Bangladesh. *World Development, 24*(4), 635–653.

Hashmi, T. I. (2003). *Failure of the Welfare State: Islamic Resurgence and Political Legitimacy in Bangladesh*. London: RoutledgeCurzon.

Hossain, N. (2012). Women's Empowerment Revisited: From Individual to Collective Power among the Export Sector Workers of Bangladesh. *IDS Working Papers, 2012*(389), 1–40.

Islam, S. S. (2001). The Politics of Islam in Bangladesh In S. C. Saha and T. K. Carr (eds), *Religious Fundamentalism in Developing Countries*. London: Greenwood Press.

Islami Bank Bangladesh Ltd. (n.d.). Concept and Ideology: Rural Financing. Retrieved from: www.islamibankbd.com/abtIBBL/cis_rural_financing.php (accessed 6 January 2012).

Islami Bank Foundation. (n.d.). Quarterly Progress Report April to June 2011. Retrieved from: http://fkprogram.org/wp-content/uploads/2011.06-IBF-Quterly-report-April-June.pdf (accessed 5 March 2012).

Jahan, R. (2005). *Bangladesh Politics: Problems and Issues*. Dhaka: The University Press.

Kabeer, N. and Mahmud, S. (2004). Rags, Riches and Women Workers: Export-oriented Garment Manufacturing in Bangladesh. In M. Carr (ed.), *Chains of Fortune: Linking Women Producers and Workers with Global Markets* (pp. 133–164). London: Commonwealth Secretariat.

Karim, L. (2004). Democratizing Bangladesh State, NGOs, and Militant Islam. *Cultural Dynamics, 16*(2–3), 291–318.

Karim, L. (2008). Demystifying Micro-credit: The Grameen Bank, NGOs, and Neoliberalism in Bangladesh. *Cultural Dynamics, 20*(1), 5–29. doi: 10.1177/0921374007088053.

Karim, L. (2011). *Microfinance and its Discontents: Women in Debt in Bangladesh*. Minneapolis: University of Minnesota Press.

Karlekar, H. (2005). *Bangladesh: The Next Afghanistan?* London: Sage.

Kearney, M. (1995). The Local and the Global: The Anthropology of Globalization and Transnationalism. *Annual Review of Anthropology, 24*, 547–565.

Khan, F. C., Ahmad, A. and Quddus, M. (2009). Preface. In F. C. Khan, A. Ahmad and M. Quddus (eds), *Recreating the Commons? NGOs in Bangladesh* (pp. xxiii–xxvii). Dhaka: The University Press.

Khan, Z. R. (2001). *From Mojib to Zia: Elite Politics in Bangladesh*. Colorado: International Academic Publishers.

Khondker, H. H. (2004). Class and State in Bangladesh: Political Economy of Authoritarian Democracy. *Journal of Bangladesh Studies, 6*, 20–34.

Khosla, N. (2009). The Ready-made Garments Industry in Bangladesh: A Means to Reducing Gender-based Social Exclusion of Women? *Journal of International Women's Studies, 11*(1), 289–303.

Kumar, A. (2009a). Jamaat and its Agenda of Islamic State in Bangladesh. *Strategic Analysis, 33*(4), 541–552.

Kumar, A. (2009b). Terror Financing in Bangladesh. *Strategic Analysis, 33*(6), 903–917. doi: 10.1080/09700160903255913.

Lewis, D. (2004). On the Difficulty of Studying 'Civil Society': Reflections on NGOs, State and Democracy in Bangladesh. *Contributions to Indian sociology, 38*(3), 299–322.

Lewis, D. and Hossain, A. (2008). A Tale of Three Villages: Power, Difference and Locality in Rural Bangladesh. *Journal of South Asian Development, 3*(1), 33–51.

Lewis, D. J. (1997). NGOs, Donors, and the State in Bangladesh. *The ANNALS of the American Academy of Political and Social Science, 554*(November), 33–45.

Madan, T. N. (1998). Secularism and its Critics. In R. Bhargava (ed.), *Secularism and Its Critics* (pp. 297–320). Delhi: Oxford University Press.

Mahmud, S. (2003). Actually How Empowering is Microcredit. *Development and Change, 34*(4), 577–605.

Maniruzzaman, T. (2001). Bangladesh Politics: Secular and Islamic Trends. In R. Ahmed (ed.), *Religion, Identity and Politics: Essays on Bangladesh*. Colorado: International Academic Publishers.

Mannan, M. (2009). Islam, NGOs and Development: The Shaping of Conflict Models in Bangladesh. In F. C. Khan, A. Ahmad and M. Quddus (eds), *Recreating the Commons? NGOs in Bangladesh* (pp. 81–106). Dhaka: The University Press.

Masjid Council for Community Advancement. (n.d.). *Annual Report 2007* (32pp.). Dhaka: Masjid Council for Community Advancement.

Mesbahuddin, T. (2010). Religion in Development: An Islamic Model Emerging in Bangladesh. *Journal of South Asian Development, 5*(2), 221–241.

Mohsin, A. and Guhathakurata, M. (2007). The Struggle for Democracy in Bangladesh. In Z. Hasan (ed.), *Democracy in Muslim Societies: The Asian Experience* (pp. 47–74). Los Angeles, CA: Sage.

Montgomery, R., Bhattacharya, D. and Hulme, D. (1996). Credit for the Poor in Bangladesh. In D. Hulme and P. Mosley (eds), *Finance against Poverty* (pp. 94–176). London: Routledge.

Muhammad, A. (2009). Grameen and Microcredit: A Tale of Corporate Success. *Economic and Political Weekly, 44*(35), 35.

Muhammad, A. (2012, May 22, 2012). RMG in Bangladesh I: Growth of Industry and Deprivation of Workers. *New Age*. Retrieved from http://newagebd.com/detail.php?date=2012-05-22&nid=11016#.UfG8dqzXuXQ (accessed 22 May 2012).

Muslim Aid. (2010). *Annual Report 2009: Microfinance and SME Programme* (48pp.). Dhaka: Muslim Aid.

Muslim Aid. (n.d.). *Cyclone SIDR Response* (27pp.). Dhaka: Muslim Aid.

Naher, A. (2005). *Gender, Religion and Development in Rural Bangladesh.* PhD thesis. Heidelberg University, Heidelberg.

Nuruzzaman, M. (2004). Neoliberal Economic Reforms, the Rich and the Poor in Bangladesh. *Journal of Contemporary Asia, 34*(1), 33–54.

Ong, A. (1999). *Flexible Citizenship: The Cultural Logics of Transnationality.* Durham, NC: Duke University Press.

Ong, A. (2006). *Neoliberalism as Exception: Mutations in Citizenship and Sovereignty.* Durham, NC: Duke University Press.

Parmar, A. (2003). Micro-credit, Empowerment, and Agency: Re-evaluating the Discourse. *Canadian Journal of Development Studies/Revue canadienne d'études du développement, 24*(3), 461–476.

Pearl, D. and Phillips, M. M. (2001). Grameen Bank, Which Pioneered Loans for the Poor, Has Hit a Repayment Snag. *Wall Street Journal, 27*(11), 01.

Pegu, M. (2011). 'Development', Capitalism, NGOs and People's Movements in Bangladesh: An Interview with Anu Muhammad. *Asia Left Observer*, 4 November. Retrieved from: http://daniellesabai1.wordpress.com/2011/04/11/development%E2%80%99-capitalism-ngos-and-people%E2%80%99s-movements-in-bangladesh-an-interview-with-anu-muhammad/ (accessed 3 June 2013).

Pitt, M. and Khandker, S. (1995). *Household and Intrahousehold Impacts of the Grameen Bank and Similar Targeted Credit Programmes in Bangladesh.* Paper presented at Credit Programmes for the Poor: Household and Intrahousehold Impacts and Programme Sustainability, Dhaka, Bangladesh.

Pitt, M., Khandker, S., Choudhury, O. and Millimet, D. (2003). Credit Programs for the Poor and the Health Status of Children in Rural Bangladesh. *International Economic Review, 44*(February), 87–118.

Prothom-Alo. (2011). Aghat Asche, Sankito Nagork Samaj (in Bengali), News report, 9 June. *Prothom-Alo*, pp. 1, 19. Retrieved from www.prothom-alo.com/print/news/160971 (accessed 9 June 2011).

Quddus, M., Ahmad, A. and Khan, F.C. (2009). An Introduction to NGOs in Bangladesh. In F. C. Khan, A. Ahmad and M. Quddus (eds), *Recreating the Commons? NGOs in Bangladesh* (pp. 3–26). Dhaka: The University Press.

Rahman, A. (1999a). Micro-credit Initiatives for Equitable and Sustainable Development: Who Pays? *World Development, 27*(1), 67–82. doi: 10.1016/s0305–750x(98)00105–3.

Rahman, A. (1999b). *Women and Microcredit in Rural Bangladesh*. Boulder, CO: Westview Press.

Rankin, K.N. (2001). Governing Development: Neoliberalism, Microcredit, and Rational Economic Woman. *Economy and Society, 30*(1), 18–37.

Riaz, A. (2003). 'God Willing': The Politics and Ideology of Islamism in Bangladesh. *Comparative Studies of South Asia, Africa and the Middle East, 23*(1–2), 301–320.

Robertson, R. (1992). *Globalization: Social Theory and Global Culture*. London: Sage.

Salmon, L. (1994). *Partners in Public Service: Government–Non-profit Relations in the Modern Welfare State*. Baltimore, MD: Johns Hopkins University Press.

Scott, J. (1990). *Domination and the Arts of Resistance: Hidden Transcripts*. New Haven, CT: Yale University Press.

Selinger, E. (2008). Does Microcredit 'Empower'? Reflections on the Grameen Bank Debate. *Human Studies, 31*(1), 27–41.

Shehabuddin, E. (1999). Contesting the Illicit: Gender and the Politics of Fatwas in Bangladesh. *Signs, 24*(4), 1011–1044.

Sobhan, R. (1997). The Political Economy of Micro-credit. In G. D. Wood and I. A. Sharif (eds), *Who Needs Credit? Poverty and Finance in Bangladesh* (pp. 131–141). Dhaka: University Press.

Stiglitz, J. E. (2002). *Globalization and Its Discontents*. New York: Norton.

Talentino, A. K. (2004). The Two Faces of Nation-building: Developing Function and Identity. *Cambridge Review of International Affairs, 17*(3), 557–575.

Tomalin, E. (2006). Religion and a Rights-based Approach to Development. *Progress in Development Studies, 6*(2), 93–108.

Van Schendel, W. (2009). *A History of Bangladesh*. Cambridge: Cambridge University Press.

White, S. C. (1999). NGOs, Civil Society, and the State in Bangladesh: The Politics of Representing the Poor. *Development and Change, 30*(2), 307–326.

Wood, G. (1997). States without Citizens: The Problem of the Franchise State. In D. Hulme and M. Edwards (eds), *NGOs, States and Donors: Too Close for Comfort* (pp. 79–92). London: Macmillan.

Wood, G. and Gough, I. (2006). A Comparative Welfare Regime Approach to Global Social Policy. *World Development, 34*(1), 1696–1712.

Wood, G. D. (2009). Clashing Values in Bangladesh: NGOs, Secularism and the Ummah. In F. C. Khan, A. Ahmad and M. Quddus (eds), *Recreating the Commons? NGOs in Bangladesh* (pp. 43–80). Dhaka: The University Press.

World Bank. (1990). *Poverty and Public Expenditure: An Evaluation of the Impact of Some Selected Government Programmes*. Washington, DC: The World Bank.

World Bank. (1995). *Bangladesh: From Stabilization to Growth*. Washington, DC: The World Bank.

World Bank. (2006a). *Bangladesh Country Assessment Strategy: 2006–2009*. Dhaka: The World Bank.

World Bank. (2006b). Economics and Governance of Nongovernmental Organizations in Bangladesh. *Bangladesh Development Series Paper No. 11*. Dhaka: The World Bank.

Yunus, M. and Jolis, A. (2003). *Banker to the Poor: Micro-lending and the Battle Against World Poverty*. New York: Public Affairs.

Zohir, S. (2004). NGO Sector in Bangladesh: An Overview. *Economic and Political Weekly* (4 September), 4109–4113.

# 3 Islamic NGOs

## New ideology and new mission in development?

The penetration of an Islamic development model into hegemonic secular development practice in the constitutionally secular state of Bangladesh is complicated. Yet Islamic NGOs have emerged as an alternative source of development providing *shari'a*-based microfinance, health and sanitation, and humanitarian assistance during natural disasters. Hence, it is imperative to explain why they emerge and what makes them different. The main aim of this chapter is to provide an insight into the ideological frameworks that inform Islamic NGOs and the way in which these frameworks inform the practice of Islamic NGOs in Bangladesh through an examination of their mission, agendas and 'successful' mobilization of rural subjects in Bangladesh. It is therefore pertinent to look at the ways in which religion and religious ideals are adopted and used in the development practices of Islamic NGOs, thus leading to an understanding of what makes them religious or Islamic. Many scholars have assumed that the people of Bangladesh would prefer a religious alternative for development support, since religion represents their inner core of life (Abecassis, 1990, p. 72; Banu, 1992; Devine and White, 2009; Hashmi, 2000; Landell Mills, 1992; Naher, 2010; Rozario and Samuel, 2010; White, 2009). Therefore, it might be asked whether these Islamic NGOs are in an advantageous position compared to their secular counterparts. Again, in a nation in which secularism is the official model of governance, a critical understanding of the emerging Islamic NGO-led model of development in Bangladesh is of crucial importance. This chapter begins with a discussion on the origin and spread of three chosen Islamic NGOs with the emphasis on the chosen programmes (e.g. humanitarian aid, *shari'a*-based microfinance and the *Hasana* programme), followed by a discussion of factors that have affected the growth and spread of Islamic NGOs (for instance, cultural proximity and sociopolitical structure), followed by a discussion on Islamic identity and its crisis in Islamic NGOs in Bangladesh.

### Islamic NGOs: making space in development practices in Bangladesh

In the first instance, this chapter needs to make it clear that this book is mostly about people's experience of development practices of NGOs, and Islamic

NGOs in particular in Bangladesh. Yet it is pertinent to explain the programmes and activities of the chosen Islamic NGOs to get some detailed information about them. The first NGO under study is Muslim Aid, a UK-based Muslim relief and development agency registered with the NGO Affairs Bureau of Bangladesh on 10 November 1991 (Registration no. NGOAB-552) (Muslim Aid, 2011, p. 46) as a Bangladesh field office of Muslim Aid UK. Muslim Aid UK[1] is one of the largest Muslim relief and development agencies providing humanitarian and emergency relief for millions in over 70 of the world's poorest countries (Muslim Aid, 2010a) with an annual budget of US$13 million (Petersen, 2012, p. 135). It was established in 1985 as a response to the African famine.[2] Muslim Aid has field offices in Bosnia, Iraq, Sudan, Somalia, Pakistan, Sri Lanka, Indonesia, Cambodia, Kenya, Gambia, Lebanon, India, Jordan and Bangladesh. Muslim Aid Bangladesh began its intervention in Bangladesh in the aftermath of the devastating tropical cyclone in 1991 which killed over 138,000 people and left as many as 10 million homeless (Muslim Aid, 2012; Phillips and Gritzner, 2007). Muslim Aid was initially involved in relief distribution for cyclone-affected people, but expanded its activities to include climate change, education and vocational training, health and sanitation, and Islamic microfinance. The activities of Muslim Aid in Bangladesh are presented in Appendix I.

The second Islamic NGO under study is the Islami Bank Foundation (IBF),[3] a subsidiary organization of Islami Bank Bangladesh Ltd,[4] which came into existence in 1991. It is registered with the Ministry of Social Welfare. It was born out of the social welfare commitment of the Bank for which it created a *Sadaqa Tahbil.*[5] The *Sadaqa Tahbil* formally emerged as an NGO, the Islami Bank Foundation, with a total fund of 38 million BDT (equal to US$4.6 million as per 30 April 2012 rates) to work in the areas of relief and rehabilitation, education and training, health and sanitation, income generation and *dawah* (preaching). A detailed list of the activities and programmes of the IBF is presented in Appendix II. This book includes the *shari'a*-based microfinance programme of the IBF funded by the Islamic Development Bank (IDB) under the *Fael Khair*[6] programme and the *shari'a*-based microfinance under the Rural Development programme (RDS) funded by the Islami Bank Bangladesh. While the IBF is responsible for managing microfinance under *Fael Khair*, microfinance under RDS is managed by the Bank itself. However, the field visit to Shyamnagar suggests that the IBF used to run the RDS programme there. Yet, to simplify, this research used both of the programmes under the banner of *shari'a*-based microfinance.

The third Islamic NGO under consideration is the Masjid Council for Community Advancement (MACCA), which began in 1999 with the efforts of Maulana Abul Kalam Azad. Inspired by the core values of Islam, MACCA, as claimed in their mission statement, strives to create an egalitarian society free from poverty, extremism and injustice by working for human security, sustainable integrated development, peace and communal harmony (MACCA, 2008). MACCA's programmes range from *zakat*-based (Islamic alms giving) microfinance programmes to education and training, orphanages, interfaith dialogue on religious harmony and HIV prevention. A detailed account of the activities of MACCA is provided in Appendix III. For the purposes of this study, I focus on the *zakat*-based community development programme called *Hasana/Parshi* through which MACCA channels *zakat* to the poor using an innovative model called *Hasana*. Since these Islamic NGOs run different programmes, I have narrowed the focus to include three different but interconnected programmes (e.g. Humanitarian Aid, Islamic Microfinance and the *Hasana* programme) of these NGOs.

### *Humanitarian aid and development*

Bangladesh is a natural disaster-prone delta, located in the lower catchment area of the Ganges and the Himalayas. Almost every year Bangladesh faces tidal surges, cyclones and flooding. As a result, it requires large initiatives both to prepare for and cope with such disasters. In such a context, initiatives from the government are not sufficient to address these problems and thus long-term rehabilitation programmes funded and implemented by non-state actors are required. However, the presence of the microcredit web of mainstream NGOs during these disasters turned out to be a burden for the rural people. For example, following the super-cyclone *Sidr* in 2007, the Government of Bangladesh had to urge NGOs to suspend their weekly instalment collection from the affected people for a period of time, since the affected people were unable to repay the loan. However, NGOs persistently wanted to collect their loans. In such a context, emergency assistance in the form of cash or food becomes critical; hence Islamic NGOs, with their interest-free and flexible credit and services for the affected people, stepped into these cyclone-affected areas (following the cyclone *Sidr* in 2007) and became very attractive options for them. This is also prevalent in the programme of activities of Islamic NGOs since, for almost all Islamic NGOs in Bangladesh, humanitarian relief activities and programmes are common and prioritized in their agendas compared to their other activities (e.g. education and skills development, health and sanitation).

As part of its disaster response, Muslim Aid Bangladesh undertook disaster assistance programmes in the super-cyclone *Sidr*-affected areas during 2007/2008. The organization implemented its disaster responses in different phases. The first phase, called 'early recovery', included a clean-up programme where human and animal bodies were buried, and debris was cleared from houses, roads, ponds and canals. Muslim Aid also supplied drinking water for 300,000 families, food for 250,000 families, emergency health services for 35,000 patients and cash for work support for 1,000 families (Muslim Aid, n.d., p. 3). In the second phase of the *Sidr* response, Muslim Aid supplied food items and non-food relief items to the victims, called 'emergency' relief. The third phase, rehabilitation, included emergency shelter construction, livelihood projects, school support programmes, mosque construction and repairs, water and sanitation support, and finally capacity-building. As part of its rehabilitation programme, Muslim Aid developed two model villages: one in Mirzaganj Upazilla in Patuakhali District where 400 shelters were set up under the name of 'Shah Paran Model Village', and the other bearing the name 'Shajalal Model Village' in Sharonkhola Upazilla in Bagerhat District. Both model villages are named after two famous Muslim saints whose tombs are located at Sylhet, a northeastern district of Bangladesh.

'Shajalal Model Village' was set up in 2008 by Muslim Aid to rehabilitate the cyclone *Sidr*-affected people in Sharonkhola in Bagerhat District. The model village consists of three smaller villages, namely Kadamtala, Lakurtala and Chal Rayenda under Sharonkhola Upazila. Six hundred permanent shelters were built in this model village. Under this model village programme, Muslim Aid also built a cluster settlement of 22 houses called 'Shajalal Polli'.

Both Muslim Aid and IBF run a major programme called *Fael Khair*, sponsored by the Islamic Development Bank (IDB). In response to the urgent need for assistance to the victims of cyclone *Sidr*, which affected the southwestern coast of Bangladesh in November 2007, and to provide long-term solutions to the recurring cyclones in this region, an anonymous donor (*Fael Khair* in Arabic) donated US$130 million to the Islamic Development Bank (IDB).[7] Out of this, US$20 million is being used to provide urgent relief in the form of agricultural support to affected farmers, fisherman and others. This Agro-Input Program is being implemented in accordance with Islamic *shari'a*. Therefore, operating NGOs are not taking any service charge or interest from the beneficiaries. Four NGOs are implementing the project: Muslim Aid, the Islami Bank Foundation, BRAC and VOSD. Unlike Islamic NGOs, BRAC does not offer any Islamic teaching among the beneficiaries.

According to Muslim Aid, the organization reached 448 villages of 13 upazilas[8] under six cyclone *Sidr*-affected districts and disbursed a total of BDT663.46 million under the *Fael Khair* Program (Muslim Aid, 2011, p. 23). The Islami Bank Foundation, along with its Rural Development Scheme from the parent Islami Bank Bangladesh Ltd, also offers *shari'a*-based microfinance. *Shari'a*-based microfinance under RDS is run by the Islami Bank's branch while other forms of microfinance programme (*Fael Khair*) are run by the Islami Bank Foundation. Under the RDS programme, they have reached 782,189 beneficiaries and disbursed BDT66,585.80 million through 208 branches in 61 districts (Islami Bank Bangladesh Ltd, n.d.). According to IBF, under the *Fael Khair* Program, they reached 77,101 beneficiaries and disbursed BDT1,984.34 million through 28 unit offices in 27 upazilas in 12 *Sidr*-affected districts up until March 2011 (Islami Bank Foundation, n.d.).

## *Islamic microfinance:* shari'a*-based financing and development initiative*

In contrast to the Grameen model of microfinance, the Islamic model of microfinance is gaining popularity among the poor. Research on the negative aspects of the Grameen model of microfinance (Goetz and Gupta, 1996; Karim, 2008; 2011, p. 72; Montgomery *et al.*, 1996; Rahman, 1999), as well as statements made by many of the officials of Islamic NGOs whom I interviewed, indicates that the conventional microcredit programmes run by secular NGOs fail to bring the desired outcome and to reach the poorest of the poor in the country. Secular NGOs provide credit to the poor (especially women) with a very high rate of interest ranging from 18 to 30 per cent (e.g. 20 per cent for Grameen Bank) (Karim, 2011, p. 72). Hence the poor are unable to repay the loan and must take out additional loans from other NGOs to repay the first loan. Therefore, they enter into a vicious circle of microcredit and subsequent poverty, with the result that conventional NGOs elevate poverty rather than alleviate it. In such a context, Islamic NGOs came forward to provide an alternative to conventional microfinance through the *shari'a*-based microfinance programme. As one of the Islamic NGO officials stated,

> If the [secular or non-Islamic] NGOs wanted to alleviate poverty, if they wanted this person to get better ... then they won't be able to continue their usury business. Rather they want to sustain their [poor women] poverty.

Muslim Aid is one of the pioneers of *shari'a*-based or Islamic microfinance in Bangladesh. Muslim Aid started its Islamic Microfinance programme in 1993 which is based on the 'Shari'a principles that emphasize equitable and justifiable resource distribution and social development' (Muslim Aid, 2010a, p. 6). Muslim Aid has two components in its *shari'a*-based micro-credit programme; one is general Islamic microfinance and the other is the Agro-based *Fael Khair* programme funded by the Islamic Development Bank. Under the general Islamic microfinance programme, Muslim Aid has thus far reached up to 69,036 families in 1,565 villages of 53 upazilas under 30 districts across the country (through 55 offices) with a total disbursement of BDT2,510.76 million (Muslim Aid, 2011, p. 23).

The Islamic microfinance products that Muslim Aid and other Islamic NGOs currently offer include the *Quard Hasana, Murabha* and *Musharaka* types of financing. The literal meaning of the Arabic term *Quard Hasan* is beautiful loan. It is a type of Islamic financing and credit delivery system which does not charge any interest. Some Islamic scholars argue that in the *Quard Hasan* system of credit delivery, the lender is also required to pay service charges or operational costs. However, this may be regarded as profit or interest, rather than as the actual operational costs (Khan, 2008). In principle, recipients are required to return the original amount they receive. In the Quran, *Quard Hasan* is mentioned several times. For example, in the Quran it states: 'Who is he that will give Allah qard al hasan? For Allah will increase it manifold to his credit' (57:11). In the *shari'a*-based microfinance programme in Bangladesh, many organizations use this mode of credit delivery system. Among the Islamic NGOs in this study, both Muslim Aid and the Islami Bank Foundation use this mode of loan delivery.

The Arabic word *Musharaka* means partnership, which in financial systems is a profit-sharing joint venture or an 'equity participation contract' (Khan, 2008, p. 13). As a type of *shari'a*-based microfinance system, it is designed for limited, long-term, production or commercial activities where the customer and credit provider contribute capital jointly and share profits or losses according to the agreed contract. Yet in the Islamic School of Legal Thought (madhhabs) they differ with regard to the ratio of profit that may be charged under *musharaka* contracts.

In the Sunni Muslim tradition there are four main madhhabs consisting of *mujtahid* (a person accepted as an original authority in Islamic law), Imams who were thus explainers, and operationalized the Quran and *Sunna* in the specific *shari'a* rulings in the lives of Muslims that are collectively known as jurisprudence (*fiqh*). These four madhhabs are Hanafi, Hanabli, Shafi and Maliki.[9] Shafi and Maliki madhhabs agree upon the sharing of profit and loss as proportional to their investment. However, the Hanafi and Hanabli madhhabs agree that the ratio could be fixed with the consent and agreement of the partners. Both Muslim Aid and the Islami Bank Foundation use this mode of loan delivery.

The Arabic word *Murabaha* means a cost-plus profit contract which is mainly used for financing assets or working capital inputs (for instance, raw materials, machinery or equipment). This is the most popular and widely used *shari'a*-based financing system due to its simple nature (Khan, 2008, p. 11). In this system of financing the bank or an organization agrees to purchase on behalf of a client who will then reimburse the bank through instalments within a stated period of time.

In all three of these sites (e.g. Bagerhat, Satkhira and Manikganj) of this research *shari'a*-based microfinance programmes have gained the most popularity. During the focus group discussions it was apparent that many people wanted to become new members of the *Islami Samity*, although the local NGO officials frequently declined due to their capacity. The branch manager for a microfinance programme of an Islamic NGO in Sharankhola told me of his struggle to attract members at the beginning, since people did not believe that the NGO would provide any interest-free credit. However, after a few years they received a high demand from the public. As he stated, 'There are many members in our organization who in their entire 50/60 years of age never took any loan from any NGOs. Now as you see, they are taking loans from us and getting benefits.' I asked again, 'Why is this so?' He simply replied, 'Because our credit is interest-free and based on Islamic ideals.' Yet rural women's participation in such microfinance and development programmes of Islamic NGOs is more complex, a subject which is discussed in Chapter 5.

## Hasana/Parshi*: a* zakat*-based Islamic model of development*

Currently, MACCA is implementing a faith-based Integrated Development, Education and Livelihood (IDEAL) village project in Manikganj District. MACCA claims that this is a comprehensive and integrated community development model. The core concept behind the IDEAL village project is *Parshi.*[10] *Parshi* is a Bengali word meaning neighbourhood or neighbour. The main motivation to use this concept, as stated in MACCA's Annual Report 2007,[11] is 'strengthening relationships among the neighbors – making them sensitive to the needs of others living in the community' (Masjid Council for Community Advancement, n.d.c, p. 13). *Parshi* is a *zakat*-[12] based programme collecting *zakat* from the rich and certain corporations; for example, Rahim Afroz (the largest energy and transport solutions industry in Bangladesh). The Annual Report for the years 2007 and 2008 termed this *zakat*-based development programme *Parshi*, while later publications termed it *Hasana*. Yet, the main idea behind the programme is the same as *Parshi*.[13] In the original *Parshi* model it was abbreviated as PARSHI, where P stands for prayer (programme component establishing *salat*), A is for assistance (establishing *zakah*), R is for rearing, raising and resourcefulness (caring), S is for societal saving (socioeconomic uplift), H stands for honesty and humanism (promotion of human qualities), and finally, I stands for investment (programme component is income generation through growth promotion) (Mesbahuddin, 2010, p. 230). Therefore the core component of the IDEAL village programme is *Parshi*. The Hasana programme in Chandirchar, Manikganj has eight such *Parshi*, involving 30 to 40 people of the same locality (neighbours) living in poverty, getting together to sort out their problems and subsequent solutions (MACCA, 2008, p. 13).

## Determining the uniqueness of Islamic NGOs in development: searching for a 'model'

One of the ways to address the emergence of Islamic NGOs is to look at the uniqueness of their development practices (e.g. the model village programmes). Islamic NGOs working in Bangladesh have institutionalized the idea of what they call the 'model village'. Therefore, the 'ideal village' of the IBF, the 'model village' of Muslim Aid and the comprehensive 'IDEAL village' (*Hasana*) of MACCA signify a thrust for a unique development model informed by the teachings and principles of Islam. This research revealed certain important characteristics of this model village, including its location, beneficiary participation in decision-making, transparency issues in distribution and management, Muslim Diaspora connections and dissatisfaction over the housing project.

The concept of a model village is not new and has frequently been used in rural development programmes in Bangladesh. However, Islamic NGOs claim that these model villages are different from conventional 'model village' programmes. One of the main ways Islamic NGOs differentiate their model village programmes is in their emphasis on religious orientation. The practice of religion is profoundly resonant for the development practice of Islamic NGOs, whether in the choice of village name, the behaviour of NGO officials or in day-to-day operations. For example, as per the operational manual of the IBF,[14] one of the stated responsibilities of programme officers is to

> provide religious teachings along with the monetary investment and inspire them [aid recipients] to observe these religious teachings to live a life as pure [*khati*] Muslims. For the beneficiaries of other religious denominations,

> [officials must] inspire them [recipients] to be of an ideal character [*adarsha chritraban*] based on the teachings of their religion.[15]

Yet other Islamic NGOs (e.g. MACCA) emphasize the creation of a caring society based on the principles of Islam (Masjid Council for Community Advancement, n.d.a).

A common feature of the 'model villages' is the practice of Islamic faith in development practices, whether designating a village and a *samity* with an Islamic name, providing Islamic teachings on site or the use of Islam in their activities. For example, Muslim Aid named its model village 'Shajalal Village' at Sharonkhola after a well-respected and famous Muslim saint Shajalal who came to Bangladesh to preach Islam, although the original names of the villages under Shajalal Model Village are Kodomtola, Chal Rayenda and Lakurtola. While I was walking to these villages, after some distance I saw a large billboard with the name of the model village, the number of shelters provided in the village and the shelter provider's name.

As I was interested to know how this model village was unique, I asked a Muslim Aid official why Shajalal was called a 'model village'. He simply replied, 'It is different from others.' Then I asked how it was different. He replied, 'No one has ever seen such a village. People who receive shelter from Muslim Aid are better than any other shelter provider (for example, BRAC, the Indian government) and people never even dreamt of such permanent settlement.' While Muslim Aid refers to the village by the name 'Shajalal', there are few official documents that mention the name of the village. The name for the model village was chosen by members of the Muslim Diaspora living in London, who are mainly from Sylhet (where Shajalal's tomb is located). The Muslim Diaspora used this name to raise funds overseas for *Sidr* victims, and used these funds to build the model village and name it after their hometown saint. The current country director of Muslim Aid argued that the name of the village does not have any importance in its work. Yet, at the local level, Muslim Aid features the name prominently on large billboards all over the villages along the main road. As one of the key informants explained,

> They give it [the village] this name, made a big display and mainly created this village along the side of this highway so that they could attract the attention of donors, the media and the government. That's because when these high officials travel on this highway, they [will see the village and] be surprised what Muslim Aid has done.

It is interesting to note that in the programmes of Islamic NGOs (e.g. the model village) as claimed by the Islamic NGOs as well as the beneficiaries, there is a shift from the profit-making business (e.g. through conventional microcredit) of conventional NGOs to serving humanity (of Islamic NGOs) through interest-free microcredit. When I asked Zhanu, an ex-member of Grameen Bank, why she had joined an Islamic NGO, she replied, 'I left [Grameen Bank] because they charge interest. We must pay interest [to Grameen Bank], since they came here to make business, thus who will pay (credit) without interest)?' This same sentiment was articulated by a Muslim Aid official in Dhaka who said, 'We came here not to make business, but to serve them'. According to Islamic NGO officials as well as beneficiaries, one of the unique elements of Islamic NGOs is their understanding of NGOs as the source of 'help and salvation (*mukti*)' – freedom from the oppression of high interest rates. Thus, the discourse that emerges from Islamic NGOs' development practice is one with an orientation towards Islamic ideology, namely to serve humanity rather than to make a business out of their NGO-ing. Whenever I asked respondents whether there is any interest of Islamic NGOs to provide free credit to them, the answer was almost the same as Zinia's, an Islamic NGO borrower, who claimed: 'They don't have any benefit, but just to serve people.'

Other Islamic NGOs emphasize innovation in their programmes. One example is the use of *zakat* in development practice (*zakat*-based microfinance). Thus the officials of MACCA claim that the IDEAL (Integrated Development, Education and Livelihood) village is one of the most unique models of development to serve the rural poor. The main uniqueness of this model is the use of *zakat* as the main source of funding, in which MACCA transfers the ownership of the money to the beneficiary. The Bengali translation of the word *zakat* (or *zakah*) means blessing, purification, increase and goodness. Technically, *zakah* is defined by a Quranic injunction as a determined portion (i.e. 2.5 per cent taken from the wealthy and allocated to the more deserving). To be clear, *zakat* is an obligatory form of alms while *sadaqa* is a spontaneous form of alms. There is another form of Islamic alms called *fitra*, which is compulsory, and is paid to the poor on the day of the breaking of the fast (*Eid-ul-Fitar*) after Ramadan. Alms giving is referred to in the Quran many times. For example, in the Surah Al-Taubah (9:103), Allah says, 'Of their goods take alms, that so you might purify and sanctify them; and pray on their behalf. Verily your prayers are a source of security for them: and God is One Who hears and knows.' *Zakat* is the third of the Five Pillars of Islam and hence rejecting it leads to disbelief, and Muslims are commanded to fight those who refrain from paying *zakat*. The Quran also says, 'And those in whose wealth is a recognized right for the (needy) who asks and him who is prevented (for some reason from asking)' (Surah Al-Ma`arij 70: 24–25).

Despite being a majority Muslim country, *zakat* collection and distribution is yet to develop systematically. Therefore, *zakat* distribution is an individual act and there is no legal framework for its institutional collection and distribution in the Bangladeshi state. This leads Islamic NGOs in general and MACCA in particular, as its programmes officer claims, to the development of a systematic way to collect *zakat* and distribute it for development. This *zakat*-based model of development is different from the secular/mainstream NGO intervention and from other Islamic NGOs' intervention in many ways. First, this is entirely *zakat* based and therefore it transfers assets (*zakat* money) to the targeted poor without any interest or service charge. Second, it corresponds to the existing social structure of rural society based on *para* or *mahalla* (neighbourhood), which is a 'single neighbourhood' which is closely tied together and celebrates both pains (e.g. natural disasters, death rituals) and pleasures (e.g. *Eid* and other religious festivals). Third, it is unique also because of its comprehensive nature which includes not only interest-free loans, but also health, sanitation, education, water supply and religious education for beneficiaries in the same single project (e.g. *Parshi*). This is, as MACCA officials claim, not available in secular NGO development practices. Finally, as MACCA hopes, if it is successful it will lead to the institutionalization of *zakat* for development practice.

One of the most important aspects, as suggested by both the officials and the beneficiaries, is the prohibition of interest in credit delivery. A significant proportion of Muslims refrain from using interest-based microfinance services for fear of breaching religious beliefs. Indeed, it is indicative from the field data that it is likely that even less religiously observant Muslims, who currently use interest-based microfinance, may prefer *shari'a*-based microfinance if available. All the beneficiaries of these NGOs whom I interviewed showed disdain towards interest. Indeed, one of the beneficiaries of the IBF at Sharonkhola reminded me that getting involved in interest is equivalent to committing incest with one's own mother.[16] Beneficiaries' understanding and subsequent strong position against interest is the result of the Islamic NGOs' mobilization of rural people against interest. It is, at the same time, important to note that being Muslim they are aware that getting into *shud* (interest) is not right. Respondents claimed that as there were no other alternatives to *shud* available to them, before the introduction of *shari'a*-based microcredit, they got involved in *shud*. But they are now even more aware of the 'punishment from Allah' and this is reinforced by the Islami *samity* not to commit such a sin. During the induction meeting and regular *samity* meetings, Islamic NGO officials focus on the implications of charging and offering interest/*riba* (in Arabic) which is strictly prohibited (*haram*) in Islam. This ultimately reinforces people's perceptions of interest or *shud*. One of the Islamic NGO officials recited a verse from the Quran about this prohibition (Surah Al-Baqarah: 275–276) during my interview with him. I also heard the recitation during the *samity* meeting regarding Islam's position about *shud* or interest. The translation is as follows: 'but God has permitted trade and forbidden usury … God will deprive usury of all blessing, but will give increase for deeds of charity: for He loves not creatures ungrateful and wicked.' All of the mainstream/secular NGOs in Bangladesh supplying credit to the poor charge a very high rate of interest. Although in some cases Islamic NGOs charge a service charge of 7.5 per cent, it is less than their secular or mainstream counterparts, as they charge between 15 and 20 per cent (e.g. Grameen Bank 20%, BRAC 15%, BUREAU 15%).[17]

The distribution of interest-free loans from Islamic NGOs similar to what Muslim Aid offers has led to an increased take-up in aid, and the data reveal a sharp rise in the number of beneficiaries of *shari'a*-based microfinance (from 257 in 1993 to 56,746 in 2009 in the case of Muslim Aid). Thus, Islamic NGOs with their interest-free credit serve two purposes: the first is avoidance of the sin of usury, and the second is the economic benefit of no interest.

It is also noteworthy that the beneficiaries of *shari'a*-based microfinance and the *zakat*-based development programme cite 'Islamic teaching' as the most important factor next to interest-free credit as their main reason to join this programme. A beneficiary of an Islamic NGO puts it this way: 'Islami Bank provides interest free loans here. The most important thing is the Quranic Teaching they give to women.' This teaching ranges from discourses around individual piety to appropriate behaviour in the public sphere, i.e. the correct performance of prayer, fasting and Quranic recitation, as well as the rights and duties as wife, husband and neighbour. Teachings also address the type of business or activity they are allowed to conduct with the money. It is imperative to ask why rural people follow such teachings. One of the obvious reasons is that they are more fearful of religion *(dhrama viru)* than religious (*dharmic)* and strive to follow a righteous religious and cultural path. At the same time this is also related to the conditions imposed by the Islamic NGOs. As one of the respondents at Tala explained, 'Islami Bank [IBF] provides the credit with certain conditions. We must pray five times a day, can't lie.' This is also echoed in the operational manual which emphasizes the 'character' [*charitra*] of the potential beneficiary in the aid selection process.

The other important aspect along with interest-free credit is the Islamic and moral training of NGO officials. I asked NGO officials where they received their motivation to serve people in a transparent and Islamic way. They referred to the initial training from these organizations when they entered the job. Since they work within the principles of Islamic teachings, they (the officials) are committed to their jobs and they tend to see their job not just as a job, but rather as a service for a greater purpose. As the operation manual of an Islamic NGO explicitly mentions, it is the very first responsibility out of the 28 responsibilities mentioned. It reads as follows: 'This work has to be taken not just as a job, but as a better worship [*Ibadat*] of Allah and a challenge. You have to dedicate yourself to the development of the poor, penniless and the oppressed.' Thus, through serving in an Islamic NGO, they are able to fulfil their duties and responsibilities as Muslims. They (Islamic NGO officials) stated that this encourages them to conduct themselves in an honest and dedicated manner towards these organizations. Therefore, all the branch managers and programme officers interviewed in this research agreed that there is no room for corruption in their organization in general, and in their respective branches in particular. However, this claim regarding honesty and corruption contradicts Ahmad's (2009, p. 196) findings which claim that religious NGOs are corrupt; for example, that bribes are offered to get funds transferred from the government, which became even worse in the case of Islamic NGOs after 9/11. For Ahmad, the other source of corruption is in the misuse and plunder of funds by religious NGO managers.

Other features, especially in the case of *shari'a*-based microfinance, that are distinct from the secular NGOs concern the flexibility in repayment or instalment (*kistee*) collection and extended grace period.[18] The repayment of credit and the subsequent approach to collect it from the beneficiaries informs the nature of coercion from the mainstream NGOs.[19] There are many sayings concerning the regular and strict repayment rules in rural areas. My respondents from all of the three locations expressed their worry and frustration. Several of the respondents at Shyamnagar and Sharonkhola shared the following saying with regard to their credit instalments:

> Brsihti pore tip tip,
> Kister Taka thik thik
>
> [Rain falls in drop by drop,
> Pay your instalments on time on time].

Contrary to the non-Islamic NGOs, Islamic NGOs have a very soft approach when collecting repayment. At the same time the ability to offer low or interest-free aid poses questions about Islamic NGOs' sources of funding (as is discussed in the next chapter). When I asked some Islamic NGO officials why they took such a soft approach, they simply replied, 'Upor theke kono chap nai', meaning 'there is no pressure from above (head office)'. The officials at Head office also said, 'we are here not to make business, but to serve people'. Hence, a strong religious motivation is a core component in their development practices. Thus, it is right to ask whether their religious orientation of development practices helped them to emerge and expand in rural Bangladesh. Is it important to have the same religious and cultural orientation between the beneficiaries and the organization for the expansion and non-resistance to the growth of these NGOs to occur? It is thus imperative to look at whether this religious or 'cultural proximity' to Bangladeshi religious culture helped these NGOs to emerge and expand without any resistance, contrary to the experience of the secular NGOs.

## Emergence of Islamic NGOs, non-resistance and cultural proximity

At some level, it is tempting to argue that since Bangladesh is a Muslim majority state, Islamic NGOs had a natural environment within which to emerge. If this is the case, then one could ask why secular NGOs preceded the development of Islamic NGOs in Bangladesh. Therefore, this simplistic explanation does not capture the complexity of the origin and spread of Islamic NGOs in Bangladesh. As this research has shown, it is imperative to focus on the reasons behind the growth of Islamic NGOs in general and *shari'a*-based microfinance programmes in particular, and why they expanded without any resistance from rural people, the clergy and religious leaders. Hence, a number of factors have been identified throughout this book to explain the emergence and spread of Islamic NGOs in Bangladesh.

The first and foremost reason for the emergence of Islamic NGOs is the same as their secular counterparts, i.e. they emerged to fill a vacuum in service provision (Devine, 2003, p. 229). Since the state is weak and hence unable to reach its poor citizens, non-state actors, including NGOs, have taken over the role of the state in service provision. Yet, the emergence of Islamic NGOs requires a more critical understanding of the popular resistance towards secular NGOs and the subsequent growth of Islamic NGOs.

Secular NGOs, particularly their policies of microcredit and women's empowerment, have produced controversy and faced a subsequent backlash from the rural traditional and religious leaders. Research on NGOs in Bangladesh has revealed conflict between secular NGOs and the rural religious elite, particularly during the 1990s (Hashmi, 2000, p. 131; Karim, 2004, pp. 292, 306; Rafi and Chowdhury, 2000, p. 20; Shehabuddin, 1999, p. 1017). However, there was no such conflict reported in the media regarding Islamic NGOs, which led me to question the reasons for non-resistance towards these organizations. Although there are many explanations of such backlashes against secular NGOs, it is clear that particular programmes of secular NGOs (e.g. women's empowerment) clashed with the traditional and religious beliefs of rural society (Devine, 2009; Naher, 2010). Thus, for example, a BRAC field officer who rides a motor bike in a rural village and parades women in front of unrelated males during street processions is anathema to rural clergy and pious Muslims. During my field visit to Shyamnagar, I listened to many popular folk sayings regarding Grameen Bank, BRAC and other major NGOs. One of these sayings describes the notion of BRAC's efforts towards women's empowerment:

> Rasta ses Truck e,
> Mayelok ses korlo BRAC e
>
> [Truck ruined the road,
> BRAC ruined the women].

Because they are aligned with Islamic religious ideals, Islamic NGOs are more easily able to operate sensitively towards Muslim beneficiaries. Therefore, 'cultural proximity' plays an important role in explaining why Islamic NGOs emerged in Bangladesh and the way in which Islam informs their work. Clarke (2008) argues that humanitarian agencies are now more aware of cultural and religious sensitivity and 'cultural authenticity' for successful relief operations. In this line, the notion of 'cultural proximity' emerged (Palmer, 2011). According to this argument it is more convenient to work with those who share the same cultural or religious background (see e.g. Benthall, 2007a; De Cordier, 2009; Palmer, 2011).

In such a context, it is important to examine whether or not the Islamic identity of both NGOs and beneficiaries has facilitated their acceptance in Bangladesh. This idea has been contested. For example, De Cordier (2009, p. 622), in agreement with Benthall (2007b, p. 7), argues, 'It is well-established that international Christian NGOs can work effectively in Christian parts of Africa through local church networks, and there is surely considerable potential for international Islamic charities to work in a similar way among Muslims.' Yet Palmer (2011, p. 106) argues with regard to Islamic Relief's activities in Bangladesh that it is 'naïve to presume that being "Muslim" will facilitate easy and effective relations between an organization and beneficiaries, an organization and host country, or between organizations' (Palmer, 2011, p. 106). Contrary to Palmer (2011), these research findings show that there are three different aspects of Muslim identity that facilitate the access, spread and implantation of Islamic NGO activities in rural Bangladesh.

First, although few officials of Islamic NGOs in this study wanted to label their organizations 'Islamic' (they preferred to call them simply humanitarian organizations), their identity as Islamic *samity* gave them an advantageous position compared to other NGOs, particularly Christian NGOs. Yet, the rural female beneficiaries believed that when a staff member from an Islamic NGO arrived in their village or house, they could more easily identify with the Islamic images and narratives that the staff member used. This confirms De Cordier's (2009, p. 614) account of international Muslim NGOs working in disaster relief on the global periphery. However, some might argue that Western donors, NGOs and Christian NGOs can also generate cultural proximity with Muslim beneficiaries through the use of Muslim staff. However, the findings of this research suggest that the trust between secular NGOs, the Western donors and the rural beneficiaries of NGOs (Islamic) has been broken, and rural people, particularly women, find it preferable to identify with the *Islami Samity*.[20]

Second, social structure plays an important role in the operation of such NGOs. The people of Bangladesh, as mentioned elsewhere following Mannan (2009, p. 98), are God-fearing Muslims or '*dharmaviru*' (religion-fearing) as opposed to the 'radical Muslim' or '*ugrapanthi*' (extremist). The rural people's lived experience of religion, which encompasses '*dharma bhiti*' (fear of religion founded on cultural fiction), has been exploited by the rural elite and the *moulivis* (religious leaders and preachers) at the micro level and by the political parties and institutions at the macro level (Mannan, 2009). Thus, at the macro level, the construction of a secular Bengali (ethno-linguist identity) and religious Bangladeshi (territorial-religious) identity was a political decision. At the macro level, in this construction of identity, the rural masses often do not participate in urban elitist secular discourse. Therefore, people's preference for *non-radical/extremist Islamic alternatives* is very natural in a social context in which people's construction of *dharma bhiti* encompasses everyday life. Thus, those who help the poor out of a sense of religious obligation are more attractive than their secular counterparts. During my visits to NGO officials (e.g. the programme manager of a Christian NGO) at Shyamnagar, they talked about rumours regarding Christian NGOs in which those organizations would take away the dead body of a Muslim beneficiary and 'convert' it to Christianity. Indeed, some of the people in the research area believed that if they accepted aid from a Christian NGO when they died, their body would be taken by the Christian NGO and stamped with a Christian seal, thus somehow converting them to Christianity.[21] Thus Rahela explained why she did not accept support from a Christian NGO:

> The money is from a Christian [NGO]. If we receive a house from CARITAS as aid, they will take away our dead body and put a Christian

> seal on it. Therefore, we will no longer remain a Muslim. Moreover, most Muslims don't want to eat in a Hindu house, but BRAC/CARITAS people do. But the Muslim Aid people never eat at anybody's house.

It is interesting to note that even in a crisis (e.g. the post-cyclone *Aila* context), religion dominates rural social structures in Shyamnagar and is intertwined in everyday lives and livelihoods. For example, one of the respondents, Feroza, who received a house from CARITAS, told me of her anxiety about accepting money from a Christian NGO. Her only son is studying in a *madrasah* (religious school) in Satkhira District town to become a *Mowulana* (religious scholar). Being the mother of a *Mowulana* and an observant Muslim, she is anxious about the uncertainty of her afterlife since receiving aid from a Christian NGO. She said, 'My son and I are now dying, thinking of what will happen to us since we have received a house from CARITAS.' Christian NGO officials thought that this rumour might have been spread by those who had failed to receive a house from CARITAS, due to its extremely fair distribution policy and management. Whenever I asked the beneficiaries of Islamic NGOs whether they had been advised by Muslim Aid and Islamic Relief staff not to get involved with Christian and other non-religious NGOs, they told me that such things did not happen there. It is still a mystery to the CARITAS staff as to who is spreading the rumour against CARITAS. In such a context of religious tension, the availability of aid from an Islamic NGO must be one of the most attractive options for rural people where there will be no fear of conversion and they can 'die in peace'.[22]

Finally, to understand the growth and acceptance of Islamic NGOs we need to explain the political construction of national identity and religion-based politics, which created increased opportunities to Islamic NGOs, even radical NGOs. By radical organization, following Clarke (2006, p. 840), I mean those which 'engage in illegal practices on the basis of faith beliefs' or, in extreme cases, engage in violent acts and use religion to justify their actions. Since the visibility and use of Islam in national political discourse has become paramount and major political parties have subsequently compromised with Islamic parties and practices in order to achieve electoral victory, the opportunity for Islamic NGOs to expand has been high. The growth of Islamic NGOs shows that most of them began their operations in the 1990s, which was the ruling period of the centre-right political party the BNP along with its Islamic allies. This is not to make a causal connection, but to argue that a supportive political infrastructure paved the way for the growth of Islamic NGOs in Bangladesh.

Alongside the religious domain and cultural proximity, other factors need to be explored to see how these NGOs have emerged and practised their development work. One of the arguments for the spread of religious NGOs is that they are cheap and cost-effective, which is also true for Islamic NGOs in Bangladesh. Working for Islamic NGOs means serving humanity (which is the slogan for Muslim Aid), and which ultimately means serving Islam. Almost all the Islamic NGO officials agreed that working for their organization has greater meaning. As an Islamic NGO employee from head office said,

> We all, from top to bottom, consider this organization as our own. Because we did not come here to do a job, but to serve, to fulfil people's demand. We're getting a benefit, too; one such benefit is that we are getting salary, promotion for our job. Second is a social commitment. Third, being a Muslim I will receive a reward for this, such a desire, such a fear drives or motivates people towards a positive direction. As a result, you will see all of my staff are dedicated as well as committed, and this is our foundation.

Those whom I interviewed claimed that because they are committed to Islam they are also 'free' from corruption. One of the Islamic NGOs referred to Quranic verse which is translated as 'You shall observe Allah; Allah is fully aware of the innermost thoughts' (Quran 5:7), which ultimately keeps him away from any corruption. This represents, at the same time, an imperative that they reduce the operational cost due to their Islamic affiliation. As one Islamic NGO official explained to me, this is why their operation costs are low and they are able to serve people for little cost:

> We have around 0.5 million mosques. So far we have trained 10,000 Imams. They reach millions of Muslims during Friday prayer sermon [*khutba*] to discuss and disseminate information on the different community development issues including HIV/AIDs. We train them once, but they work on the development for a long time. Thus you can work for millions of people with a minimum cost. This is also a unique approach in our organization.

In the above case, where there are huge numbers of volunteers (e.g. Imams at the mosque) working for Islamic NGOs (e.g. the spread of knowledge about HIV prevention), it significantly reduces their operational costs. Since these NGOs are cheap to operate, official donors (Western) also prefer to channel their funds through these NGOs. For example, Muslim Aid receives funding from the European Union (e.g. through ECHO), MACCA (for a faith-based approach to HIV/AIDS prevention) from USAID (Masjid Council for Community Advancement, n.d.; Muslim Aid, 2012).

Although Western donors (e.g. the World Bank and DFID) have engaged with the issue of religion, this has not been conducted on an equal basis among NGOs. They have mostly engaged with Christian rather than Muslim NGOs (McDuie-Ra and Rees, 2010). Therefore, the emergence of Islamic NGOs in Bangladesh is more to do with the availability of funding from the Middle Eastern Muslim states. For example, the current programme under study, the *Fael Khair* programme, is funded by an anonymous Saudi donor (IDB, 2013).[23] Most of the banned Islamic NGOs in Bangladesh are of Middle Eastern origin. Kumar (2009) claims that funds for the Islamic NGOs in Bangladesh come from countries like Libya, Abu Dhabi, Saudi Arabia, Qatar, Kuwait, Iran and Egypt. The emergence and engagement of transnational Muslim FBOs has been connected to the general increase in transnational NGOs since the Second World

War, the so-called Islamic resurgence that gave an ideological basis to these NGOs and an escalation in oil prices in 1979 (Petersen, 2012, p. 113).

The above discussion on Islamic NGOs has emphasized how the Islamic ideology informed both the development practices of Islamic NGOs and the related sociopolitical structures to explain the non-resistance and consequent growth of Islamic NGOs. The following section will focus on the construction of Islamic identity and its problems for Islamic NGOs in Bangladesh.

## Islamic identity in development: from legitimacy to crisis

In the Introduction, I defined any formal organization as Islamic, whose identity and mission are self-consciously derived from the teachings of Islam (including any subsect of it), and which operates following the Islamic principles and on a voluntary and non-profit basis. I have already discussed some of the unique characteristics that differentiate Islamic NGOs from their secular counterparts. This section will analyse visual and symbolic representations and practices of Islam in the operation of these NGOs, followed by an exploration of the crisis in Islamic identity for such organizations.

### *What makes them Islamic: visual representation*

As Pink (2007, p. 10) notes, images are 'inextricably interwoven with our personal social identities, narratives, lifestyles, cultures and societies, as well as with the definitions of history, space and truth'. The representation of such NGOs through visual images, as well as in the practices of religion in organizational operations, along with the practices of officials and beneficiaries, form the core component of the identity of Islamic NGOs. Therefore, it is imperative to explain the visual and symbolic representation of these and other NGOs which represent any religious connotation. The Islamic NGOs under study represent an Islamic identity in their logos and names. These will be explained in order. In the case of Muslim Aid,[24] the logo represents a drop of water which symbolizes life, underscored by a crescent to emphasize the fact that Muslim Aid is driven by the humanitarian spirit of Islam. In the case of the IBF, the logo represents the Arabic calligraphy of 'Bismillah ar-Rahman ar-Rahim'; i.e. in the name of Allah, the Most Beneficent and the Most Merciful. Masjid Council for Community Advancement is abbreviated to MACCA,[25] which represents the holiest city in the religion of Islam. In Bangladesh as elsewhere, one of the cherished dreams of the Muslim is to visit Macca for Hajj. The logo contains the map of Bangladesh inside the mosque. For the two local NGOs, in their logo the names in the Arabic language also represent the language of the Holy Quran; hence representing the signs and symbols of the Islamic religion. Presenting themselves in such fashion is due to their inclination to show people that they are Islamic. Yet Arabic is not the language used in Bangladesh, and most of the people in the country do not read or write Arabic. However, Muslims are required to recite the Quran in Arabic. Therefore, the writing of NGO names in Arabic gives them credibility and meaning among Muslims (Table 3.1).

*Table 3.1* Logos of Islamic NGOs

| *Muslim Aid*[a] | *IBF*[b] | *MACCA* |
|---|---|---|
| Old logo | Old logo | Masjid Council for Community Advancement |
| | Islami Bank Foundation | |
| New logo | New logo | |
| Muslim Aid Serving Humanity | Islami Bank Foundation | |

Source: Annual reports of Muslim Aid and MACCA, and IBF website.

Notes

a Muslim Aid's old logo collected from their previous annual report logo, 1999, and in 2003 they changed their logo.

b Old logo was used on the IBF website under Islamic Bank Ltd. website, until IBF have its own website.

In the case of the donor and programme under study (e.g. the Islamic Development Bank and *Fael Khair* programme), the name and logos explicitly contain Islamic connotations. In addition, most of the local, national and international Islamic NGOs working in Bangladesh represent their religious orientation through unambiguous names and logos. For example, Islamic Relief is one of the largest Islamic NGOs in the world and its logo is a symbol of a mosque with two minarets encompassing a globe, with the name of the organization in the middle. Most Islamic NGOs of Bangladeshi origin prefer to choose an Islamic name. For example, out 104 Bangladeshi Islamic NGOs, 67 have a Muslim name (e.g. Al-Fala Aam Unnayan Sangstha, Al Amin Social Welfare Organization, AL Kuba Islami Welfare Organization, Hilful Fujul Samaj Kallyan Sangstha).

Contrary to the above visual representation, Islamic NGOs included in the study were keen to demonstrate a non-discriminatory policy to the beneficiaries other than Muslim. All the NGO officials, especially at the beginning of the interviews, talked about their non-discrimination policy and showed me how they maintain this. Even in their publications they are concerned to demonstrate their openness through visual representation; for example, in the Muslim Aid Annual Report. In the 2009 Annual Progress Report of Muslim Aid on the *Fael Khair* Program, of the first three photos of beneficiaries (on page 12), two are images of Hindu women. The whole report contains 40 photos of beneficiaries. Most of them are female (33), and 16 of the photos are of Hindu women.

At one level, it is easy to ascertain the Islamic orientation of these NGOs from their unequivocal names and logos. Yet, determining the true context of these organizations' religiosity and Islamic identity is a much more complex task and requires including the impressions from both the staff members and the beneficiaries and non-beneficiaries of these NGOs, and a close observation of religious practices in the activities of these NGOs.

## *Islamic ideology or religion in practice*

As has already been argued, it is necessary to focus on the activities as well as the impressions of the staff and beneficiaries and non-beneficiaries in the study in order to explore the way in which religion or Islamic principles inform the practices of these organizations. Although it is easy to ascertain the religious orientation from the organization's unambiguous name and logo, the identification of the extent of religiosity of these Islamic NGOs is not straightforward (Palmer, 2011, p. 99). Yet this may be done through an examination of the frequency of their references to and practice of Islamic *shari'a* or Quranic injunctions in their programmes and activities, including promotional and fund-raising activities. For example, all of the three Islamic NGOs under this study frequently quoted the Quran to raise funds. One of these NGOs, in its funding appeal for the orphan children programme, known as the Children Welfare Program, talked about their frequent references to the Prophet Muhammad being an orphan both to stipulate their (NGO) responsibilities to orphans as well as for donors to give money to help the orphans. For the poverty alleviation programme, the same NGO, along with many Quranic verses, also referred to Prophet Muhammad's sayings: 'if any individual of any village wakes up in the morning having passed the night starving, Allah [SWT] does not take the responsibility of existence and protection of the village' (Masjid Council for Community Advancement, n.d., p. 8).

Muslim Aid, IBF and MACCA, within their credit programmes, provide Islamic teachings to the beneficiaries as part of the programme; for instance, providing religious education in *samity* meetings or, in the case of MACCA, Quran training as part of their *Hasana* programme. However, NGO staff at their head office said they don't have any religious programmes/teaching components in their *shrai'a*-based credit programme, while the Annual Report of the Muslim Aid's *Fael Khair* Program states: 'members will meet weekly and take part in religious, education, capacity-building and awareness promotional programs' (Muslim Aid, 2010b, p. 8). I participated in nine beneficiaries' centre meetings (*samity* meetings), which opened with a recitation from the Quran and then provided some Islamic teachings from the *Hadith* (sayings of Prophet Muhammad) and the Quran. Yet, NGO officials did not want to term it an Islamic or religious education programme. Rather they preferred the term 'moral education'.

Although a high official in Muslim Aid stated that there was no instruction given from head office to local branches to conduct moral or Islamic education, he agreed that some local branch staff members may use moral education to run their programmes more smoothly. As one of the high officials stated,

> Morality comes from religion. Actually what happens, when you give money to poor people, even if you give it to rich people, it is difficult to handle the money. When you get the money, then you will try to spend it in different ways. Even rich people, because there are lots of needs ... [therefore] if you develop the morality of people, then you know ... they may pay back the money. In that sense as morality relates to religion, in some cases our staff look at it as strategy, you know, if you follow the guidance of Islam ... then it will help to keep the morality, something like this ... but we are not preaching any Islam.

In contrast to his statement, another high official from the same organization noted,

> Actually, we had some religious education/teachings in our programme. You will see among our old beneficiaries, as a Muslim they need to know *faraj* of Odhu, at least five *surah*, necessary Islamic rules and principles. Knowing one's own religious rules and regulations means that these were our components. Afterwards, we noticed that local NGOs who run on a different concept wanted to call us fundamentalists because of these words. For this reason, we kept these activities [Islamic teachings] out of our agenda. Yet, our staffs still want to keep beneficiaries aware of these issues.

As a sister concern of the Islami Bank Bangladesh Limited, it is obvious that the IBF runs under *shari'a* principles. One of the high officials of the IBF does not see any problem being identified as an Islamic organization and referred to the exponential growth in Islamic banking throughout the country.[26] He particularly mentioned three aspects of their development programmes, namely economic, social and spiritual. With regard to spiritual development, he emphasized the issues of day-to-day affairs (e.g. the duty of a wife to her husband, how she should behave). During the interview with him he cited an example of one of his beneficiaries from Barishal who became happier in her conjugal life after joining the IBF. This was possible, he claimed, because of the IBF's teachings of Islam. Among the three NGOs under study, MACCA is the one who in all its circulations mentioned that it is a faith-based organization. In its mission statement for its 2010 Annual Report, the organization claims,

> MACCA is faith-based development, humanitarian and campaigning organization working for human security, sustainable integrated development, peace and communal harmony. Inspired by the core values of Islam, MACCA strives for creating an egalitarian society free from poverty, extremism and injustice.

During the visit to the Head of the NGO in Dhaka and the field office in Manikganj, officials of the NGO emphasized the teachings of Islam in their activities. One of the field officers told me,

> Those who used to do interest-based activities are now doing profit-based business. Along with this, [MACCA is] providing Islamic education, hygiene education and moral development for them.

During interviews with one of the high-level officials of the Islami Bank Foundation who is also involved in the management of the *Fael Khair* Program and the Rural Development Scheme (RDS), I spent the whole day from 10 a.m. to 7 p.m. at this office. During my stay, I observed the activities of the officials. They offered prayers three times in a group (*Jamaat*) along with their director and following each prayer time there was a discussion (*boyan* in Bengali) from the *Hadith* and the Quran. Here the intention is not to explain individual piety, but this research is instead interested in the religious practices of the organization as it relates to the Islamic identity of that organization.

At the beneficiary level, Islamic identity was more important. For the beneficiaries the common name for these three organizations under investigation is *Islami samity*.[27] Whatever they may call themselves in head office or in the official documents, for the rural people these NGOs are just *Islami samity*, though in certain cases some of the interviewees mentioned the name of the NGO (e.g. Muslim Aid, Islami Bank rather than IBF and Masjid Council). Yet, during the interviews and stays in these areas, people always labelled these NGOs as *Islami samity*, and even many beneficiaries could not tell me the name of the NGO from where they received humanitarian help or *shari'a*-based microfinance. They just knew that they received assistance from *Islami samity*.

During participation in the *samity* meetings, I observed that when the field officer arrived at the centre, he entered saying loudly, '*As Salamu Alikum*' (Peace be upon you). My experience from observing many secular NGO meetings in my native village in the 1990s as well as from a research report (Naher, 2010, p. 319) was that women would stand up and salute the young sirs (NGO officers). Contrary to the mainstream secular NGO fieldworkers, Islamic NGO officials approach women in an Islamic way. Moreover, women tend to call the Islamic NGO field officer *bhi* (brother) contrary to sir for the secular NGO field officer. Some women still call the Islamic NGO officials 'sir' due to their long practice with the word for secular NGO officials during their involvement with such NGOs. The different (Islamic) way of approaching women or beneficiaries also made them distinctive. Therefore, from approaching the beneficiaries to running the programme activities, the practice of Islam is very explicit, which a beneficiary called Bokul of the IBF at Sharankhola expressed in the following way:

> First they ask us to recite *surah*, and then they discuss some Islamic topics. They talk about the prophets and the rights of a wife towards her husband, what to do, and not do, and give *salam* to others. How to offer prayer? They

> correct our *surah* ... behave nicely, talk about Allah ... therefore, we practise more prayer and fasting than before.

Some beneficiaries even went further to describe the intentions of such NGOs. As a MACCA beneficiary at Manikganj explained:

> We know that they came from a Muslim country to teach us prayer and Islamic teachings. Since the people of our region are illiterate, they came to teach us prayer and Islamic teachings and to bring us to the path of Islam.

Thus an Islamic identity and practice and the prescription of Islam from these NGOs have a profound impact upon strengthening the Islamic identity of the rural population through religious duties (e.g. prayer, fasting), behaving in a certain way and leading an Islamic lifestyle.

## Crisis, hesitation and problems in Islamic identity

Construction and deconstruction of the Islamic identity of the organization and its beneficiaries reflect the crisis, hesitation and uncertainty at the organizational and grassroots level. During the fieldwork, none of the Islamic NGOs wished to identify themselves as 'Islamic', since they work with both Muslims and non-Muslims. During the interview with one of the high-level officials at Muslim Aid he emphasized the issue of justice when it came to the question regarding the role of religion or Islam in their identity. He stated, 'Islam is important in our motivation, but as an international NGO we do not discriminate.' Other Islamic NGOs did not even want to talk about the issue of Islamic identity (e.g. the Islami Bank Foundation, MACCA, AMWAB). They were more inclined to show what they stated were their unbiased development activities. This book has used 'self-identification'[28] methodology, meaning whether the organization considers itself to be a religious NGO and therefore 'whose identity and mission are self-consciously derived from the teachings of one or more religious or spiritual traditions' (Berger, 2003, p. 16). In the case of the Islamic NGOs under study, their self-identity is unambiguous, at least in their names and logos, and frequent references to the Quran and *Hadith* in their programmes, agendas and activities (Berger, 2003; Petersen, 2012). However, these NGOs were not comfortable with being identified or labelled as Islamic NGOs. This discomfort could be a result of strict surveillance by the state.

### *State surveillance and perceived threat: war crime, Islamist and Jamaat connections*

The current centre-left government led by the Bangladesh Awami League, after resuming power in December 2008 through a landslide electoral victory, has exposed its strict crash programme to hunt Islamic militants as one of their election manifestos. Recent actions of the Awami League government and its predecessor caretaker government took action against the country-wide terror bombing by the militant Islamic group Jamaatul Mujaheden Bangladesh (JMB) in 2005, and subsequently executed some of the top Islamic militants. At the same time, the stricter commitment of the present government to bring secularism back to the Constitution and send war criminals for trial has produced anxiety among Islamic political parties. Since Islamic NGOs are also connected with Islamic political parties, as in the case of IBF and MACCA, it became a source of worry to have an Islamic identity. From several news reports, it was evident that there were allegations against Islamic NGOs working in Bangladesh for their alleged connections with the Islamist militants through funding. The *Daily Star* and *New Age* have reported on this alleged terrorist funding and listed suspected Islamic NGOs.[29] Therefore, the present government has announced a more intense scrutiny of the sources of foreign funds of NGOs, since the present Finance Minister A. M. A. Muhith believes that 'there are some investments in the country that patronise militant activities'. He also stated, 'When Mr Mujahid [Ali Ahsan Mohammad Mojahid, Jamaat-e-Islami, Secretary General and former social welfare minister] was in charge a number of new NGOs popped up.... If we look into these NGOs, we might get to know something (*Daily Star*, 2009).

As was mentioned elsewhere, a dividing line between the secular and pro-Islamic political party and its supporters has become so explicit that when a secular party is in power there is a perceived threat among the pro-Islamic party. This crisis in identity therefore lies at the nexus between secular and religious issues in national politics. The national discourse on secularism is complex where all major political parties use religion for political legitimacy and electoral victory. Moreover, the issue of secularism, one of the four fundamental principles of the state as per the 1972 Constitution, was subsequently amended by the military regime. Use of religion in politics and the subsequent division of the polity into a secular and religious block (e.g. the Awami League as pro-secular and the BNP as pro-Islamic) led to a flexibility in operations during BNP rule and to a tightening of Awami rule. The pro-Islamic party often blames the secular political party for destroying Islam; the pro-Islamic party portrays itself as the vanguard of Islam while the pro-secular party blames its counterpart for nurturing Islamist militants.

At the same time, international pressures, particularly after 9/11, ensure that the Bangladesh government does not harbour any Islamic fundamentalist or terrorist organizations (Ahmad, 2009, pp. 188–189). Therefore, in recent times we have seen the Bangladeshi government sign treaties with the USA, and particularly with India, to curb terrorism[30] and Islamic militancy. For example, during the recent visit of the US Secretary of State Hillary Rodham Clinton, the Bangladeshi Prime Minster assured Secretary of State Clinton of her zero tolerance policy towards terrorism (*Daily Star*, 2012b). Moreover, some western donors have disbursed aid for Bangladesh only on the condition that it does not shelter any Islamic terrorist organizations (Ahmad, 2009). In such a context, state surveillance becomes an issue in exposing the Islamic identity of these NGOs.

Therefore, the Islamic identity of these NGOs, has been a source of worry for the officials who work for them and the beneficiaries who receive loans or other services from them. This anxiety was manifested at all levels from top to bottom of the NGO administration. Yet NGO fieldworkers, particularly branch managers-in-charge, were the ones facing the most problems. The main concern over this anxiety was their alleged connection with the Islamist militants and Jammat-e-Islam, the right-wing and the largest Islamic political party in Bangladesh. Whenever I asked NGO field officials they told me of their concerns over police and detective interrogations. The branch managers of Islamic NGOs at Sharonkhola talked about their concerns over police interrogation. During their interrogations, they had to give details of their activities, funding and with whom they worked. The branch manager of an Islamic NGO at Sharonkhola stated,

> We do have the same pressure, too. We have the problem with our Islam, where there is morality, there comes the most hit ... there is no such torture on others [BRAC] ... what we have on Muslim NGOs ... NSI [National Security Intelligence] has interrogated me for two to two and half hours ... he showed me a list and through me they tried to know whether I know about OMAI, Islamic Relief, Islamic Aid.... They have surveillance over Islami Bank ... Muslim Aid too.

This was almost the same statement I got from other local Islamic NGO officials in three of the study areas. Moreover, at the beneficiary level, some of them were concerned about problems in identifying themselves as beneficiaries of such NGOs. For example, one beneficiary of MACCA named Jamiruddin put it this way: 'They think we belong to Jamaat, but we are not. That's why many people mistrust us. They tend to think someone belongs to Jamaat, if they wear a cap.' However, many respondents told me that they are linked to or supporters of Jamaat. For example, an IBF beneficiary at Shyamnagar claimed that 'Especially those who support Jamaat-e-Islam, they are in this organization ... most of them ... you can say 80 per cent'. Contrary to this beneficiary, the IBF official at Sharonkhola disagreed regarding the number of Jamaat supporters; rather he focused on their Hindu beneficiaries. I heard the same argument from a Hindu member, Bithi at Sharonkhola, who said, 'We [Hindu and Muslim] are human beings, and live in the same area, hence we didn't believe that the Islamic NGOs would discriminate against us'. Yet other beneficiaries (e.g. Nahar of IBF at Satkhira) referred to their connection with Jamaat. Because of the connection with Jamaat, they trust the IBF. In response to the question why she trusted IBF, she simply replied, 'They are the supporter of Jamaat and we are also the supporter of Jamaat'.

Yet some among the non-beneficiaries and key informants offered mixed impressions of the alleged connection of these Islamic NGOs with Jamaat Islam and any other militant outfit. One of the key informants at Sharonkhola told me, 'we have proof that they are having connections with a particular political party [Jamaat] and they give preference to the supporter of this particular political party in aid delivery'. On the contrary, a beneficiary of a secular NGO gave me her impressions, saying:

> I did not get any aid from them … I don't know much about them. But, I think, they give mostly to the Jamaat supporter. [I asked her: Why does she think so?] Because our *hozur* [a term used to identify a religious scholar] runs the *samity*. His wife is also a *rukun* [member] of Jamaat.

However, I was interested to see how secular NGOs perceive the activities of Islamic NGOs (for example, whether these Islamic NGOs are connected with any radical political party or religiously biased). One of the respondents who is a high official of a local NGO in Shyamnagar told me 'I am not sure about their connection with Jamaat, but they might have religious bias in case of beneficiary selection'. Contrary to this opinion, a secular NGO official in Sharonkhola gave an interesting insight which represents a professional commitment not to comment on other NGOs (i.e. Islamic NGOs). When I asked him to comment on the Islamic NGOs, he replied: 'I am sorry, I can't comment on them [Islamic NGOs]. We work in the same area. We are colleagues. It is out of my professional ethic to comment.'

The recent issue of the war crime trials held by the International Crimes Tribunal (ICT) needs attention in this regard. ICT was set up by the present government to try those who were involved in the war crimes of 1971 during the independence struggle of Bangladesh. Subsequently, some of the top leaders of Bangladesh Jamaat-e-Islam were arrested for trial as they are alleged to have been involved in war crimes. Some of them have already received death sentences. Although none of the officials of IBF was directly involved in war crimes, their Jamaat connection makes them vulnerable. People who run the Islami Bank also run IBF, and belong to Jamaat. In the case of MACCA, the Chairman of the NGO, Abul Kalam Azad, was accused of war crimes and subsequently received a death sentence from the war crime tribunal. He was a *rokun* (member) of Bangladesh Jamaat-e-Islam who fled the country on 4 April 2012 after the ICT issued an arrest warrant against him. In the case of Muslim Aid, a recent newspaper report[31] shows that Chowdhury Mueen-Uddin who lives in London, is director of Muslim spiritual care provision in the NHS, a trustee of the major British charity Muslim Aid and a central figure in setting up the Muslim Council of Britain

> was allegedly the 'operation-in-charge' of the killings of intellectuals during the Liberation War … led the Dhaka unit of Al Badr, one of the forces created to help the Pakistani occupation army and opposed the pro-liberation forces during the war.
>
> (*Daily Star*, 2012a)

The main argument of this chapter is that there is an effort by Islamic NGOs to reconstruct Islamic identity at the grassroots level through the spread of

Islamic practices in their development models. This chapter has revealed that the Islamic ideological orientation of these NGOs informs the development practices of Islamic NGOs. Islamic NGOs develop and adopt particular ways to act, run and implement their programmes among rural people, whether through naming a particular village in an Islamic way, or using an Islamic ideals-based financial system or a *zakat*-based programme. This chapter has also established that due to the religious/cultural proximity of Islamic NGOs with Bangladeshi religious culture, it is easy for the Islamic NGOs to expand as well as succeed in their programme activities. Thus Islamic NGOs are in an advantageous position compared to their secular counterparts due to their Islamic identity. However, this chapter has also revealed the way in which there are contradictions in identity at the organizational level resulting from polarization in the national political discourse into Islamic vs. secular. Contradictions in identity were revealed as well with the recent rise of militant Islam, the consequent labelling of Islamic NGOs as funders of extreme militants or having connections to Jamaat by the media and secular intelligentsia and subsequent stricter state surveillance.

## Notes

1 For details on the activities of Muslim Aid UK, see www.muslimaid.org/.

2 For details on the origin, see 'Speech by Sir Iqbal Sacranie, Chairman, Muslim Aid' on the occasion of its Twenty-fifth Anniversary held in London, UK, available at www.muslimaid.org/index.php/media-centre/25th-anniversary/launch-speech/409-speech-sir-iqbal-sacranie (accessed 27 April 2012).

3 For a detailed account of the Islami Bank Foundation see www.islamibankbd.com/foundation/preface.php.

4 Islamic Bank Bangladesh Limited is the first Islamic Financial institution in Bangladesh as well as in Southeast Asia. It was established on 13 March 1983. It is run strictly by Islamic *shari'a* principles. For details, see www.islamibankbd.com/index.php.

5 *Sadaqa* is an Islamic term which means voluntary charity, and *Tahbil* means fund; hence *Sadaqa Tahbil* stands for voluntary charity fund. There are numerous *hadits* (sayings of the Prophet Muhammad) on *Sadaqa* in Islam.

6 *Fael Khair* is run by the Jeddah-based Islamic Development Bank, while four Bangladeshi NGOs – BRAC, VOSD, Muslim Aid and the Islami Bank Foundation – have implemented this programme in the 12 cyclone *Sidra*-affected districts of Bangladesh since 2008.

7 The anonymous donation of US$130 million for the cyclone *Sidr* victims was made by a Saudi citizen through the Islamic Development Bank based in Saudi Arabia. It is the single largest donation ever made by an individual to Bangladesh. Source: The Financial Express, available at www.thefinancialexpress-bd.com/more.php?news_id=105624 (accessed 1 May 2012).

8 The upazilas/thanas are the second lowest tier of a four-tiered local government in Bangladesh. These include divisions (seven), districts (64), upazilas/thanas (509) and union parishads (4,466) (Bangladesh Bureau of Statistics, 2011).

9 The Hanafi madhhab (named after the Persian scholar Abu Ḥanifa an-Nu'man ibn Thabit, 699–767) is the predominant school in South Asia, Central Asia, the Caucasus, the Balkans and Turkey. Maliki madhhab was founded by Malik bin Anas (711–795) and was followed mostly in North Africa, West Africa, the United Arab Emirates, Kuwait, parts of Saudi Arabia, Oman and many Middle Eastern countries,

as well as parts of India. Abu Abdillah Muhammad ibn Idris al-Shafi'i (767–820) founded Shafi'i madhhabs. Ahmad bin Muhammad bin Hanbal Abu `Abd Allah al-Shaybani (780–855) founded the Hanbali madhhab.

10 Recently, MACCA changed the name of the group model from *Parshi* to *hasana*. *Hasan* means best deeds. Although they have changed the name of the group, the motto and objectives of the programme remain the same. Through personal communication with one of the officials at MACCA I came across a clash over the concept and model of *Parshi* with regard to whether Dr S. M. Ali Akkas of the Policy Leadership Unit of the Ministry of Women's and Children's Affairs of the Government of Bangladesh first conceived the idea.

11 During my field visit in June 2010 to February 2011, this was the latest available Annual Report.

12 *Zakat*, sometimes *Zakah*, is one of the Five Pillars of Islam. Literally, *Zakat* means growth and development since in providing *zakat* to the needy, Allah will increase one's wealth. However, *zakat*-eligible Muslims are obliged to give 2.5 per cent of their possessions (surplus wealth) to charity, generally to the poor and needy.

13 The *Parshi* Model of development was developed by Akkas (n.d.), and MACCA has been implementing this since the beginning (Meshbauddin, 2010).

14 I obtained the operational manual in printed form from one of the high officials of the IBF at their Dhaka office.

15 The Bengali word *charitra* (character in English) has great significance and is a very important component in religious education. To be a *charitraban* [good character], one must possess virtues such as respectful conduct, honesty, kindness, modesty, chastity, patience and forgiveness.

16 When I asked her why she became involved with *shari'a*-based microfinance, she replied: 'Don't you know that getting involved in interest is equivalent to committing incest with one's own mum?' Upon return from the field, I checked whether there is any such thing in the Quran or *Hadiths* and found the following in the *Hadiths* narrated by Abu Hurayrah: 'The Prophet, peace be on him, said: "Riba has seventy segments, the least serious being equivalent to a man committing adultery with his own mother" ' (Ibn Majah, cited in Chapra, 2006, p. 11).

17 These data are based on an interview with one of the high officials of an Islamic NGO.

18 Grace period is the time allowed to a beneficiary for the non-payment of an instalment after receiving credit; for example, instalments for the conventional NGO start just after the beneficiaries receive the loan, while in the case of *shari'a*-based microfinance beneficiaries receive 15 to 30 days' grace before the first instalment is due.

19 Details on coercion by secular NGOs and the Islamic alternative will be the focus of Chapter 6.

20 During my interviews with the female beneficiaries of microfinance programmes of the Islamic NGOs and particularly the Islamic Bank Foundation and Muslim Aid's programme beneficiary, I have called these NGOs the '*Islami samity*' rather than calling them Muslim Aid or IBF.

21 During my field visit at Shyamnagar, I also consulted with Christian NGOs like CARITAS. I had a meeting with five field officers and a programme manager at Masudermor, under Nil Domor of Shyamnar, where they expressed their thoughts on the people's concern about conversion to Christianity among rural Muslims in that area on 5 August 2010.

22 This is one of the cherished desires among Muslims that they want to die in peace. Thus 'Shanti te Morte Chai' (die in peace) expressed by the women in Shyamnagar depicts their acute concern about the activities of Christian NGOs as well as their piety.

23 According to the IDB (2013), 'an anonymous donor (*Fael Khair* in Arabic) has entrusted to the Islamic Development Bank (IDB) a generous donation of US$130

million' for cyclone *Sidra* victims in Bangladesh. None of the official documents I came across mentioned the country of origin of this donor. Yet my respondents from IDB and Islamic NGOs told me the donor was from Saudi Arabia, though some of my respondents said he was from the Middle East.

24 In 2003 Muslim Aid decided to update its logo to reflect the growth and success that Allah has bestowed upon its humanitarian work. Muslim Aid's logo reflects our humble intention to serve God by 'serving humanity'. People, of course, remain at the heart of our effort to save lives, alleviate suffering and to combat abject poverty and injustice. But it is humanity that we are seeking to reach out to, regardless of race, religion, nationality or gender. The drop of water that is at the centre of Muslim Aid's logo symbolizes life, underscored by the crescent to emphasize the fact that we are driven by the humanitarian spirit of Islam. The green colour represents hope and joy, and in many Muslim cultures is associated with Islam (quoted in www.muslimaid.org/index.php/child-sponsorhip-rf/5-where-we-work/639-a-new-look-for-muslim-aid-on (accessed 2 April 2012).

25 The Bengali word Macca is spelled Mecca in English. It is the birthplace of the Prophet of Islam Muhammad and a site where the verses of the Holy Quran were ascribed to the Prophet Muhammad. Mecca is regarded as the holiest city in the religion of Islam, and a pilgrimage to Mecca known as the Hajj is *farge* (obligatory) upon all Muslims who can afford it.

26 This interview was conducted with one of the high officials of an Islamic NGO in his office at Dhaka on 14 December 2010. This was one of the longest interviews in my field research.

27 As per the guidelines of credit disbursement, all NGO beneficiaries are grouped around a certain *samity* (association in English). Every *samity* has around 30 to 40 members who are divided into groups or five or six, to ensure maximum accountability and loan repayment. A *samity* is generally located in one of the beneficiary's houses/premises known as a centre. In every *samity* there is a centre leader and deputy leader.

28 For a detailed discussion on self-identification, see Benedetti (2006); Berger (2003); Petersen (2012).

29 See the details on Islamic NGOs and terror funding at www.atimes.com/atimes/South_Asia/GI22Df01.html, www.ctc.usma.edu/posts/the-funding-methods-of-bangladeshi-terrorist-groups, www.thedailystar.net/newDesign/news-details.php?nid=80287.

30 During several meetings at ministerial level, Bangladesh and India denounced extremism, violence and terrorism, and agreed to cooperate proactively in combating terrorism, as well as agreeing to complete the long-awaited extradition treaty at the earliest opportunity (Bhattacharya, 2012).

31 Mohammad Abdul Hannan Khan, chief investigator of the International Crime Tribunal in Bangladesh, told the Bangladeshi English daily newspaper the *Daily Star* that 'We have made substantial progress in the cases against them [Chowdhury Mueen-Uddin and Ashrafuzzaman Khan].... It could take a couple more months to move the charges [to the International Crime Tribunal]' (*Daily Star*, 2012a). However, he denied all the allegations against him, terming them as 'politically motivated' and false. This news also appeared in major newspaper in the UK. For details, see Daily Mail Online, 15 March 2012 at www.dailymail.co.uk/news/article-2130108/British-Muslim-leader-faces-war-crimes-charges-Bangladesh-possible-death-penalty-hes-convicted.html (accessed 8 May 2012); *Sunday Telegraph* print version of 16 April 2012 or the Telegraph at http://blogs.telegraph.co.uk/news/andrewgilligan/100151195/chowdhury-mueen-uddin-to-be-charged-with-war-crimes-5/ (accessed 8 May 2012).

## References


Abecassis, D. (1990). *Identity, Islam, and Human Development in Rural Bangladesh.* Dhaka: The University Press.

Ahmad, M.M. (2009). For God's Sake: The Religious Non-governmental Organizations in Bangladesh. In F. C. Khan, A. Ahmad and M. Quddus (eds), *Recreating the Commons? NGOs in Bangladesh* (pp. 183–206). Dhaka: The University Press.

Banu, U. A. B. R. A. (1992). *Islam in Bangladesh.* Leiden, The Netherlands: E. J. Brill.

Benedetti, C. (2006). Islamic and Christian Inspired Relief NGOs: Between Tactical Collaboration and Strategic Diffidence? *Journal of International Development, 18*(6), 849–859.

Benthall, J. (2007a). Islamic Charities, Faith-based Organizations, and the International Aid System. In J. Alterman and K. von Hippel (eds), *Understanding Islamic Charities.* Washington, DC: CSIS Press.

Benthall, J. (2007b). The Overreaction against Islamic Charities. *ISIM Review, 20*, 6.

Berger, J. (2003). Religious Nongovernmental Organizations: An Exploratory Analysis. *Voluntas: International Journal of Voluntary and Nonprofit Organizations, 14*(1), 15–39.

Bhattacharya, P. (2012). Dhaka, Delhi Agree to Sign Extradition Treaty. *Daily Star.* Retrieved from http://archive.thedailystar.net/newDesign/news-details.php?nid=233275.

Chapra, M. U. (2006). The Nature of *Riba* in Islam. *The Journal of Islamic Economics and Finance, 2*(1), 7–25.

Clarke, G. (2006). Faith Matters: Faith-based Organisations, Civil Society and International Development. *Journal of International Development, 18*(6), 835–848. doi: 10.1002/jid.1317.

Clarke, G. (2008). Faith-based Organisations and International Development: An Overview. In G. Clarke and M. Jennings (eds), *Development, Civil Society and Faith-based Organisations: Bridging the Sacred and the Secular.* Basingstoke: Palgrave Macmillan.

Daily Star. (2009). NGOs under Scanner for Funding Militancy. Available at www.thedailystar.net/newDesign/news-details.php?nid=8028 (accessed 3 January 2011).

Daily Star. (2012a). War Crimes Probe Targets 'Butchers': Charges to be Pressed Against Chowdhury Mueen-Uddin, Ashrafuzzaman in 2 months. Available at www.thedailystar.net/newDesign/archive.php?date=2012-04-16 (accessed 14 August 2012).

Daily Star. (2012b). Zero Tolerance for Terrorism: Hasina assures Hillary. Available at www.thedailystar.net/newDesign/news-details.php?nid=232915 (accessed 6 May 2012).

De Cordier, B. (2009). Faith-based Aid, Globalisation and the Humanitarian Frontline: An Analysis of Western-based Muslim Aid Organisations. *Disasters, 33*(4), 608–628.

Devine, J. (2003). The Paradox of Sustainability: Reflections on NGOs in Bangladesh. *The ANNALS of the American Academy of Political and Social Science, 590*(1), 227–242.

Devine, J. (2009). Organizational Success and the Informal Politics of Social Change. In F. C. Khan, A. Ahmad and M. Quddus (eds), *Recreating the Commons? NGOs in Bangladesh* (pp. 107–128). Dhaka: The University Press.

Devine, J. and White, S. (2009). *Religion, Politics and the Everyday Moral Order in Bangladesh.* University of Birmingham, International Development Department, Religions and Development Research Programme.

Goetz, A. M. and Gupta, R. S. (1996). Who Takes the Credit? Gender, Power, and Control over Loan Use in Rural Credit Programs in Bangladesh. *World Development, 24*(1), 45–63.

Hashmi, T. I. (2000). *Women and Islam in Bangladesh*. Basingstoke and London: Macmillan.

IDB. (2013). The Program. Available at http://fkprogram.org/the-program/ (accessed 24 June 2013).

Islami Bank Bangladesh Ltd. (n.d.). Rural Developement Scheme. Available at www.islamibankbd.com/prodServices/rdsScheme.php (accessed 24 June 2013).

Islami Bank Foundation. (n.d.). Quarterly Progress Report April to June 2011. Available at http://fkprogram.org/wp-content/uploads/2011.06-IBF-Quterly-report-April-June.pdf (accessed 5 March 2012).

Karim, L. (2004). Democratizing Bangladesh State, NGOs, and Militant Islam. *Cultural Dynamics, 16*(2–3), 291–318.

Karim, L. (2008). Demystifying Micro-credit: The Grameen Bank, NGOs, and Neoliberalism in Bangladesh. *Cultural Dynamics, 20*(1), 5–29. doi: 10.1177/0921374007088053.

Karim, L. (2011). *Microfinance and its Discontents: Women in Debt in Bangladesh*. Minneapolis: University of Minnesota Press.

Khan, A. A. (2008). Islamic Microfinance: Theory, Policy and Practice. Available at http://reference.kfupm.edu.sa/content/i/s/islamic_microfinance_theory__policy_and__84883.pdf (accessed 9 April 2012).

Kumar, A. (2009). Terror Financing in Bangladesh. *Strategic Analysis, 33*(6), 903–917. doi: 10.1080/09700160903255913.

Landell Mills, S. P. (1992). *An Anthropological Account of Islamic Holy Men in Bangladesh*. Unpublished Ph.D. thesis, University of London.

Mannan, M. (2009). Islam, NGOs and Development: The Shaping of Conflict Models in Bangladesh. In F. C. Khan, A. Ahmad and M. Quddus (eds), *Recreating the Commons? NGOs in Bangladesh* (pp. 81–106). Dhaka: The University Press.

Masjid Council for Community Advancement. (n.d.a). *Annual Report 2008*. Dhaka: Masjid Council for Community Advancement.

Masjid Council for Community Advancement. (n.d.b). *Annual Report 2007* (p. 32). Dhaka: Masjid Council for Community Advancement.

Masjid Council for Community Advancement. (n.d.c). *Annual Report 2009–10* (p. 42). Dhaka: Masjid Council for Community Advancement.

McDuie-Ra, D. and Rees, J. A. (2010). Religious Actors, Civil Society and the Development Agenda: The Dynamics of Inclusion and Exclusion. *Journal of International Development, 22*(1), 20–36.

Mesbahuddin, T. (2010). Religion in Development: An Islamic Model Emerging in Bangladesh. *Journal of South Asian Development, 5*(2), 221–241.

Montgomery, R., Bhattacharya, D. and Hulme, D. (1996). Credit for the Poor in Bangladesh. In D. Hulme and P. Mosley (eds), *Finance against Poverty* (pp. 94–176). London: Routledge.

Muslim Aid. (2010a). *Annual Report 2009: Microfinance and SME Programme* (48pp.). Dhaka: Muslim Aid.

Muslim Aid. (2010b). *Fael Khair Program for Victims of SIDR Cyclone in Bangladesh: Annual Progress Report (May–December 2009)* (32pp.). Dhaka: Muslim Aid.

Muslim Aid. (2011). *Annual Report 2010: Microfinance and SME Programme* (58pp.). Dhaka: Muslim Aid.

Muslim Aid. (2012). *Annual Report 2011* (52pp.). Dhaka: Muslim Aid.

Muslim Aid. (n.d.). *Cyclone SIDR Response* (27pp.). Dhaka: Muslim Aid.

Naher, A. (2010). 'Defending Islam and Women's Honour against NGOs' in Bangladesh.

*Women's Studies International Forum, 33*(4), 316–324. doi: 10.1016/j.wsif. 2010.02.005.

Palmer, V. (2011). Analysing Cultural Proximity: Islamic Relief Worldwide and Rohingya Refugees in Bangladesh. *Development in Practice, 21*(1), 96–108.

Petersen, M. (2012). Islamizing Aid: Transnational Muslim NGOs after 9.11. *Voluntas: International Journal of Voluntary and Nonprofit Organizations, 23*(1), 126–155. doi: 10.1007/s11266–011–9185–5.

Phillips, D. A. and Gritzner, C. F. (2007). *Bangladesh.* New York: Infobase Publishing.

Pink, S. (2007). *Doing Visual Ethnography* (2nd edn). London: Sage.

Rafi, M. and Chowdhury, A. M. R. (2000). Human Rights and Religious Backlash: The Experience of a Bangladeshi NGO. *Development in Practice, 10*(1), 19–30.

Rahman, A. (1999). Micro-credit Initiatives for Equitable and Sustainable Development: Who Pays? *World Development, 27*(1), 67–82. doi: 10.1016/s0305–750x(98)00105–3.

Rozario, S. and Samuel, G. (2010). Gender, Religious Change and Sustainability in Bangladesh. *Women's Studies International Forum, 33*(4), 354–364. doi: 10.1016/j.wsif.2010.02.009.

Shehabuddin, E. (1999). Contesting the Illicit: Gender and the Politics of Fatwas in Bangladesh. *Signs, 24*(4), 1011–1044.

White, S. C. (2009). Beyond the Paradox: Religion, Family and Modernity in Contemporary Bangladesh. *Religions and Development (RaD) Research Programme*. University of Bath, UK.

# 4 Governing rural life

## From neoliberal governmentality to sacralized governmentality

The main aim of this chapter is to explore changing patterns of governmentality through the intervention of Islamic NGOs in rural Bangladesh. The chapter evaluates the ways in which Islamic NGOs shape the local governance of rural villages with their programmes of activities. The main argument revolves around explaining how Islamic NGOs use neoliberal governmentality, or a form of neoliberalism called 'pious neoliberalism', to deliver a new hybrid form of governmentality. This chapter analyses how and why Islamic NGOs adapt Islamic principles of charity to promote neoliberal practices like financial investment, entrepreneurship, self-help strategies and management practices, and hence produce a hybrid form of governmentality which I call 'pious governmentality'. Therefore, this chapter deals systematically with different types of NGOs (e.g. Islamic and secular) to highlight the compatibility of or intersection between neoliberal governmentality and religion rather than considering Islamic NGOs as antithetical to globalization, modernity and neoliberalism. To explore this issue I explain the perceptions of rural people as well as NGO officials on the performance, transparency, corruption, and accountability of Islamic NGOs compared to mainstream NGOs. Therefore, it is based on people's constructions of *Islami samity* or Islamic NGOs that correspond to Islamic religious practice. The chapter opens with an explanation of the existing understanding of neoliberal governmentality and 'pious neoliberalism', followed by a discussion of what really makes neoliberal governmentality 'pious governmentality'. The next section explores the pious governmentality of Islamic NGOs with an emphasis on rhetorical constructions of the entrepreneurial *Homo economicus*, manageralism and professionalism. Next, the chapter analyses the funding of Islamic NGOs to explore how transnational NGOs and donors contribute to 'pious governmentality'.

### Neoliberalizing development and hybrid governmentality: where do the Islamic NGOs stand?

Neoliberalism, as it was discussed in Chapter 1, represents a regime of policies and practices in which

> a valorization of private enterprise and suspicion of the state, along with what is sometimes called 'free-market fetishism' and the advocacy of tariff elimination, currency deregulation, and the deployment of 'enterprise models' would allow the state itself to be 'run like a business'.
>
> (Ferguson, 2009, p. 170)

Neoliberalism in its strictest sense refers to a macroeconomic doctrine and a regime of policies and practices related to this doctrine, while Nikolas Rose and other 'Anglo-Foucauldians' tend to emphasize the techniques of government that work through the creation of responsible citizen-subjects (Ferguson, 2009, p. 173). Therefore, neoliberalism as a policy framework represents a shift from Keynesian welfarism towards the primacy of markets, leading to the state's withdrawal from the provision of public goods and services, and thereby forcing the government to abandon its commitment to the welfare state through subjugating the state to deregulation, marketization and privatization (Larner, 2000).

### *From neoliberalism to pious neoliberalism, neoliberal governmentality to pious governmentality*

Contrary to the above-mentioned neoliberalism, a new form of neoliberalism is emerging around the Muslim majority states that may be termed 'pious neoliberalism' (Atia, 2012), where there is a marriage between neoliberalism and Islam or a tendency to restructure neoliberal ideals with those of an Islamic discourse. For Atia, 'pious neoliberalism' is 'the discursive combination of religion and economic rationale in a manner that encourages individuals to be proactive and entrepreneurial in the interest of furthering their relationship with the God' (Atia, 2012, p. 809).

Although Islamic NGOs are also adherents of neoliberal principles of economic development, their on-the-ground practices are different from secular NGOs in that they blend religious and neoliberal principles into a new form of neoliberalism, sometimes referred to as the 'spiritual economy' (Rudnyckyj, 2009, 2010) or 'pious neoliberalism' (Atia, 2012). Thus, an emerging trend among the academics analysing Muslim societies emphasizes the compatibility between Islam and neoliberalism. For example, Osella and Osella (2009, p. S205) explained the term 'social mindedness' – a combination of piety and economic calculation among the Kerala Muslim Entrepreneurs from India who position their business practices within the framework of 'ethics and moral responsibilities deemed to be Islamic'. They are also committed to reorientating local Muslim subjectivities (for example, self-transformation through education) and practices towards the requirement of contemporary capitalism. Several other researchers (e.g. Hefner, 1998, 2012; Sloane, 1999; Soares, 2005) focus on the reorientation and reproduction of Muslim subjectivity through a combination of politico-religious orientation and economic practice. Rudnyckyj (2010, p. 21) shows that in Indonesia, 'Islam was reconfigured according to calculative rationality insofar as Islamic values (such as hard work, honesty, transparency, and self-discipline) were promoted because of their economic benefit. Enhanced religious practice was seen as conducive to greater profitability.' This tends to lead pious neoliberal subjects towards this worldly material success as well as towards spiritual success in the afterlife.

Whether it is neoliberalism, pious neoliberalism or spiritual economy, all share the core principles of economic rationality, management principles practice and profitability. Based on the Foucauldian concept of neoliberal governmentality, I introduce 'pious governmentality' that includes a discursive combination of the application of Islamic rhetoric in the procedures, application and techniques of neoliberal governmentality. I use this concept to explore how NGOs manage or control the behaviour of the population to make them successful and pious private entrepreneurial beings based on economic rationality and calculative reasons. It is an assemblage of the techniques and practices of governance that integrates the neoliberal principles of accountability and transparency, as well as 'personal responsibility' and 'self-care' by the entrepreneurial, competitive and rational economic individual (*Homo economicus*) with that of religious values and piety. This idea corresponds with that of Atia (2012, p. 823), who used neoliberalism as both policy and governmentality. With the idea of pious neoliberalism in mind, she examines a context-specific manifestation of neoliberalism to describe the interplay between Islam and religion with economic logic. She focuses more on the policies and programmes of faith-based organizations in order to bridge Islam with neoliberal ideology. Yet, the way in which she describes the activities of faith-based development organizations and a televangelist reflects governmentality; that is, the creation of a social condition to govern and transform the individual that is conducive to neoliberalism. Therefore I think it is better to use 'pious neoliberal governmentality' or simply 'pious governmentality' as an analytical term rather than pious neoliberalism. Indeed, as Hamann (2009, p. 38) argues, 'the central aim of neoliberal governmentality is the strategic production of social conditions conducive to the constitution of *Homo economicus*, a specific form of subjectivity with historical roots in traditional liberalism'. In neoliberal governmentality, '"the conduct of conduct" bring together the government of others (subjectification) and the government of one's self (subjectivation); on the one hand, the biopolitical governance of populations and, on the other, the work that individuals perform upon themselves in order to become certain kinds of subjects'. In that sense, 'pious governmentality' is an appropriate term here to see how it works within the framework of neoliberalism in conjunction with Islamic principles and piety.

Therefore, this book explains how Islamic NGOs with their emphasis on *halal vs. haram* (prohibited vs. approved), submission to Allah, avoidance of sin (e.g. through avoidance of usury or *shud*), regular prayer and modesty as well as rewards in the life hereafter help to sustain neoliberalism. Argued this way, this book does not claim that only Islam is uniquely suited to neoliberal governmentality; rather other faiths have the same potential (e.g. Christianity). Therefore, Islamic NGOs or FBOs in general govern the neoliberal subject through both their service provision (for instance, *shari'a*-based microfinance and humanitarian aid in my research) as well as governing the individual self. I am aware of the challenge that defining pious governmentality in this way poses to the dominant paradigm of modernization, secularism and development, as does the revival of Islamic piety as an alternative to that of neoliberalism in the Muslim world. Therefore, in this book I deal systematically with the different types of NGOs and their relation with neoliberalism in the context of Bangladesh. Yet, the main emphasis in this book is on the compatibility of neoliberalism and Islamic NGOs in Bangladesh.

## Why pious governmentality: is this distinctive?

What makes the governmentality approach of Islamic NGOs distinctive from their secular counterpart is the use of Islamic principles while regulating conduct. It is obvious that Islamic NGOs which operate microcredit programmes use the same group approach model in their programmes, but the inclusion of the Islamic *shari'a* principles differentiates the governmentalities of an Islamic from a non-Islamic NGO. For example, the operational manual[1] of the *Fael Khair* Program of an Islamic NGO listed 28 duties of a programme officer. The first duty is:

> This work [working with the Islamic NGOs] has to be considered not just a job, rather the best worship (*Uttam Ibadat*) and a challenge. You have to dedicate yourself to improve the economic conditions of the oppressed, the poor and the penniless.

Unlike secular NGOs, Islamic NGOs emphasize their reliance on the Islamic principles to be corruption-free, committed and eventually cost-effective. I have mentioned elsewhere in this book that Islamic NGOs emphasize the religious motivation for their employees and beneficiaries to manage the programme as well as its employees and beneficiaries. Therefore, it is important to note how devotion and commitment arose from moral and religious motivation, making Islamic NGOs, as the Islamic NGO officials argue, effective in operation and cost. This is how one of the high officials of an Islamic NGO explained it: 'if you develop the morality of the people, then you know … they may pay back the money. In that sense morality relates to religion, and in some cases our staff took it as a strategy.'

Another NGO official also believes that religious and moral motivation would make their poverty alleviation or development intervention successful. As an Islamic NGO programme officer argues,

> There are two types of poverty: one is economic poverty and the other is moral poverty. You can alleviate economic poverty without any motivation. Yet, to bring changes in his behaviours there is no other way but to provide moral elements in development.

The use of religious rhetoric in development practices of Islamic NGOs is mainly to make their programme successful and control the targeted population

– the rural people, and women in particular. It is obvious from the field that Islamic NGOs are very successful in doing so. For example, Maksuda at Shyamnagar, who received a loan from an Islamic NGO, explained why she wanted to repay the loan regularly:

> I have taken the loan, don't I have to repay it? Is it right not to repay? Don't I have to die? I offer prayer five times a day. Wouldn't I have to repay? I have got the just money; I have to return this just money, otherwise how I will account to Allah.

The orientation of beneficiaries to the religious principles of any religion is evident in the activities of Islamic NGOs towards Muslim and non-Muslim beneficiaries. For non-Muslims they emphasize following their 'own religion', be it Hinduism or another religion which ultimately gives the Islamic NGO greater control over its targeted population (i.e. the beneficiaries of *shari'a*-based microfinance). It is therefore important that recipients should not be a-religious; rather they should be religious to some point.

Besides, another distinctive practice of Islamic NGOs is their emphasis on the *halal vs. haram* (approved vs. prohibited) in everyday life, ranging from types of business to people's behaviour. Through the imposition of *haram vs. halal* Islamic NGOs control the population to decide what to do (business activity) and what not to do (for example, not to cheat in weight in their grocery shop or the right form of dress code). Islamic NGOs clearly emphasize the development of entrepreneurship, however, through a *halal* means. For example, during the interviews, NGO officials as well as beneficiaries emphasized their involvement in *halal* practices. For example, Zinia, an Islamic NGO member at Shronkhola, offered an example of strictness with regard to *halal* activities in its programme.

> In our centre, there was a member who took a credit from our *samity* and lent out for interest. Meaning that she would get interest on that money, while lending the money to another. Therefore, she was expelled from the *samity*, since none can lend the money for interest (*shud*).

Another respondent at Manikganj explained the conditionality on *halal* business as instructed by her overseeing official.

> Our sir told us not to get involved in any activities that Islam does not permit. For example, I cannot raise *shukor* [pig]. You know … it is not even allowed to speak this word [*shukor*], if you use this word your mouth will be putrid [*napak*] for 40 days. So, I set up a grocery shop with the money I got from them. Sir also told us not to cheat on the weight and measure in my shop since it is a sin. If I do so, I would be deprived of *barakat* [blessing] in my wealth and my life and Allah will not accept my *du'aa* [request/supplication]. This will ultimately lead me to hell fire.

Therefore, I asked all the local NGO officials how they ensure that these women invest the money in some *halal* or *shari'a*-approved activities. One of the Islamic NGO officials replied:

> Before the induction, we conduct 10 to 12 meetings and get to know them ... in the beginning we try to make sure but it is not possible to become 100 per cent successful. After one year of transaction we become mostly certain whether they are getting involved in unapproved activities.

At the same time another Islamic NGO official explicitly mentioned, among others, that one of the responsibilities of the unit-in-charge (manager) is 'to ensure use of *shari'a* in the investment procedure and ensure the appropriate use of this investment'. This *hala/haram* differentiation results in conducting the beneficiaries' behaviour whether personal, social or entrepreneurial.

Although Islamic NGOs also adopt neoliberal principles, they use Islam to justify actions both at the beneficiary level as well as at the official level. Neoliberal rationality in Islamic NGOs has sometimes been compromised with the Islamic rhetoric of 'Allah's Willing', which in the long run helps to regulate beneficiaries' spiritual as well as economic behaviour. For example, one of the respondents at Manikganj who owns four cows with the money loaned from the NGO explained what she would do and how the NGO would treat her if her cows died. She said, 'If the cows die, it is Allah's will. If Allah takes away the cows, there is nothing we can do.' She then explained how she would repay the money if the cows died: 'I don't have to repay the money. If Allah takes away something, what can they do? Instead, they would help us again.' The Islamic NGO official who was in charge of that area also validated her claim. He told me the same story. This motivates the individual recipient to strengthen *iman* (belief) in Allah on the one hand as well the NGO's 'generosity' which may make this NGO distinctive from other NGOs.

At other points, Islamic NGOs are not different from their secular counterparts when it comes to their intentions; for example, in the motivations behind the selection of women as beneficiaries. As I discuss in Chapter 6, secular NGOs select women as beneficiaries because they are easily accessible, manipulable and more vulnerable to the loss of their shame and honour. The same motivations are also held by the Islamic NGOs. For example, when I asked the branch manager of an Islamic NGO at Sharonkhoal about the gender composition of its beneficiaries, he informed me that although the centre had been male-only in the beginning, the organization had been forced to change its strategy within the first year of operation. This is how he explained such changes:

> We started with a male centre in this area ... in 2009 a decision was made not to increase the male centre. Since the beginning, male centres were not good ... our success would be impossible if it was based on the male. For example, when a male is a member of an NGO and takes the loan, women in the family don't have any headache. Some could make business out our

> loan and leave the *samity* without repaying the loan. But if it's a female, wherever she goes, she stays at home and returns the instalment.

Another official of an Islamic NGO also said that the organization had similar reasons for selecting female beneficiaries, although it also had male beneficiaries. The reasons were that women were understood to be more easily accessible, more susceptible to *lojja* (shame) and *ijjot* (honour), and that they were more likely to repay the money quickly.

## Secular NGOs and neoliberal governmentality

Scholars who insist that NGOs further neoliberal development agendas often argue that 'individual entrepreneurial freedoms and skills' (Harvey, 2007, p. 2) are enhanced through the creation of institutional frameworks, which correspond to neoliberal ideals of the privatization and marketization of public goods. Moreover, the empowerment mantra of the NGOs, as Kamat (2004, p. 170) argues, surely lead to the marketization of social identities and relations. Neoliberal notions of empowerment, as Kamat (2004, p. 170) argues, are 'individualizing the process of empowerment where each has to build his/her capacities to access the marketplace [and] reduces the concept of public welfare to private interest'. Thus one of the important aspects of neoliberal governmentality is to regulate the individual self, to transform people into self-responsible and self-caring individuals. In the discussion which follows, I emphasize certain particular issues in order to see how neoliberalism is working in the NGO sectors in Bangladesh with particular focus on Grameen Bank, BRAC and their microfinance programmes.

### *Privatization of the individual self*

Neoliberalism works through a number of calculative technologies intended to ensure that individuals conduct themselves according to the norms of enterprise and self-responsibility, and these have been extended to the domains of NGOs. In the discussion which follows, I explain how the mainstream NGOs (e.g. Grameen Bank and BRAC) adopted the neoliberal strategy of infusing market values into everyday aspects of social life and shifted responsibility onto individuals in rural Bangladesh.

Grameen Bank mentions on its website that it believes that 'charity is not an answer to poverty. It only helps poverty to continue. It creates dependency and takes away the individual's initiative to break through the wall of poverty.'[2] Therefore, poor people need financial help (e.g. microcredit) to be self-employed. Muhammad Yunus, in an interview with *The Kathmandu Post*, explains why microcredit is important and how it works to harness individual potential to combat poverty through practices and policies (e.g. microcredit):

> First, the [existing] financial system doesn't work for the poor. They can't go to a bank and take a loan. That system is created for the people who

> already have lots of money. We needed a system which works for the poor. With microcredit, they can borrow and start a business. Also, it creates self-employment. I can't find a job, so I create my own job. I start a little business, and it generates employment. It works wonderfully for the woman, because it means she doesn't have to go to the factory. She doesn't have to go to the city, which is very difficult for her. She stays home and starts a business like raising chickens, doing embroidery she can sell. And it empowers the women too.[3]

The Grameen Bank model, as Karim (2008, p. 14) argues, 'rests on the idea of the individual entrepreneur who, with the help of micro-credit, becomes self-employed, owns private property (the assets she builds with loans), and sells her labour on the market'. This is clearly tied to the ideology of neoliberalism. Most NGOs that deliver microcredit and other services strongly hold this view. NGOs use microcredit as a form of governmental strategy which attempts to cultivate a subjectivity of the rational economic being that 'might function efficiently and sustainably in the domain of market' (Rankin, 2001, p. 30).

BRAC also emphasizes the individual potential and argues that 'initially limited to encouraging self-employment, our Microfinance Programme has progressively moved towards supporting small enterprise development'. One of the most significant things to note here is whether Grameen, through its 'social business' or BRAC's 'social enterprise' model, have restructured relationships with the poor and created a new social identity[4] to accomplish the desired restructuring 'consistent with the financial stability of the lenders and an ideal of self-regulating markets' (Rankin, 2001, p. 28). Therefore, the participation of women in the credit programme was believed to enhance the financial sustainability of the microcredit programmes as women have a higher propensity to return the loan due to social and cultural obligations. Thus these poor women are valued because, as Muhammad Yunus argues, 'not only capitalism is good for the poor', but 'the poor are good for capitalism' (Yunus, 2007, cited in Karim, 2008, p. 14). Yet, these women are obliged to act in accordance with the values of 'discipline, efficiency and competitiveness' (Karim, 2008, p. 6). This resembles what Nikolas Rose has similarly argued with regard to social welfare reform in the West: 'In this system, each individual is solicited as an ally of economic success through ensuring that they invest in the management and success of their own economic capital' (Rose, 1996a, p. 338).

Therefore, NGO-led development initiatives have pushed the poor to become clients of many NGOs concurrently as well as searching for better NGO options for their economic success, as they are responsible for their own success and failure as a result of the state's withdrawal of welfare provision. One of the respondents, Mir Ali Khan, a 51-year-old farmer at Tala, who was once a member of Uttaron (a national NGO) for 20 years, joined BRAC in 2006 due mainly to the inability of Uttaron to provide him with large amounts of loans. He maintains a family of five and spends at least 20,000 Taka per month. He explains why he moved out from Uttaron and how BRAC helped him to be a successful farmer and entrepreneur:

> I earn only 25/30,000 Taka. I am also the group leader. I want to leave the NGO, but they won't let me. I took a loan of 120,000 Taka from BRAC and a 'good loan' of 30,000 Taka. A good loan is awarded to those who repay the loan in a regular and timely manner consistently. I pay 15 per cent interest on BRAC's loan, so I have to pay back 13,800 with a monthly instalment of 11,500. [He tells me why BRAC's terms are better.] For example, I needed 50,000 Taka, if I want to loan it from people I will have to mortgage my land for two years or otherwise sell it. I could not go to the bank, as it might be a lengthy process as well as involving a bribe. I could take a loan from *Islami Samity*, but they only give 10/20,000 Taka which is a very little amount for my agriculture. But BRAC gave 50,000 in the beginning, then 80 and 120,000 three times in the last four years. I can't tell whether people in my area are getting better or not with the help of NGOs, but I myself benefited. With the money from BRAC, I started cultivating potatoes and eggplants on rented land. I bought two *bigas* of land after joining BRAC. With the help of BRAC, I bought a water pump and a tractor to cultivate my land as well as renting them out. Now I don't have to look back. I could not study, but my children did. I am making profits from my cultivation. I don't need any more help from NGOs. I am now self-reliant. Now people in my village respect me, come for advice on production, storage and marketing of vegetables. Among all the NGOs working in my area BRAC is better. Their environment is very good; there are no foul talks in transaction. Both the condition of the office and the transaction is very clear. They behave well when I go to their office.

While the welfare state takes the responsibility (e.g. health care, education, credit, employment) for its citizens, the withdrawal of the state brings in NGOs to take over these responsibilities. However, NGOs as adherents of neoliberalism transfer these responsibilities (e.g. credit, employment) to the individual. NGO clients are thus constructed as responsible clients and the 'onus for development falls squarely on their shoulders, and their citizenship manifests not through entitlement but through the "free" exercise of individual choice' (Rankin, 2001, p. 29). It became clear when the respondent told me:

> Don't eat the money', big [*boro*] sir told me before I go to get the money from the other small [*choto*] sir. [I asked her what it meant.] She replied: sirs want us to invest money in business or agriculture, but not buy *Shari-goina* [shari or ornaments], or even rice to eat. They asked us to invest the money in business. Thus I gave the money to my husband to set up a grocery shop. [Then, I asked, what will happen if they incur loss in their business. She reluctantly replied], what else … I have to pay the money back … no other way. It is now our responsibility to make the business a success.

In addition, a number of case studies are provided in all of the annual reports of both secular and religious NGOs to demonstrate the success of rural female entrepreneurs in particular. These NGO clients are now meant to be self-regulated and responsible for their actions in their businesses or activities related to their livelihood. Although NGO clients have now been transformed into self-caring, rational entrepreneurs, it is important to ask whether this transformation would ultimately result in progress. Yet, the NGO discourse on progress or success becomes illusive and some NGO officials are sceptical about this 'progress'. During my fieldwork, most of the non-Islamic NGO clients I interviewed were members of several NGOs at the same time. A BRAC branch manager expressed her worries regarding these beneficiaries as well as how they are transferring their responsibilities to the poor client:

> They are not progressing; ultimately what happens, is that our money is revolving. You will be surprised. I have been here for the last three years, I haven't seen anyone who progressed a lot ... apparently, we charge 15 per cent interest, but out of a 20,000 Taka loan, they receive 19,000 Taka, since we deduct 50 Taka per 1,000 as savings. Though this 1,000 Taka she gets back afterwards (usually at the end of the year), but when we are giving them the loan we say we are giving them 20,000, but in reality we are giving them 19,000. Since she is giving 15 per cent interest which altogether makes it 3,000, therefore she is giving us 4,000 Taka more. Again, when she is repaying eight or 10 instalments before two or three months, how much then is the interest rate? Many people understand this, but the poor people have no other options.

She then cited an example from a newspaper article about microcredit which she had saved. The article was from the popular Bengali National Daily *Prothom-Alo*:

> You will find the picture of development in rural Bangladesh, when you see boys and girls are going to school in groups. Now kids from most all the families starting to go to school. I want to mention a small thing here. When, for the first time, as a BRAC worker I go to a Village Organization (VO) meeting in an area, then I see 30/40 men and women there. All of them sat on the mat in a courtyard. My colleague and I went there and we had shoes on our feet. We took off our shoes and sat on the mat. Outside of the mat, there were only our shoes. But in 2010 we went to a same kind of area and saw that everybody came to us wearing shoes and nice clothes. Therefore, doesn't this prove that the poor people of the village are progressing?

Interestingly, she asked me whether someone wearing shoes means that person has progressed. This is a picture of the secular NGO-led development practices in rural Bangladesh where the NGO subject just becomes the mere neoliberal element for success, though success is far distant for many. It is therefore important to mention the way in which NGOs make aid recipients into *porojibi* (meaning parasite, a term used by one of my key informants), where beneficiaries become dependent on NGO aid and where the NGO transforms them into a passive recipient by binding them into a long-term reciprocal relationship. Whatever success they achieve, all the beneficiaries of such NGOs follow the written and unwritten rules and prescriptions of such NGOs that teach them to be self-helped, self-regulated and self-responsible.

All of the microcredit NGOs in Bangladesh use solidarity groups, and in particular a female solidarity group approach (i.e. women form a group of five or six likeminded women from the same area and each *samity*/centre has five to six groups) which works as collateral against their credit from the NGOs. This group is ultimately used by the NGOs to strengthen the financial sustainability of microcredit programmes and to contribute more effectively to the broader goals of deepening financial markets (Rankin, 2001, p. 28). Therefore, women's participation in microcredit turns into a mechanism for 'slash[ing] administrative costs', 'motivating repayment' and 'introducing financial discipline through peer pressure' (Yaron, 1991, p. vii). Rhyne and Otero (1992, p. 1564) nicely depict how the group mechanism helps the sustainability of the microcredit financial market:

> The group plays a role in reducing the cost of gathering information about the borrower, but its more important role is in motivating repayments through shared liability for default. Lenders can shift some of the loan processing and loan approval tasks onto groups because the groups have better access to information on the character and creditworthiness of potential borrowers.

During interviews with BRAC and Grameen Bank beneficiaries, all of them informed me that NGOs gave the credit to them after an initial screening which was carried out by existing members of the NGOs. As a BRAC beneficiary at Tala said: 'before providing me with the loan, they [BRAC] collected detailed information from neighbouring members of the centre to decide whether we could be provided with the credit'. This form of peer review of credit worthiness may be understood as a type of client surveillance mechanism that ensures the return of loans, since each and every person in the group is responsible for everyone else's default. In this way peer pressure is a source of policing over other members so that they conduct themselves in line with the desires of NGOs.

Individual entrepreneurship is the most significant goal that the microcredit programme of the NGO wants to achieve through restructuring the rural financial system. Many respondents who are beneficiaries of Grameen Bank and BRAC narrated a different story on the use of the money which also goes against the idea of a rational economic being. Although the beneficiaries of microcredit are overwhelmingly women, it is unequivocal that the loan is used by the husbands or male members of the family. When I asked, 'you have received the credit, so why don't you use the money?', the response of one BRAC beneficiary at Sharonkhola was:

> I borrowed the money. But I don't know how to make a business out of this money. Thus my husband told me to give him the money so that he could buy a van [a kind of rickshaw]. I gave it to him.

The same kind of explanation of the use of money by the male members of society is prevalent in all of the study areas.

On the other hand, during the interview with Shakila at Shyamnagar, she said that she would lend some money to one of her relatives who would repay the loan on her behalf and she would buy a cow with the rest. Then I asked her how one could buy a cow with half of the money. She replied, 'I will not actually buy a cow. I will spend half of it to repay the loan from another NGO.' Then I asked her what would happen if she was caught by the BRAC officer. She replied, 'if sirs come to see my cow I would borrow my neighbour's cow. It's not that difficult for me to manage.'

Moreover, secular NGO officials also know that many of their clients will not use the money for the intended activities. What makes the officials happy, as some respondents claimed, is the timely return of the money. Thus these officials are much more concerned about the disbursement and timely recovery rate than about rational use and the consequent progress made by the beneficiaries. Thus it is not always true that secular NGO beneficiaries will represent a 'rational economic man' or will apply a rational and calculative means to use the money. Therefore, being part of a secular NGO does not always guarantee that a beneficiary will turn into an entrepreneur *Homo economicus*. What is therefore imperative here for NGOs is the hidden purpose of the group approach which is to strengthen the financial health of their microcredit programme, rather than the social citizenship or welfare of the rural poor people that corresponds with neoliberal capitalism's goal. Yet, the success of their programme of activities also depends on efficient managerial expertise and an emphasis on accountability of the NGOs' staff and beneficiaries.

## *Managerialism, accountability and participation*

Neoliberalism works through a number of mechanisms intended to ensure that individuals conduct themselves according to the norms of enterprise and self-responsibility. This has been extended to the domain of NGOs through a range of practices (e.g. audits, targeting, financial management and business planning) that are justified and promoted through the concept of accountability (MacKinnon, 2002, p. 309; Rose, 1996). Therefore, some scholars have argued that NGOs, through their increasing emphasis on managerialism and professionalism, serve as 'transmission channels' for the new techniques of managerialism (Townsend *et al.*, 2002, p. 830). In the context of the Global South, this results in new patterns of 'governability, which seems to be the goal of donors, not poverty reduction as stated' (O'Reilly, 2010, p. 183).

The practices of NGO accountability, as Najam (1996) argues, are threefold. First, NGOs are accountable to patrons, which implies an 'upward accountability'

(Edwards and Hulme, 1996b, p. 967). This includes the realm of the relationship with the donors' (internal and external) foundations and governments. In this mode of accountability, donors held NGOs responsible for the 'spending of designated money for designated purposes' (Najam, 1996, p. 342), thereby invoking the possibility of controlling the policies of funded NGOs. Second, NGOs are accountable to their clients, which implies the relationships with the 'groups to whom NGOs provide services' (Najam, 1996, p. 346) and, possibly, the community and regions indirectly in the catchment of NGO activities, which may be termed 'downward' accountability (Edwards and Hulme, 1996b, p. 967). The mechanism of ensuring accountability to the client is through the participation of beneficiaries in the decision-making process of NGOs. This, in turn, compels clients to agree to what the NGOs had already intended to do (Khan, 2003, p. 270). Finally, NGOs are held accountable to themselves, meaning internal accountability which includes NGOs' responsibilities to their goals, mission and to the staff.

During my interviews with the managers of different secular NGOs (e.g. BRAC, Shushilan, Progoti, Gonoshokti, Agrodut), they all told me that they followed the same procedure to maintain accountability to the donor as well as to the government. For BRAC, funded projects are audited both by international and government approved local auditing firms. The annual and audited reports are sent to the government as well as to the donors to ensure their accountability to the government and mainly to the donors. Ensuring accountability to their donors guarantees in most cases the further extension of the project/programme as well as increasing the opportunity to attain new projects. Yet, the small local NGOs are also held accountable to the Upazila Nirbahee Officer (UNO), the administrative head of the local upazila, who ensures the participation of NGOs in the monthly NGO coordination meeting and whenever necessary.

During the interviews, I was interested to learn how the NGOs, both secular and religious, ensure their accountability to their clients which is, as my research argues, a grey area of NGO accountability (Ahmad, 2009; Ebrahim, 2003; Edwards and Hulme, 1996a; Khan, 2003). Accountability to clients is one of the main mantras in development practices. All the NGOs in the study repeatedly told about their commitments towards accountability to their clients. Thus, in response to how they ensure accountability to their clients, all the NGO officials emphasized the issues of transparency and participation of their beneficiaries in their meetings and programmes, and the opportunities to make any complaints to the manager of the local branch of an NGO. However, in practice, none of the beneficiaries of NGOs (as they told me) made any formal complaints against the activities of the staff to the manager, whether it was a secular or an Islamic NGO. This was because power relations between the beneficiaries and the secular NGO staff are vertical, so that NGOs can govern the conduct of their clients. In such a context, it is right to ask whether it is different for Islamic NGOs. Do Islamic NGOs exercise power over the conduct of their beneficiaries? Do they use different forms of rhetoric (e.g. principles of Islam) to justify their 'conducts of the conduct'? In the next section, I explore how Islamic NGOs use the rhetoric of neoliberal governmentality in their development practices in Bangladesh within the framework of *sacralized governmentality* or what I call *pious governmentality*.

## Islamic NGOs and neoliberal governmentality: the emergence of pious governmentality

In this book I am interested in examining the welfare provision of Islamic NGOs and the dynamic interplay between religious rhetoric and neoliberal economic policy preferences in the development practices of NGOs. As this research contends, secular economic provisions are sacralized to form a union between the religious and the economic and political rationalities – a combination of piety and economic calculation. This new assemblage is seen not as excluding but as reinforcing one other. Thus I explain how neoliberalism also works in Islamic NGOs but in a different way. In making such an argument, I am at the same time aware of the fact that Islamic NGOs in Bangladesh are different from each other in terms of their approach to the programmes, patterns and nature of activities, sources of funding and networks. Thus, arguing that all Islamic NGOs follow the same path of sacralized neoliberal governmentality would lead to a danger of over-generalization. Therefore, this book explains how neoliberal governmentality is working differently for different Islamic NGOs in Bangladesh.

### Homo economicus, *piety and Islamic NGOs*

I have already mentioned elsewhere how secular NGO-led development practices in Bangladesh cultivate neoliberal rationality towards individualism, self-improvement, productivity and entrepreneurship. Likewise, Islamic NGOs also emphasize the same discourse of development, as Muslim Aid (2010a, p. 7) states:

> Our borrowers, most of whom are women, use these loans to engage in various income generating activities to improve their socio-economic condition. Primarily limited to encouraging self-employment, our microfinance program has progressively moved towards supporting small enterprise development. This expansion focus stems from a growing recognition of the multiplier effects of enterprises through employment generation, as well as backward and forward linkages with many economic activities.

This is also obvious in all Muslim Aid's published materials. For example, the annual report of one Islamic NGO provides success stories of the SME (Small and Medium Enterprise) businesses, and the titles of these stories read as 'SME Success Story 1: Harun-ur-Rashid is now self-reliant' and 'SME Success Story 2: Rani Begum from housewife to entrepreneur', 'Golapi Begum of Nageswary is self-relient by beef fattening'. Another annual report of Islamic NGOs produced the same kind of 'self-reliant' women's stories: Momotaz Begum expanded her business', 'Purno Laxmi defeated poverty', Morium Begum lightened by fish culture', and 'Rita Rani is now self-reliant through bamboo basket cottage industry'. These cases represent Islamic NGOs' endeavour to turn women into successful entrepreneurs and thus be self-reliant. The case studies that follow exemplify the cultivation of the neoliberal subjects who work towards self-improvement, productivity and entrepreneurship, and who combine piety and Islamic practices. Therefore, these recipients are constructed not as victims of neoliberalism but as active participants in their success through driving for material benefits in their present life and spiritual success in the life hereafter (*Akherater lov*).

Materials produced by Islamic NGOs give plentiful examples regarding the success of beneficiaries of *shari'a*-based microfinance and *Hasana* programmes, with illustrations of the ways in which Islamic NGOs provide them with both material success in this world and spiritual benefits in the afterlife. For example, one of my respondents has been a beneficiary of IBF's interest-free loan at Hazrat Abu Bakar centre since its inception in Shyamnagar. He is a Quran-e-Hafiz,[5] teaches at the local mosque and is a successful honey trader. He claims that he is 'considered one of the biggest honey traders in the region'. He explains how he became a successful honey trader:

> I took a 60,000 Taka loan from IBF. I have two books [account] with IBF, one in my wife's name and other is in my name. I need more than hundreds of thousands of Taka for my business ... I became successful with the money, because I did not spend the money on buying the daily necessities. To the best of my knowledge, I did not spend even to buy a kilogram of rice with this money; I rather invested in my business, and worked hard to become successful. On an average, I collect 800 to 1,000 kg of honey. I collect this amount of honey in three ways: due to people's trust in me I get hundreds of thousands of Takas-worth of honey on credit; I collect hundreds of thousands of Taka from others and as well from IBF. I am doing a *halal* business with the halal money, and Allah showered me with the due blessings.

During the interviews with a female member of the Ma Amena centre (centre no. 35) of IBF at Shajalal Model Village, a 50-year-old bearded man in a long *panjabi* and topi joined in our conversation and introduced himself as the husband of my respondent. He and his wife told me the story of his success and how he became self-reliant with credit from the IBF. He is the head of the household of four children and spends BDT10,000 per month to live a decent life. He is a small entrepreneur who sells fish (shrimp), collecting them from the local market and sending them to Dhaka where they are sold at a high price. His wife received two loans from the IBF: one for BDT10,000 (around US$120) and another for BDT13,000. Using this money he invested in buying shrimp from the shrimp farmers and the local market, and selling to the wholesale market in the capital, Dhaka. Along with the money, he needs to invest all of his time to buy cheap shrimp from the surrounding areas. For him, all is Allah's willing; Muslim Aid is just a medium (*usila*). He said to me, 'Allah will not change the condition of a nation until they change what is within themselves' (Surah Ar-ra'ad: 11). I asked whether the IBF helped him to change his mindset. He replied:

> They just don't give us the loan, they help us decide what sorts of business we should choose and encourage us to work hard to make a profit. They help us to buy the materials for our business and monitor our activities. Therefore, there is very little chance for us to spend the money on worthless activities other than business.

During an interview with one of the Islamic NGO officials at Sharonkhola he provided me with the success story of a beneficiary named Setara. The NGO official wrote down this story to send to head office for media coverage on the success of the organization's *shari'a*-based microfinance. This story was as follows:

> Setara Begum won the poverty. She is 49 years old. Her husband's name is Shahjahan Gazi. He is a small wood business man, and can barely support his family. He was very affected by *Sidr* and lost his means of living. Although he was very poor and disaster affected, no aid reached him. Therefore, Setara Begum decided to help her husband. But how could she do this? She thought for a while and decided to raise goats to earn some money. Yet, she did not have the financial capital to do that. She knew that Muslim Aid helped through providing people with interest-free small loans. She invited six women and organized a group to join Muslim Aid. Then, through the centre leader, she got the loan proposal and subsequently was granted a loan of 15,000 Taka each. Setara Begum bought eight goats with the money we provided. After six months her five goats gave birth to 10 kids. However, due to cyclone Aila, four goats died. She then sold all the remaining goats. She took 20,000 Taka from us again. This time she bought 10 goats with the money. After six months five of her goats gave birth to 11 kids. Now every day she gets two kilograms of milk she sells to the neighbour and the market. Part of the money she earns from selling the milk pays for her instalment from our loan and she spends on consumption and savings for her family. She is very happy with her husband and children and she is no longer worried about her livelihood. She thanks Allah and Muslim Aid for the help.

There are plenty of stories of successful entrepreneurs in Muslim Aid's microfinance programme. The success of such entrepreneurship is dependent upon the nature and management of the project, including monitoring beneficiaries and their activities. This has a positive impact on the beneficiaries which helps them to achieve their goals.

Successful entrepreneurship is very evident in the case of MACCA too. All of the respondents from MACCA agreed that they had benefited through MACCA in their business and agriculture, and had become self-reliant. One of the respondents, Hasan, told his story about how he became successful.

> I live with my parents and a sister. I joined MACCA five years ago and became a member of *Hasana* no. 4. Until now, I have borrowed 214,000 Taka from MACCA, with which I bought cows and a tractor and a water pump. I use the tractor and water pump to plough and for irrigation for the other people. With these I am making good money. Look at [as he asked me] our houses. They look so good now. We did not have a toilet before, now we do. I even bought a motor bike for myself. I could not study, but my young sister is going to the *madrasah*. My mother offers prayer regularly, and my father moderately observes religious duty. I myself try my best to observe these. You know, to be established and respected in the society, you need money. MACCA gave me this opportunity to make money in *halal* way. I don't need to seek others' help. They led me to work hard, not sit idle. They used to tell me those who work hard and follow the right path, Allah will bless them with success in this world and will give rewards for my honesty after my death.

Like Hasan, other respondents also shared with me their desire to be successful in their respective jobs, whether it was a small business, agriculture or cattle fattening. Since they are not allowed to be involved in interest-based activities, they are rather encouraged to use capital accumulation and reinvestment in the *shari'a*-approved business. It is imperative to note that few of my respondents reminded me that 'our prophet (PBUH – Peace be upon Him) was a very successful and honest businessman and we must follow the path that our beloved prophet followed'.

NGO staff members were very passionate in explaining why their beneficiaries are successful in business or entrepreneurship. The branch manager of an Islamic NGO at Sharonkhola reported:

> We just don't give them the money; we also provide them with the training. That's why our results are good. We have almost no defaulters. During the training, we discuss some motivational and consciousness-raising issues that are concerned with how to change their economic condition, what to do and how to do it with this money. This motivation is so strong that once one of my beneficiaries left for Chittagong, and became sick. She neither contacted us nor repaid the loan. After a few months, she suddenly appeared and returned 2,500 Taka which is half of the loan. We did not pressure her like other NGOs; she was just highly motivated by us and returned the money. If she did not repay the loan willingly, we could not collect it. This is how our Islamic teachings make our beneficiaries more responsible and accountable to the *samity*.

The message he was trying to convey is that a strong motivation in line with religious doctrine improves the performance of the beneficiary which in turn benefits the NGO to run smoothly. It is interesting to note how the beneficiaries as well as the NGO staff express their piety and Islamic morals as a source of their success in the programme and in successful entrepreneurship. Thus, whenever I asked beneficiaries why they considered themselves to be successful in their business or in agriculture, the very quick and common answer was, 'this money has blessings [*barakat*]' from Allah. Yet, contrary to this argument, one of the secular NGO officials at Sharonkhola claimed that people who go to Islamic NGOs do not think about Islam. They just consider it as interest-free. She reminded me of a local saying: '*Chore na shone dhormer kowtha* [the story of religion does not heal], meaning that religion is not important in this context, but the money. They will try to get money from wherever they can get it.'

Yet, to achieve this material success Islamic NGOs under study emphasized the issue of accountability, transparency and participation like their secular counterpart. What makes it different from their secular counterpart is their emphasis on conforming to Islamic ethics and morals which gives more opportunity for staff, beneficiaries and the organizations themselves to perform more efficiently in their service delivery. The next section questions whether the neoliberal practices of transparency, accountability and participation are practised in a different way from secular NGOs, or whether there is any religious implication in the practice of such principles in Islamic NGOs that promote the managerial skills of the organization, and subsequent productivity.

### *Accountability, transparency and corruption in Islamic NGOs*

As discussed earlier in this chapter, Islamic NGOs, like their mainstream counterparts, also emphasize people's participation as core values in their development practices. Although participation in development practices has several different meanings, at one level 'participation refers to information about a planned project being made available to the public', which may include consultation with community leaders and members; yet the decision is being made by the NGOs. At another level, participation could mean public involvement in actual project-related activities (Ebrahim, 2003, p. 818). Since the contemporary neoliberal rule strives to 'govern through community' (MacKinnon, 2002, p. 309), I was interested to see how managerial technologies are actually deployed by Islamic NGOs through targeting, local consultation and community appraisal which, in turn, enable them 'to render local communities visible and calculable as "objects' of government"' (MacKinnon, 2000; 2002, p. 309; Ward and McNicholas, 1998). Therefore, people's participation or community participation in Shajalal Model Village in Bagerhat, the IDEAL Village in Manikganj and in *shari'a*-based microfinance programmes in all three districts, including Satkhira, was particularly investigated to measure the nature of participation and what it means for NGO officials and beneficiaries.

In the case of humanitarian aid for cyclone *Sidr*-affected people under the Shajalal Model Village in Sharonkhola, Muslim Aid incorporated a community-based approach to ensure the participation of their beneficiaries. At the level of the design of the shelter project, the consultant (appointed by Muslim Aid) met with a wide range of shelter actors in Bangladesh as well as in Sharonkhola from 5 to 22 January 2008, and worked with affected community people to identify their preferred shelter design, and to explore the feasibility of implementing a community-managed programme. Thus Muslim Aid explains:

> In implementing all these shelter projects the community participation approach was used involving the community from the beginning to the end of the project; in the shelter design, the purchase and procurement of materials and the monitoring and evolution of progress and performance.
>
> (Muslim Aid, n.d.a, p. 6)

The main aim of the community managed approached was to:

1 Empower beneficiary groups, as well as the community.
2 Ensure the quality of work through the beneficiary.
3 Arrange safe custody of construction materials by the community and build ownership of the project.
4 Develop an example of community- as opposed to agency-managed programmes for Bangladesh (Muslim Aid, n.d.b, pp. 1–2).

The IDEAL Village programme of MACCA under the *Hasana* programme seeks the active participation of beneficiaries with the vision to 'solve the community problems through community leadership and preferably through community resources' (Masjid Council for Community Advancement, n.d.a, p. 15). Through this participation, MACCA will help to:

> Increase management capacities of the members to make them efficient managers of their own institution. *Hasana* groups are self-managed institutions and are implementing a number of interrelated activities not only for their own welfare but also for the overall development of the community they are living with.
>
> (Masjid Council for Community Advancement, n.d.b, p. 10)

*Shari'a*-based microfinance programmes, in all three Islamic NGOs under study, follow the group-based approach, where the women and their peers form a group of five or six women to be included in the *samity*. However, at the initial level, NGOs themselves, with the help of the local community, select their beneficiaries based on their targets. Thus the beneficiary selection and group formation for the *shari'a*-based microfinance programme of *Fael Khair* of Muslim Aid use a community approach to ensure that all eligible and interested people can participate in their programme. As Muslim Aid (2010b, p. 13) states,

> The beneficiary identification mechanism is participatory. Muslim Aid community level staff were given the primary responsibility to select the beneficiaries in consultation with the community and the local government. A seven-member community level Project Implementation Committee (PIC) was drawn from the existing social structure of the cyclone *Sidra* population from members of the local community – a teacher, a businessman; a Union Parishad member, a religious leader, a community-based organization (CBO) representative, a beneficiary representative and a woman from a woman headed household to encourage women's participation.

It is unequivocal that the official version of participation may be different from that of the programme participants. At some point, participation was not as clear as the NGOs claims. NGO programme participation indicates inclusion of the beneficiaries, but it acts as well as a source of exclusion for many others in the same area of operation, due to diverse reasons. During the interviews with non-beneficiaries of Islamic NGOs they claimed that they wanted to be members of the Islamic NGO, but the officials did not want to take them on. Therefore, I asked why they (the Islamic NGO officials) did not include certain people. All of them replied with the same answer, which mainly referred to their limited capacity. It is obvious that the resource limitation is one of the underlying factors in the exclusion. Yet, the respondents told of many other reasons for the exclusion of other participants along with the religious and political orientation of the beneficiaries. Although the Islamic NGOs promise to reach the poorest of the poor with their microfinance, some of them are still left behind or intentionally excluded due to the fact that they are not 'business worthy' or 'bankable'. This was manifested during the focus group discussion and interviews with respondents at Shyamnagar, most of whom rely on the forest for their livelihood and are virtually landless, since they live on the government's *khas* land. This was particularly evident during the interview with Jalil, one of my respondents at Shyamnagar, who claims: 'they [*Islami Samity*] are giving to the rich. Those who have 50 *bighas* of land are with the Islamic NGOs. I am a poor man; but they will not give it to me.' The tendency towards exclusion and preference for a certain group of people has an important implication for the participation mantra, and accountability and transparency towards their beneficiaries.

NGO-led development discourse revolves around the idea of accountability to ensure that the practice is people orientated, and that the grassroots people's desires and demands are leading to a better development outcome. Therefore, accountability as one of the core values in development practices is also prevalent in the practices of Islamic NGOs. Like the mainstream NGOs, their accountability is more oriented to their beneficiaries.

Muslim Aid is a member of the Humanitarian Accountability Partnership (HAP)[6] and believes it is accountable to the beneficiaries for delivering all its services and interventions in a timely and orderly manner by maintaining the quality of deliverables. Information sharing with beneficiaries and their involvement in the process of planning, implementating and monitoring Muslim Aid's interventions was ensured through community meetings, training, public information boards, signboards, banners, bulletins, stickers, posters, T-shirts and other media. Muslim Aid implemented a systematic complaints-handling mechanism which enabled beneficiaries to easily convey their concerns through suggestion/complaint boxes established in the project offices to receive suggestions or complaints from the beneficiaries and other stakeholders.

Muslim Aid introduced a complaint and response mechanism with a proper feedback system during the project period. The following procedure was adopted:

- Finalizing the focal/contact person from male and female staff from the field offices of the NGO and informing the beneficiaries of the name of the contact person through community meetings. Beneficiaries were assured that the complainant's details would be confidential and not revealed to project staff.
- Introducing complaints and suggestion boxes in visible and easily accessible places for the beneficiaries who were informed of the time when the box would be opened. Contact addresses, including the phone numbers of the contact persons, were communicated to beneficiaries through pass books, beneficiaries files, information boards, and leaflets and community meetings.
- All complaints and suggestions were recorded in the register and a reply was given to the complainant within three days, either individually or in group meetings and/or by taking appropriate action on the complaint (Muslim Aid, n.d.a).

Muslim Aid installed display boards, information boards, billboards and signboards, and also distributed printed news bulletins, leaflets and stickers. Providing contact details of Muslim Aid staff to beneficiaries enabled them to have access to all information regarding Muslim Aid and its emergency operations.

Other Islamic NGOs in the study also revealed their commitment towards accountability and transparency. During the interviews with the NGO officials at their head office and at the local branches in particular, they repeatedly emphasized how transparent and accountable they are in their operations and with their beneficiaries. To ensure their transparency and accountability, NGO workers referred to their accountability to the management at the district or zone level. At the same time, they also referred to their monthly reports and meetings with the local administration (e.g. with the Upazila Nirbahee Officer) and local the management committee formed by the NGOs where they report on their activities, progress and problems.

At the beneficiary level, the concept of transparency and accountability is not clear, though, when I asked, respondents focused on whether they had to spend money or provide something else in exchange for the services. All of the respondents agreed that they did not spend a single penny or use their kinship network to receive services from Islamic NGOs. Yet, a few key informants insist that Islamic NGOs provide services to certain special or likeminded people. As a local government representative at Sharonkhola claims,

> Those who work with Muslim Aid UK Bangladesh chapter … majority of them are from a religious-fundamentalist political party and we also identified it here. People who belong to Jamaat-e-Islam, along with some other fundamentalist circle, are representing/running Muslim Aid in Bangladesh.

However, none of the local branch managers or programme officers of Islamic NGOs agreed with this claim, but rather emphasized their non-discriminatory policy. As an official of an Islamic NGO at Sharonkhola describes it:

> A renowned face of this area, whose name I don't want to tell you, once told me that we were providing houses selectively and only to the Jamaat. I replied, if this is the case, then please come with me one day, to see how many centres we do have at Jamaat-e-Islami's house, how many at Awami League's house and how many at BNP's house. Yes, we have a centre at Jamaat-e-Islami's house, but how many are they? On my way to a centre, a person who is not our member told me that we are making people militant, helping only Jamaat. Then I replied to him, if we are converting all the people to Jamaat, then how come we have 200/250 Hindu members? Moreover, we have such centres where all 30 women are Hindu.

Yet this contradicts the claim of some Islamic beneficiaries who state that in their *samity* more than 80 per cent are supporters of Jamaat-e-Islam, which proves the allegation of the local government representative challenging their bias towards 'special party people' as he terms it. Therefore, it is very complex as to how they maintain transparency and a corruption-free service delivery. It is quite possible that if they had provided services to likeminded people there would be less accountability towards the beneficiary. It is important to note that whenever I asked the Islamic NGOs' beneficiaries what they had to do in case of any complaint they had one common answer, namely to inform the branch manager (*boro* sir).

All the officials of these Islamic organizations at local level repeatedly claimed that they never even drink a glass of water at the beneficiary's house. By saying this, they wanted to show the transparent nature of their transactions with the beneficiaries. As one official at Sharonkhola put it, 'nobody can ever claim that we had a cigarette, betel leaf or even a glass of water from any beneficiaries'. The beneficiaries also told me the same thing. Almost all the beneficiaries told me that it's a desire that their 'bhi' ('sir') should have something at their home, but they said no Islamic NGO official agreed to eat or drink anything at the beneficiary's house.

During my participation in the *samity* meeting, one of the respondents, who is also the centre leader, requested that the officials have breakfast with them. She became desperate to feed us, since the officer and I arrived at the *samity* meeting at 7.20 a.m. She insisted that I have breakfast or at least some *muri* (puffed rice) or biscuit at her home which, as she said, would give her pleasure and be seen as an honour to feed me (since I am a university professor). I said to her, okay, give me some *muri* and just water. Interestingly, the NGO officer did not accept anything. I asked him why he did not even want to drink a glass of water at this beneficiary's house. His simple answer was, 'there is no rule to eat or drink at a beneficiary's house'. When I asked why, he replied, 'because it might create the opportunity to be close with the beneficiary, resulting in bias and corruption on both sides'. Although their intention may indicate their unbiased attitude towards the beneficiaries and their promise against corruption, it is unlikely that this strict commitment helps them to achieve a successful loan recovery, since getting close to the beneficiary may lead the NGO worker to be flexible in collecting the repayments.

Yet transparency at the micro level may not reflect what is happening at the macro level, namely at the organizational level. As Ahmad (2009) argues, the RNGO in his study is to some extent corrupt. Contrary to his findings, I did not find endemic corruption in Islamic NGOs, although there is some evidence of corruption to a lesser extent. Although their annual reports contain the certified accounts which let people know where the money is coming from and where they are spending it, there were no details on the category of 'donation' (i.e. who is giving the donation). Yet some contradictions exist between the beneficiaries' and the officials' opinion with that of non-beneficiaries and what key informants discovered in the study areas. Some of them said that, particularly in the case of humanitarian aid, they had to bribe the local leaders to get the shelter or house for them. However, all the officials denied this claim when I interviewed them in the field. Whatever the real issue, all the officials tended to embody their commitment towards accountability and transparency, which represents their professionalism, and to use hidden tools to discipline the conduct of the subject.

## Governmentality, the disciplinary mechanism and Islamic NGOs

Professionalism, as is evident in the accountability, transparency and efficiency rhetoric in NGO practices, resembles the disciplinary mechanism which, following Foucault, may be termed 'the conduct of conduct'. NGO rhetoric on professionalism, therefore, is used to 'regulate the autonomous conduct of the employees through the articulation of competence' (Fournier, 1999, p. 282). Although we usually think of NGO accountability as downwards (i.e. to the client), at the organizational level people at the bottom of NGOs (e.g. fieldworkers) are accountable to their superior authority. Irrespective of the religious orientation of NGOs, the programme manager or branch manager who is in charge of a local unit of an NGO is always accountable to a higher authority and is seldom able to influence the decision making at the upper level. To take control of and keep them accountable, local in-charge/branch managers always set a target to disburse a certain amount of money to the potential beneficiary (e.g. in the case of microfinance). They are always under pressure to meet this target to prove their competence, as this is related to their future promotion and job security. One of the respondents at an Islamic NGO head office claimed that he disbursed 240 million Taka within the first six months of 2010. Thus, it is obvious that all the local officials must meet the target of disbursement of specific amounts of money during a certain period. One of the respondents at Tala expressed his concern over the disbursement, saying, 'In this month I have got a *target* to disburse 15 million Taka (BDT)'. In addition, all relevant employees of NGOs are obliged to increase the activities and performance of their NGOs. For example, at the IBF under the *Fael Khair* programme, every programme officer, as the operational manual suggests, 'has to establish 10 centers within six months and six groups in each center within nine months'. This conditionality puts pressure on local-level officials to increase their programme networks as well as to disburse and collect the money from the field to prove their efficiency and performance. In this way they are able to secure their job and future promotions.

Moreover, although the NGOs consider themselves to be autonomous (which in practice does not exist due to their upward accountability), the field-level officials do hold the power to influence decisions from the higher authority. All the NGO officials at the local level told me that they had received training and orientation on the principles and programmes of their NGOs, and that they were motivated and guided by those principles. During the interviews with the field-level officers of NGOs they explained how they are following these instructions to achieve successful operation in the field. One branch manager of an Islamic NGO told me how the training they received from head office helped him to follow the righteous path, away from corruption, leading ultimately to the successful operation of the NGO. When I asked what led them to follow the virtuous path and become corruption-free, one of the respondents replied:

> Look at you [pointing towards me], you are fasting.[7] You can eat something secretly while fasting; none in this world can trace it out. But you don't. Because, you believe, I am fasting from fear of Allah. This fear drives people in positive directions and this is the particular uniqueness of faith-based organizations.

To govern the conduct of employees of Islamic NGOs, some principles of Islamic religion have been adopted that, it is believed, bind the employees together and allow them to work more efficiently and in a committed manner. Yet one of the respondents, who is Project Implementation Officer at an international Islamic NGO, expressed his inability to provide information regarding a programme intervention. I asked him whether they have any microfinance components in their programme. He replied, 'I don't know, my upper officials can tell you, even if I know, I am not allowed to tell you.' Therefore, the removal of power from those at the middle levels or at the bottom of an organization helps the management authority at head office to control them as well as monitoring their behaviour.

At the beneficiary level, governing the conduct of the NGO subject is very evident. Previous research on mainstream secular NGOs has spelled out disciplinary mechanisms to 'control' the targeted population who are meant to be their 'clients' or beneficiaries (e.g. Karim, 2008, 2011). It has clearly been argued that '*development* [emphasis in original] deployment in rural villages in Bangladesh resembles the deployment that took place in European societies when what Foucault refers to as "disciplinary power" was established' (Bhuiyan *et al.*, 2005, p. 349). What I want to mention here about the disciplinary mechanism that has been used to control the population is the 'group' collateral approach. Since the microcredit programme is based on the idea that those people who don't have the ability to provide any financial or material collateral are excluded from the formal credit system, the NGOs used this opportunity to provide credit for them. Although there is no financial or material collateral, they use the group responsibility to ensure and manage their businesses of credit. Therefore, if any of the members of the group cannot pay their weekly instalment, the group has to take the responsibility to pay that instalment. This group collateral also acts as a vigilance and surveillance tool to control the conduct of the beneficiary; for example, for what purpose is she spending the money? Therefore, each member of a group keeps an eye on others' activities to serve her purpose better so that she doesn't have to shoulder the responsibility to repay the loan. This is one way to ensure that the beneficiary pays back the money and follows the rules of the NGOs as well as to control the population for their benefit. The benefit to the beneficiaries is to secure further loans while for the NGOs the benefit is a more efficient performance, as well as reducing their operational costs. One of the respondents, Zinia at Sharonkhola, explained how this group collateral works for them:

> There is no possibility of missing an instalment from any member in our centre. Since I am the centre leader I have the responsibility to look after anyone who is becoming a defaulter in my group as well as in my centre. If anyone faces any problem and misses any instalment in my group, all of us help her to pay the money back. But Alhamdulillah (all praise to Allah) during the past two years none of our group members have faced such a problem yet.

Yet the NGO may have different motives. NGOs see the group approach as an effective mechanism to recover their investment easily. One of the Islamic NGOs demonstrates its vision:

> If any investment receiver becomes a defaulter, members of the group will take measures to collect the money. Since the group members have selected the members of their choice to form a group and provided mutual guarantees in a written form, all the members must return the default loan without any delay.

As per the programme manual of IBF for *Fael Khair* programme, one of the duties of the programme officer is to ensure that 'if any one who is a member of any other NGO wants to join *Fael Khair* project, she has to refund all the debts of other NGOs and bring a debt clearance certificate and she has to *promise* that she will not take any interest based credit in future'. This was also evident during my interviews with local people.

One beneficiary at Tala expressed his opinion on the conditionality of Islamic NGOs, claiming that the 'Islami Bank (*Islami samity)* is giving money to the people on some conditions'. I asked what these conditions were. He replied, 'Need to offer prayer five times a day, can't lie, and can't be involved in antisocial activities.' During the interviews I asked the respondents how they had become members of Islamic NGOs. This potentially excludes those who are not very strict observant Muslims. In response to this question, Ranu, an IBF beneficiary at Tala, told her story of how she became a member:

> There was a *hojur* [Islamic scholar] named Abdus Salam who told us that we would make members of our NGO those who would support Jamaat-e-Islam, and respect Jamaat. He (my husband) offers prayer regularly and goes with Salam. Salam also said those who would pray will get money from the *Islami samity*. Since he is devoted to Islam and goes to the meetings related to Islam, hence I got the opportunity to get into the *samity*.

If any members of the NGOs were unable to meet the conditions, they might get expelled from the programme. For example, it is explicitly mentioned in the operation manual that 'if any member behaves beyond the project-rules, through a discussion within the centre meeting she would be expelled', and 'if any member is absent from three weekly meetings without any emergency cause, she would be expelled from the group after a consultation with the centre leader and the group leader'. Besides, this Islamic NGO believes that

> everybody must strictly follow the rules of the project and the centre. If even a little relaxation in the rules and discipline happens, all the activities of the project are bound to be jeopardized. As a result the aims and objectives of the programme would be interrupted.

## Funding NGOs and governmentality

In the context of neoliberal governmentality there has been a shift in the pattern of governance from state to non-state actors (e.g. transnational organizations), leading to the theorization of transnational governmentality (Ferguson and Gupta, 2002). Transnational governmentality, as Ferguson and Gupta (2002, p. 990) argue, includes not only new strategies of discipline and regulation, exemplified by the WTO and the Structural Adjustment Programmes implemented by the IMF, but also transnational alliances forged by activists and grassroots organizations, and the proliferation of voluntary organizations supported by complex networks of international and transnational funding and personnel.

This complex nature of governance through a network of NGOs relates to what Bhatt (2007, p. 1075) calls 'hypergovernance'. Hypergovernance, Bhatt (2007, p. 1075) argues, 'exemplifies how the very near and the very far, the very large and very small become intertwined in transnational relations of power and domination'. This governance process, Humphrey (2012, p. 146) argues, 'involves global projects, Western and Islamic, acting at the local level, articulated through global discourses – rule of law, human rights, humanitarianism and Islamic radicalism'. Therefore, it is imperative to analyse the practice of neoliberal governmentality through examining the complex web of (transnational) networks and hence the funding of NGOs in Bangladesh as well as their emphasis on the nature and pattern of programmes, agendas and mobilization of the grassroots people to manage the population or the 'conduct of the conduct'.

### *Funding NGOs in Bangladesh: constructing the discourse*

Although there is much discussion regarding the sources of NGO funding, there is frequently no strong evidence for it. Different perspectives on Islamic NGO funding prevail in the government and the academic and popular media discourse. For example, Islamic NGOs in Bangladesh, as Ahmad (2009, p. 200) argues, 'are suspected of having links with international Islamic terrorist organizations' through which millions of Takas are channelled into the country to several Islamic NGOs in the absence of an effective state monitoring system. Although 'there are no records of the funds arriving in Bangladesh, but according to one estimate, the amount ranges from BDT four to five billion [US$61.5 million to US$79.6 million] per year' (Kumar, 2009, p. 905). Kumar also argues that the funds come from different countries in the Middle East (e.g. Libya, Abu Dhabi, Saudi Arabia, Qatar, Kuwait, Iran and Egypt). Another author, Barkat (2006), who claims that the complex web of terror financing networks explains the 'economics of fundamentalism', argues that besides the regular inflow of foreign funds, extremist outfits have solidified their financial base and make a net yearly income of US$200 million. Of this total income, the second largest contributor after financial institutions (e.g. Islamic banks, insurance and leasing companies) is the NGO sector, contributing 20.8 per cent of the net profit. Yet during an interview with another economist in an Islamic organization he questioned the objectivity of the data presented by Barkat (2006) and regarded this as politically biased and manipulated.

In contrast to the funding of Islamic NGOs, funding sources of secular NGOs are mainly based in the Western developed countries. These secular NGOs, therefore, as Mannan (2009, p. 89) argues, 'operate as an avenue for putting Western development policies, theories etc. into practice in the local and village society' of Bangladesh. This is a process he refers to as the 'indigenization of Western culture'. Similarly, some researchers, particularly with leftist orientations (e.g. Muhammad, 2009), argue that Western capitalism and imperialism is sustaining through funding these local NGOs in Bangladesh where clients (e.g. consumers of microcredit, *polli* (rural) phones, hybrid chickens or seeds) are dependent upon their patron NGOs (Karim, 2008, 2011).

The political and religious divide in the Bangladeshi media has constructed the image of Islamic NGOs differently. While some of the mainstream news media (*Daily Star*, *Prothom-Alo*, *New Age*) perceive Islamic NGOs as financed by Islamists, other news media such as the *Daily Naya Dignta, Sangram*[8] portray them as not financed by Islamists. These news media rather focus on the success of Islamic NGOs. As a sister concern of Islami Bank Bangladesh Ltd, the IBF has come to the media's spotlight since the government states that the Islamic Bank is channelling its 8 per cent of total profit towards Jahidi activities and this is being channelled through the IBF in the name of social welfare (*Daily Star*, 2009). Contrary to this, during the interviews with officials of Islamic NGOs I was shown many newspaper clips about their activities, particularly those published in the *Daily Naya Dignta* as well as telecast by Dinganta Television, both of which are owned by a Jamaat leader Mir Kashem Ali, who is currently held on charges of committing war crimes against humanity during Bangladesh's 1971 independence war. This is, as I argue, due to the fact that Bangladeshi state and nation is divided along religious–political lines.

Following the country-wide terror bombing on 17 August 2005 the then military-backed government and the present centre-left government accused some of the national and international NGOs of funding terrorism in Bangladesh. For example, on 19 March 2009, following the Finance Minister's remarks on terror funding through Islamic NGOs, the *Daily Star* provided a list of such suspected NGOs which included 'Rabita Al-Alam Al-Islami, Al-Muntada Al-Islami, Society of Social Reforms, Qatar Charitable Society, Islamic Relief Agency, Al-Forkan Foundation, International Relief Organisation, Kuwait Joint Relief Committee, Muslim Aid Bangladesh, Dar Al-Khair, Hayatul Igachha and Tawheed-e-Noor' in their suspect list (*Daily Star*, 2009; Azad, 2009, p. 57). A recent report published by the US Senate Permanent Subcommittee on Investigations on 17 July 2012 alleged that the Islami Bank Bangladesh Ltd (IBBL) and the Social Islami Bank Ltd (SIBL) have links to terrorist financing that also exposed British banking giant HSBC's internal governance failure to control flows of suspect funds. It is also important to note that 37 per cent of the share of Islami Bank Bangladesh is held by the Saudi Arabian AL-Rajhi family and its different enterprises; for example, Al-Rajhi Bank (the world's largest Islamic Bank). Research undertaken by Barber (2011, p. 5) and Ehrenfeld (2005, pp. 45–51) shows that Islamic banks (e.g. Al-Rajhi Bank) are involved in the financing of Islamic terrorism through *shari'a*-compliant financing structures and mechanisms. While the present centre-left government is very critical of the Islamic NGOs, the previous centre-right government was more relaxed towards them, as some of its prominent leaders have allegedly patronized the Islamists in Bangladesh (Azad, 2009, pp. 50–51; Kumar, 2009, p. 908).

### *People's perception of the funding of Islamic NGOs*

Contrary to the media, academic and political discourse on funding, my research shows that very few beneficiaries of either secular or Islamic NGOs could provide me with any ideas regarding the sources of funding and why these NGOs are serving them. Yet the key informants (e.g. local government representatives, schoolteachers) in the study areas could only vaguely envisage the sources of funding, particularly for the religious NGOs. This is, as this research has found, due to the *lack of access, awareness and availability* of the information about the sources of the funding to the beneficiaries as well as the unwillingness and inefficiency of NGO officials to deliver the information on the sources of funding. This gap in information eventually led people to assume and cultivate different stories on funding, particularly about the Islamic NGOs. For example, during the field visits, I have noticed a clear distinction people used between the money they receive from their respective NGOs. Beneficiaries of Christian NGOs tend to think the money is coming from the Christian and the local church, while the Islamic NGO beneficiaries consider their money comes from overseas Muslims and Islam. Contrary to these two categories, people tend to think the money for the secular NGOs (e.g. BRAC) is coming from foreign countries, though sometimes they relate it to the Christian source of funding.

Likewise, some of the respondents also adhere to the idea that there are people in foreign countries who help them, though in most cases they are not sure who those people are. Yet few people assumed that, since they are Muslim and there are some rich Muslim countries, there is a kind of obligation to help other poor Muslims. At the same time, a few people tended to believe that some Bangladeshi people are collecting *zakat* in foreign countries to help them.

During interviews with Amirul Islam at Tala, a beneficiary of BRAC's interest-free loan (the same as other Islamic NGOs funded by the *Fael Khair* programme of IDB), he revealed his awareness of the sources of the funding of the programme in which he is participating and explained to me his worries and ideas about such funding:

> Sometimes I think why are they giving us interest-free loans and from where have they got the money. I think there may be some powerful and rich people in a foreign country. It may be that they donate or provide *zakat*. Instead of giving to a single poor person, they distribute the money through a process.

Since he assumed the money came from a Muslim, I asked him, if the money came from a Christian, what he would do. He showed a very interesting insight:

> I do not have any trouble with the money whether it is from a Christian or a Muslim. Whether the money is from a Muslim or non-Muslim, I am not paying and getting any interest. For this, I do not have any responsibilities (as I am not committing a sin). However, when it comes to interest, whether it is from Muslim or Christian, I am affected.

Yet, in the same area, an IBF beneficiary, Mohsena, who does not know who is funding the NGOs, told me that she wouldn't ever take the money if it came from a Christian. Although she does not know the source, she strongly believes that the money is coming from the kind Muslims living in a foreign country. When I asked whether she could imagine any such country, she replied, 'I think they are from Saudi'. Then I asked why Saudi Arabia. She replied: 'Saudi Arabia is number one Muslim country; they are pious and kind to Muslims.'

A similar viewpoint was expressed by a shelter beneficiary in Sharonkhola. Thus Salenur, a MABFO shelter beneficiary at Sharonkhola, believes that 'there was a rich man who was Christian. He earned lots of money and property and became a Muslim. Suddenly he became very kind in his mind, and wanted to do something for the Muslims and sent the money to help us.' As I understood it, she was referring to Muslim Aid founder Cat Stevens, the folk singer and Christian convert to Islam.

Contrary to these vague answers to the question of funding, only a few respondents, particularly those who belong to MACCA, could identify the original source of the funding of the NGO. For example, Zhinu, a MACCA beneficiary, told me about her ideas regarding the funding of their NGO: 'we heard the money is coming from the *zakat* and they are giving us the money as *zakat*. Those who are bringing and maintaining these *zakat*, they are giving this money to us as *zakat* and will not ask us to pay back the money.' In saying this, I am not arguing that all the beneficiaries of MACCA know the source of the funding. When I asked the president of the *Hasana* programme at Manikganj whether he knew the source of the money he said he only knew that the money was from *zakat*, but he had no idea who was paying this *zakat* or from whom MACCA was collecting the money. As he said, 'We don't know this, but our Chairman Abul Kalam Azad (founder of MACCA), he is giving us the money, but we don't know from where he is bringing the money.'

During the research it became clear that though the beneficiary or the non-beneficiary could not tell me the sources of the funding for Islamic NGOs, they could certainly tell me the purpose of the money. Khadija, a member of Grameen Bank (at Tala) who also received Islamic microfinance, told me she does not have any idea where the money came from but she only knows that this money came for Islam, so that people can learn and understand Islam. Maksuda at Tala, a Muslim Aid beneficiary, also told me the same thing: 'I don't know, people told me this is Islam's money.' I asked Khadiza, an IBF beneficiary at Sharonkhola, whether Islamic NGOs told them why they were helping them and from where they got the money. She replied, 'No.' When I asked her again whether she wanted to know about the source of their funding, she replied that she did not want to know. She only knows that the *Islami samity* gives them the money for *sawab*.[9]

Thus almost all of the respondents in this research could not tell me about the source of funding for their NGOs. Some respondents, on the contrary, even asked me how and why they needed to know about the NGOs' sources of funding. For example, IBF beneficiary Nodia at Sharonkhola told me when I asked her where the funding came from, 'How do I know from where and how the NGO got the funding?' In most cases respondents did not show any interest in the sources of funding for their NGOs. For example, Kashem at Sharonkhola, who is a beneficiary of Muslim Aid, mentioned the name of the immediate contact person at Muslim Aid who was looking after their Rainbow Family programme. He did not feel any necessity to know the source of funding as he says: 'I don't need to know much information [on funding]. I just know that they came to help us.' At some point, I found that these poor people feel it is difficult and 'deemed improper' to ask about the sources of the NGOs' funding due mainly to the unequal power relations, as beneficiaries feel they may be excluded from the financial benefits they are supposed to receive from the NGOs.

In addition to this, there is also evidence that NGO officials did not inform the beneficiaries about the sources of funding. Bokul of the IBF told me that she did not ask the NGOs where they got the money and the NGO did not tell her. I asked Romela, a Muslim Aid beneficiary, whether Muslim Aid had informed her about the source of their funding and she said it had not done so. Then I asked whether she had questioned Muslim Aid about this. She said,

> When we went to the office at Rayenda, we asked them, as we felt since it is interest free, if there happened to be any problem in the future, and they [Muslim Aid] assured us that there is no problem with the funding. But they did not tell us from where they got the money.

The lack of information on the issue of funding also reveals the NGO officials' unwillingness and inefficiency to deal with it. For example, during a visit to the local branch office of Islamic NGOs at Tala, I interviewed its branch manager and programme officers, and asked them to tell me whether they had encountered any problems running their programme. All of them agreed that when they go to the field, 'many people asked why this is without interest. Many comment who is there to provide loan without interest in this time.... What is their intention.... Some make good comments, but some make bad comments.' Then I asked them how they explained their source of funding. One of the field officers, Hamid, replied:

> We try to explain it in different ways. Sometimes I say, this is from Islami Bank since they know it just as Islami Bank. They do not know about IBF. So I make a kind of advertisement for the Bank (Islami Bank). Then I tell them that since Islamic Bank is making huge profits, for example, this year the Bank has made a profit of 11,000 crores Taka, so they are sending the money to *Sidr*- or *Aila*-affected areas. Sometime I say that there is a share of IDB, so IDB is helping us, therefore you have to return the money. So we are giving the money for the time being to help you.

Then I asked them whether it would be better to explain to the people about the IDB, who they are and why they are providing funding. The manager of the branch explained:

> There is some hidden problem. So we do not directly spread information that the money is from a donation/charity [*daner* Taka]. If we tell them it is *daner* Taka, they will not return the money. That's why we try our best to conceal the real source of the funding, since they will not pay the money back at all.

This lack of access to information eventually led people to construct their own stories regarding the issue of funding, particularly for the Islamic NGOs. For example, one of the respondents who is programme officer at an Islamic NGO told me an interesting story about people's construction as to the source of funding. He went on:

> People think that the money belongs to Jamaat Islam. One of the sons of Golam Azam, the Ammer of Jamaat-e-Islam, is Abul Kahair. They therefore thought this money [of the *Fael Khair* programme] is the money of Golam Azam's son's, since the name of the programme is *Fael Khair*.

Even key informants in the study areas have created their own stories about sources of funding. Whenever I interviewed a key local person, such as Abdul Malek, a schoolteacher, they did not know who these Islamic NGOs were, or from where they were getting their funds. Abdul Malek just assumed that Muslims or some Muslim countries together are funding these NGOs. During an interview with a member of the local government he told me what he knows about the funding of these NGOs. He explained:

> I asked them from where they are managing this aid. Then they said, what we distribute to you we beg [*chyea ani*] it from other people. Members of our organization beg for you from foreign countries like London, Canada. Some donate willingly and we beg from some. Besides, there are many people of us abroad who help us. Therefore, we beg these [funds] from foreign countries and distribute them to you.

The perspectives on the sources of funding for Islamic NGOs differ one from the other, leading to a controversy. What is, however, pertinent is the active presence of the transnational donors on programmes, agendas, and the operation of these Islamic NGOs in Bangladesh. In the following section, I explain how donors and transnational funding networks, including diasporas, shape and control the pattern of activities of local NGOs as well as exercising power through transferring funds, knowledge and expertise that reinforces neoliberal ideology.

## Transnational networks, funding and governmentality: the case of Islamic NGOs

The obvious relation between funding and neoliberal development is that of funding (e.g. from transnational donors) through NGOs, leading to a shift from state governance to governance by non-state actors. These non-state actors (e.g. NGOs) must follow the donor prescription to continue with the existing funds as well as to keep open the prospect of any further funding. One of the high-ranked officials of an Islamic NGO expressed their obligation to their donor in this way: 'Well, if our donor is saying this is the way they wish their work to be carried out, then we follow this.' One of the respondents who is also President of the NGO Coordination Committee at Sharonkhola and a recipient of BRAC's funding for informal education told me how the donor controls them through funding:

> We have to abide by the rules of the donors. There is no way to get out of this. For example, once the European Commission funded BRAC for a non-formal education project. As a condition, EC suggested to BRAC to increase the salary. But BRAC said, I run the non-formal education, so it will run the way it was run before. For this reason, this project was held up for two years. Then BRAC had to agree with whatever the methodology they [EC] want to run the project, and finally they agreed to fund BRAC's non-formal education project.

This is not very different from the case of Islamic NGOs. Although secular and religious NGOs are both the vehicle of neoliberal policies and practices through which they replace the state in service delivery, for example, whether it is disaster relief, microfinance or education, many have tended to see the work of Islamic NGOs as a reaction to neoliberalism (International Crisis Group, 2005). This is due to the tendency among Islamic NGOs to 'contest the influence of "the West" and secularized and Westernized elites, including capitalist rent-seeking behavior, individualism, and lack of solidarity' (Kaag, 2008, p. 4). This is not always the case, as Islamic NGOs, on the one hand, adopt the Islamic notion of charity and the humanitarian principles of Islam as their prime mover; yet, on the other hand, they practise the neoliberal principles of the market economy to create successful entrepreneurial subjects through self-improvement, productivity and individualism. In this regard access to funding for the secular donor plays an important role in the nature and pattern of activities of Islamic NGOs. For example, Hopgood and Vinjamuri (2012) claim that:

> To access public funds, it [Islamic Relief] must operate in a secular manner (e.g. not proselytize or discriminate in aid giving or hiring).... If IR seeks to grow, it will need to secure public money or widen its appeal to large numbers of non-Muslims; growth, in other hands, depends on maintaining a degree of secularization.

In this research, Muslim Aid and MACCA repeatedly showed their non-discriminatory policies towards other religious adherents, particularly the Hindus and their secular donors (e.g. ECHO, USAID and the World Bank). For example, one of the high officials of an Islamic NGO claimed, 'as an international NGO and as a Muslim NGO we do not discriminate. So, 30 per cent of our beneficiaries in Bangladesh are non-Muslim.' Thus the source of public funding pushes Islamic NGOs to negotiate their organizational identity. It is therefore Islamic NGOs, like Muslim Aid and MACCA in this study, which try to balance the secular mainstream discourse on development (e.g. sustainability, accountability, participation, empowerment and gender) with the principle of justice and compassion in Islam. Other Islamic NGOs (e.g. IBF) are more orientated towards all-encompassing Islam in their practice, activities and organizational identity. While it is easy for large NGOs to resist donors' prescriptions to some extent, for smaller NGOs it is much more difficult because of the critical importance for their survival of receiving a grant. Thus many NGOs survive only through the support of their funders, and are consequently compelled to follow the prescriptions of the donors to adopt particular programmes and patterns of activities. This essentially undermines the NGOs' accountability to its aid recipients.

### *Muslim diaspora: imagined community and building a just society*

Muslim diasporas, particularly from Pakistan and Bangladesh, have contributed strongly to the development of Muslim charities in the West. For example, Muslim Aid UK is founded by British Muslims, predominantly Pakistani and Bangladeshi diasporas in London (Clarke, 2010). In 2007, there was a total of 78 staff in the Muslim Aid Headquarters in London, of whom around 70 per cent were of Pakistani and of Bangladeshi origin.

This effort of diasporas has an important influence on the sociopolitical and cultural construct in their country of origin. As Clarke (2010, p. 517) argues, 'Ideologically, many [people associated with Muslim Aid] were influenced by the social justice agendas of Jamaat-e-Islam, a political party which campaigns for the (peaceful) introduction of *shariah* law' in both Pakistan and Bangladesh. At the same time, the construction of the conservative current of Jamaat-e-Islam strongly influenced Muslim Aid's ideology. Since its inception, for example, 17 trustees of Muslim Aid adhered to such a conservative ideology and influenced the 'relations between the London head office and the Muslim Aid's thirty thousand regular donors'. The same was true for another of the largest Islamic NGOs in Britain called Islamic Relief. Islamic Relief, like Muslim Aid, was founded by Pakistani and Bangladeshi Muslim immigrants among others in London. However, there is a lack of research on the role of Bangladeshi migrants in the Middle East about the spread of political Islam. However, media reports claimed that the funding of militants and the spread of Islamic (radical) ideas in the country related to the migrants in the Middle East.

However, public funding that comes from Muslims, particularly the diasporas, also pushes Islamic NGOs to be committed towards maintaining Islamic identity. Therefore, Bangladeshi Muslim migrants in the West, particularly in Britain, and their role in shaping the Islamic way of life is not as yet identified by any research. However, following the cyclone *Sidr*, a UK-based Bangladeshi

TV channel named 'Channel S' raised funds for housing in the *Sidr*-affected areas. This funds were channelled through Muslim Aid.

> Channel S Fundraising department is dedicated to delivering a professional service to Mosques, Islamic Institutes, International Charities and Community Organisations. The department aims to maximise fundraising by raising awareness and providing good programming for the local and international community.[10]

Therefore, 'Shajalal Model Village' in Sharonkhola was named and funded by Channel S, which compelled Muslim Aid to adopt the name of the relief and rehabilitation site as Shajalal Model Village in Sharonkhola and Sha Paran Model Village in Patuakhali. When I asked why Channel S had used an Islamic name, NGO officials told me that this was just to attract immigrant Bangladeshi, Pakistani and other Muslims to raise funds to build a model village.

Another partner of Muslim Aid, Bangladesh is ECHO (Educational, Charitable, and Humanitarian Organization)-USA, a Bangladeshi diaspora charity organization based in California, USA which collects money from donations, *zakat* or *Qubani* and channels it through NGOs like Muslim Aid Bangladesh. Like ECHO-USA, BDesh Foundation, a Virginia, USA-based charity run by the expatriate Bangladeshi, collects *zakat, sadqah* and donations, and channels them to the NGOs (e.g. MACCA) to 'serve humanity and seek almighty Allah's pleasure through natural disaster relief, poverty alleviation, health and sanitation and educational projects'.[11] Likewise, individual donations, particularly during the Arabic month of Ramadan, to help poor people in their home country are abundant throughout the developed world such as Australia, the USA and the UK. During the month of Ramadan, they use many Quranic references to collect *zakat* and *sadqah* to help their fellow human beings. For example, BDEsh Foundation in its donation collection through its website, along with other verses from the Quran, mentioned Al-Baqara, Verse 215:

> They ask you as to what they should (in charity). Say: Whatever wealth you spend, it is for the parents and the near of kin and the orphan and the needy and the wayfarer, and whatever good you do, Allah surely knows.

The Foundation used Imam Magid in a video call to donate *zakat* to the organization during a fundraising dinner in 2011.[12]

Thus the activities of the Bangladeshi diaspora reflect upon their quest to tie themselves to their country of origin which forms an 'imagined community' that obliges them to work for their fellow human beings or the Muslim *ummah*.

### *The Fael Khair programme: anonymous donor and source of funding*

Moreover, transnational Islamic NGOs, aid communities and individual funding are the long-lasting and most efficient sources for Islamic NGOs in Bangladesh.

For example, The *Fael Khair* programme under study is the initiative of the Islamic Development Bank funded by a Saudi donor. In the case of MACCA, one of the main sources of the funding was *zakat*, most of which was donated by a corporation. In the case of IBF, alongside the IDB, Islami Bank Bangladesh was the main donor. Therefore, if the donor had a wish to follow a particular prescription, for example, naming the programme or the selection of a beneficiary, they had to follow this wish. During an interview with the *Fael Khair* project manager at the Islamic Development Bank he told me about the IDB's preferences and agendas for Islamic NGOs.

For the Islamic NGOs under this study, two of them (e.g. Muslim Aid and the Islamic Bank Foundation) secured funding from the IDB under the programme called *Fael Khair* to provide agro-input for the cyclone *Sidr*-affected people in the southwestern districts of Bangladesh. Out of a total of US$130 million, the *Fael Khair* programme was allocated US$20 million which was distributed among four NGOs.

As mentioned elsewhere in this chapter, the source of funding comes from an anonymous donor from Saudi Arabia who donated US$130 million for the *Sidr*-affected people in Bangladesh to the Islamic Development Bank, a Jeddah-based international organization. The IDB chose its partner to distribute the money to the affected people. It is also interesting to note that, among the four NGOs, two are secular and the other two are Islamic, and the majority of the money went to the Islamic NGOs (i.e. 60 per cent of the total donation). During interviews with IBD officials at their offices, they offered an interesting insight into how these NGOs operated and why IDB selected two Islamic (IBF and Muslim Aid) and two secular NGOs (BRAC and VOSD), and why the majority of the money went to the Islamic NGOs. One programme officer at IDB told me that the selection was based on the performance and reputation of the selected NGOs. I then asked why there were two Islamic and two secular NGOs. He replied:

> Actually, IDB prefers those who run their organization according to Islamic *shari'a*. For this reason, IDB preferred IBF and Muslim Aid in the beginning. But, afterwards, this raised some issues and controversy regarding the observance of *shari'a* principles. Because it is for the *Sidr*-affected people, you cannot abide by *shari'a* principles. For this reason, to make it neutral and to balance the programme operation, they selected BRAC and VOSD [secular NGOs].

Yet IDB officials disagreed that they have a preference for any specific beneficiary and religious activities.

Whether this new form of governmentality could ultimately produce better outcomes for rural people in Bangladesh requires attention. All the NGOs, regardless of their religious orientation, claim success over the development process in rural Bangladesh. Yet there are of course some differences that have led people to choose Islamic NGOs as an alternative to secular NGOs. The insight provided about the NGO sector in terms of its private funding mechanism suggests that Islamic NGOs are stimulating the development of a private social welfare system for the ultra-poor. This system is being developed with a sensitive approach driven from the humanitarian spirit of Islam for justice and equitable development. It is imperative that an emerging trend in the neoliberal practice of governmentality in the Islamic NGO sector is the introduction of religious rhetoric in development practice. However, it is not yet the time to estimate the extent of change it may bring to the existing social structure of rural Bangladesh, but it definitively poses a new approach to the control of development practices as well as to rural people, and to women in particular. Therefore, the blending of religious values with development Islamic NGOs is promoting a kind of female empowerment through which they govern the life of rural Muslim women, as I discuss in detail in Chapter 5.

## Notes

1 Operation Manual of the *Fael Khair* programme was supplied to me during my interview with one of the high officials of an Islamic NGO at Dhaka on 14 December 2010.
2 What is Microcredit? Available at www.grameen.com/index.php?option=com_content&task=view&id=28&Itemid=177 (accessed 2 January 2013).
3 Muhammad Yunus claims this during an interview with the *Kathmandu Post*, December 2012. Available at http://muhammadyunus.org/In-the-Media/the-kathmandu-post-interview-of-professor-yunus-all-the-institutions-and-policies-support-the-rich/ (accessed 7 January 2013).
4 For example, access and membership to a formal organization and the consequent identity of self-maximizing women entrepreneurs (Mayer and Rankin, 2002, p. 806).
5 This term is used for someone who has completely memorized the Quran.
6 The Humanitarian Accountability Partnership (HAP) International is a multi-agency initiative working to improve the accountability of humanitarian action to people affected by disasters and other crises. See www.hapinternational.org/ for details. According to Muslim Aid Bangladesh field office, Muslim Aid is a member of HAP and ensures accountability to beneficiaries. This ensures delivery of all the items in a timely and orderly manner but does not compromise on quality.

> Information sharing with the beneficiaries and their involvement in the process of planning, implementation and monitoring of Muslim Aid's interventions was ensured through community meeting, training, public information boards, signboards, banners, bulletins, stickers, posters, t-shirts and other media.
>
> (Muslim Aid, n.d.a, p. 23)

7 Since the interview was held in the Muslims' Holy Month of Fasting (Ramadan), it is a common belief that I may be fasting due to my Muslim identity.
8 Connected with the rightist political party Bangladesh Jamaat-e-Islam.
9 *Sawāb*, an Arabic term frequently used in Bengali meaning 'reward' accrues from the performance of good deeds and piety.
10 Details on Channel S may be found at www.chsuk.tv/charity/.
11 Available at www.bdeshfoundation.org/about/ (accessed 3 September 2012) For details on BDesh Foundation visit www.bdeshfoundation.org.
12 See the Imam's call on YouTube at www.youtube.com/watch?v=dI7WGojlhVo (accessed 3 September 2012).

## References

Ahmad, M. M. (2009). For God's Sake: The Religious Non-governmental Organizations in Bangladesh. In F. C. Khan, A. Ahmad and M. Quddus (eds), *Recreating the Commons? NGOs in Bangladesh* (pp. 183–206). Dhaka: The University Press.

Atia, M. (2012). 'A Way to Paradise': Pious Neoliberalism, Islam, and Faith-based Development. *Annals of the Association of American Geographers, 102*(4), 808–827.

Azad, A.K. (2009). Funding Terrorism: Can It Be Stopped? In I. Ahmed (ed.), *Terrorism in the 21st Century: Perspectives from Bangladesh* (pp. 33–68). Dhaka: University Press.

Barber, S. (2011). New Economy of Terror: The Financing of Islamist Terrorism. *Global Security Studies, 2*(1), 1–13.

Barkat, A. (2006). Economics of Fundamentalism and the Growth of Political Islam in Bangladesh. *Social Science Review, 23*(2), 1–30.

Bhatt, C. (2007). Frontlines and Interstices in the Global War on Terror. *Development and Change, 38*(6), 1073–1093.

Bhuiyan, A. H. A., Faraizi, A. H. and McAllister, J. (2005). Developmentalism as a Disciplinary Strategy in Bangladesh. *Modern Asian Studies, 39*(2), 349–368.

Clarke, G. (2010). Trans-faith Humanitarian Partnerships: The Case of Muslim Aid and the United Methodist Committee on Relief. *The European Journal of Development Research, 22*(4), 510–528. doi: 10.1057/ejdr.2010.22.

Daily Star. (2009). NGOs under Scanner for 'Funding Militancy'. Available at www.thedailystar.net/newDesign/news-details.php?nid=80287 (accessed 3 January 2011).

Ebrahim, A. (2003). Accountability in Practice: Mechanisms for NGOs. *World Development, 31*(5), 813–829.

Edwards, M. and Hulme, D. (1996a). *Beyond the Magic Bullet: NGO Performance and Accountability in the Post-cold War World.* West Hartford, CT: Kumarian Press.

Edwards, M. and Hulme, D. (1996b). Too Close for Comfort? The Impact of Official Aid on Nongovernmental Organizations. *World Development, 24*(6), 961–973.

Ehrenfeld, R. (2005). *Funding Evil: How Terrorism is Financed and How to Stop it.* Chicago, IL: Bonus Books.

Ferguson, J. (2009). The Uses of Neoliberalism. *Antipode, 41*(S1), 166–184.

Ferguson, J. and Gupta, A. (2002). Spatializing States: Toward an Ethnography of Neoliberal Governmentality. *American Ethnologist, 29*(4), 981–1002.

Fournier, V. (1999). The Appeal to 'Professionalism' as a Disciplinary Mechanism. *The Sociological Review, 47*(2), 280–307.

Hamann, T.H. (2009). Neoliberalism, Governmentality, and Ethics. *Foucault Studies*, 37–59.

Harvey, D. (2007). Neoliberalism as Creative Destruction. *The ANNALS of the American Academy of Political and Social Science, 610*(1), 22–44.

Hefner, R. W. (1998). *Market Cultures: Society and Morality in the New Asian Capitalisms*. Boulder, CO: Westview Press.

Hefner, R. W. (2012). Islam, Economic Globalization, and the Blended Ethics of Self. *Bustan: The Middle East Book Review, 3*, 91–108.

Hopgood, S. and Vinjamuri, L. (2012). Faith in Markets. In M. Barnett and J. Stein (eds), *Sacred Aid: Faith and Humanitarism*. New York: Oxford University Press.

Humphrey, M. (2012). Counter-militancy, Jihadists and Hypergovernance: Managing Disorder in the 'Uncompleted' Postcolonial State of Pakistan. *Arab Studies Quarterly, 34*(3), 144–157.

International Crisis Group. (2005). Islamist Terrorism in the Sahel: Fact or Fiction? *ICG Africa Report, 92*. Dakar and Brussels: International Crisis Group.

Kaag, M. (2008). Transnational Islamic NGOs in Chad: Islamic Solidarity in the Age of Neoliberalism. *Africa Today, 54*(3), 3–18.

Kamat, S. (2004). The Privatization of Public Interest: Theorizing NGO Discourse in a Neoliberal Era. *Review of International Political Economy, 11*(1), 155–176. doi: 10.1080/0969229042000179794.

Karim, L. (2008). Demystifying Micro-Credit The Grameen Bank, NGOs, and Neoliberalism in Bangladesh. *Cultural Dynamics, 20*(1), 5–29. doi: 10.1177/0921374007088053.

Karim, L. (2011). *Microfinance and its Discontents: Women in Debt in Bangladesh*. Minneapolis: University of Minnesota Press.

Khan, M. M. (2003). Accountability of NGOs in Bangladesh: A Critical Overview. *Public Management Review, 5*(2), 267–278.

Kumar, A. (2009). Terror Financing in Bangladesh. *Strategic Analysis, 33*(6), 903–917. doi: 10.1080/09700160903255913.

Larner, W. (2000). Neo-liberalism: Policy, Ideology, Governmentality. *Studies in Political Economy, 63*(autumn), 5–25.

MacKinnon, D. (2000). Managerialism, Governmentality and the State: A Neo-Foucauldian Approach to Local Economic Governance. *Political Geography, 19*(3), 293–314. doi: 10.1016/s0962–6298(99)00086–4.

MacKinnon, D. (2002). Rural Governance and Local Involvement: Assessing State–Community Relations in the Scottish Highlands. *Journal of Rural Studies, 18*(3), 307–324. doi: 10.1016/s0743–0167(01)00048–1.

Mannan, M. (2009). Islam, NGOs and Development: The Shaping of Conflict Models in Bangladesh In F. C. Khan, A. Ahmad and M. Quddus (eds), *Recreating the Commons? NGOs in Bangladesh* (pp. 81–106). Dhaka: The University Press.

Masjid Council for Community Advancement. (n.d.a). *Annual Report 2007* (32pp). Dhaka: Masjid Council for Community Advancement.

Masjid Council for Community Advancement. (n.d.b). *Annual Report 2009–10* (p. 42). Dhaka: Masjid Council for Community Advancement.

Muhammad, A. (2009). Grameen and Microcredit: A Tale of Corporate Success. *Economic and Political Weekly, 44*(35), 35.

Muslim Aid. (2010a). *Annual Report 2009: Microfinance and SME Programme* (48pp.). Dhaka: Muslim Aid.

Muslim Aid. (2010b). Fael Khair *Program for Victims of SIDR Cyclone in Bangladesh: Annual Progress Report* (May–December 2009) (32pp). Dhaka: Muslim Aid.

Muslim Aid. (n.d.a). *Cyclone SIDR Response* (27pp.). Dhaka: Muslim Aid.

Muslim Aid. (n.d.b). Participation in Shelter Project – From Design to Implementation and Monitoring, 6. Available at www.hapinternational.org/pool/files/ma-participation-in-shelter-project-from-design-to-implementation-and-monitoring.pdf (accessed 19 June 2010).

Najam, A. (1996). NGO Accountability: A Conceptual Framework. *Development Policy Review, 14*(4), 339–354.

O'Reilly, K. (2010). The Promise of Patronage: Adapting and Adopting Neoliberal Development. *Antipode, 42*(1), 179–200.

Osella, F. and Osella, C. (2009). Muslim Entrepreneurs in Public Life between India and the Gulf: Making Good and Doing Good. *Journal of the Royal Anthropological Institute, 15*(s1), S202–S221.

Rankin, K.N. (2001). Governing Development: Neoliberalism, Microcredit, and Rational Economic Woman. *Economy and Society, 30*(1), 18–37.

Rhyne, E. and Otero, M. (1992). Financial Services for Microenterprises: Principles and Institutions. *World Development, 20*(11), 1561–1571.

Rose, N. (1996a). The Death of the Social? Re-figuring the Territory of Government. *Economy and Society, 25*(3), 327–356. doi: 10.1080/03085149600000018.

Rose, N. (1996b). Governing 'Advanced' Liberal Democracies. In A. Barry, T. Osborne and N. Rose (eds), *Foucault and Political Reason: Liberalism, Neo-liberalism and Rationalities of Government* (pp. 37–64). Chicago, IL: University of Chicago Press.

Rudnyckyj, D. (2009). Spiritual Economies: Islam and Neoliberalism in Contemporary Indonesia. *Cultural Anthropology, 24*(1), 104–141.

Rudnyckyj, D. (2010). *Spiritual Economies: Islam, Globalization, and the Afterlife of Development*. Ithaca, NY: Cornell University Press.

Sloane, P. (1999). *Islam, Modernity and Entrepreneurship among the Malays*. New York: St Martin's Press.

Soares, B. F. (2005). *Islam and the Prayer Economy: History and Authority in a Malian Town*. London: Edinburgh University Press.

Townsend, J. G., Porter, G. and Mawdsley, E. (2002). The Role of the Transnational Community of Non-government Organizations: Governance or Poverty Reduction? *Journal of International Development, 14*(6), 829–839.

Ward, N. and McNicholas, K. (1998). Reconfiguring Rural Development in the UK: Objective 5b and the New Rural Governance. *Journal of Rural Studies, 14*(1), 27–39.

Yaron, J. (1991). *Successful Rural Financial Institutions*. Washington, DC: World Bank.

# 5 Islamic NGOs, piety and changing gender relations

This chapter deals with constructions of gender by Bangladeshi Islamic NGOs through an analysis of discourse. Gender issues in general and the promotion of women's rights in particular have long been considered as a 'secular enterprise' in the development practices of Western NGOs and their counterparts in the Global South (Kirmani and Phillips, 2011, p. 87). However, with the return of religion in development practices in the 1990s and the increased presence of faith-based organizations (FBOs), particularly Islamic NGOs in the Muslim world, academics and researchers have reconceptualized the perceived antagonism between religion and feminism. While research (e.g. Ghodsee, 2007) shows that Islamic NGOs typically advocate a return to more conservative gender roles, some Muslim FBOs argue for more liberal rights in their practice. Therefore, both the emergence of Islamic NGOs and the rise of 'Islamic Feminism' (Moghadam, 2004) in many parts of the Muslim world require urgent attention in order to critically explore the way in which gender functions within Muslim societies like Bangladesh (Badran, 2001).

This chapter explores the role of Islamic NGOs in changing gender relations in rural Bangladesh through a focus on the practices of everyday religion. This is to see how Islamic NGOs are governing and redefining piety in order to construct the 'ideal woman' as well as one who is a successful entrepreneur. The chapter begins with an examination of the issue of women and gender in Islam and the way in which Islamic NGOs use gendered discourse in their practices. This is followed by an exploration of gender issues, identity politics and development practices in Islam as it is practised in Bangladesh. The chapter concludes with a discussion of the changes in gender relations due to the intervention of Islamic NGOs in Bangladesh, with a particular focus on Muslim women's agency and resistance.

## Women and gender in Islam

An in-depth understanding of gendered discourse in Islam and Muslim societies elucidates the way in which women are constructed in a Muslim majority state like Bangladesh. The question of whether Islam empowers women has become a central focus for many Islamic feminist scholars (e.g. Abu-Lughod, 2002;

Ahmed, 1992, 2011; Mahmood, 2005; Mernissi, 1992). Yet there is a great diversity of opinion and a tendency among scholars to focus on the contentious relations between Islam and the West. Moreover, challenges brought about by the resurgence of Islamist movements against secular-liberal politics has led feminist scholars to envisage 'a whole host of uneasy associations such as fundamentalism, the subjugation of women, social conservatism, reactionary activism, cultural backwardness, and the rest' (Mahmood, 2001, pp. 202–203). Some feminist scholars have focused more positively on Islam, attempting to understand gender relations in Muslim societies through the notion of freedom and human agency (e.g. Ahmed, 1992; Helie-Lucas, 1994; MacLeod, 1992; Mahmood, 2001, 2005; Mernissi, 1992; Mir-Hosseini, 1996). Therefore, some scholars note that involvement in Islamist movements (for example, the Mosque Movement in Egypt) can provide women with opportunities to exercise agency and achieve real gains (e.g. Ahmed, 1992; Mahmood, 2005). Some authors even speak of the growth of an 'Islamic feminism' in Muslim societies, which argues for women's access to universal human rights on the basis of the Qur'an and *Hadith* (Badran, 2001; Moghadam, 2004).

In academic discourse, particularly colonial 'feminism' as Leila Ahmed (1992, p. 244) argues, some have suggested that traditional and gendered customs prescribed by Islam are patriarchal in nature and hence oppressive to women; for example, the invocation of the veiling of Muslim women and subsequent women's subjugation (Moghissi, 1999; Winter, 2001). Therefore, there is a belief among colonists, as Ahmed (1992, p. 154) argues, that in order to 'save' Muslim women, Islam must wipe out all 'native religions, customs, and dress,' because European or Western society is superior. The unveiled women became the signifier for empowered women free from patriarchy. Therefore, the modernist discourse and its counter-Islamist discourse have focused on the marker of Muslim women's identity – the veil in Arab culture – and their bodily presence in public constitutes the most significant part of the debate over women's empowerment and disempowerment in Muslim societies (Abu-Lughod, 2002, p. 785). This is despite the wide variation in Muslim societies, due to the tendency that 'the cultural articulation of patriarchy (through structures, social mores, laws and political power) is increasingly justified by reference to Islam and Islamic doctrine' (Shaheed, 1994, p. 999).

Moreover, there is a growing literature that moves to delink Islam from patriarchy (e.g. Barlas, 2002) and argues that the disempowerment and subjugation of women in Islam is overstated (e.g. Fernea, 1998; Hessini, 1994). This strand of thought argues that historically in Islam, women were respected for their intellect and stood shoulder-to-shoulder with men (for example, the Prophet's wives Aisha and Umm Salama). It also suggests that the issue is the Muslim elite men who manipulate religious texts to disprove women's rights in Islam. While some feminists see the veil as an impediment to women's empowerment, other feminists argue that it could help women 'carve out legitimate public space' where they can interact with men 'without cost to their reputation' in societies that are beginning to integrate the public spheres (Ahmed, 1992, p. 224). Consequently, as feminist Leila Ahmed argues, the veil can 'declare women's presence in public space to be in no way a challenge to or a violation of the Islamic sociocultural ethic'. The 'portable seclusion' – a term used by anthropologist Hanna Papanek (1982 cited in Abu-Lughod, 2002, p. 785) for the *burqa* worn by Pakistani women – symbolizes women's liberation, since women can navigate a segregated living space while following the norms of Muslim society and protecting themselves from interaction with non-kin males. Other feminists working with Muslim women (e.g. Mahmood, 2001, pp. 202, 214) show that new forms of dress as a '*critical* marker' [emphasis in original] of public piety, adopted by women in Egypt, reflect their cultivation of 'the ideal virtuous self' and the '*ineluctable* [emphasis in original] means by which one trains oneself to be pious'.

A parallel explanation for the adoption of an Islamic dress code among Muslim women is also prevalent in academic literature. As Abu-Lughod (2002, p. 786) argues, 'The modern Islamic modest dress that many educated women across the Muslim World, have taken on since the mid-1970s now both publicly marks piety and can be read as a sign of an educated urban sophistication, a sort of modernity'. Research on Bangladeshi Muslim women suggests that most of the women who wear the *hijab* are young, educated and modern, and represent an image of 'modern Muslim women' in the public space (Hussain, 2010, p. 331). Rozario (2006) nicely depicts why a significant proportion of 'mobile women' (for example, university students and middle-class urban women) have adopted the veil as part of the increasing prominence of the Islamist movement in Bangladesh while posing both positive (for example, women's agency) and negative (for example, reinforcing gender stereotypes) implications for gender relations. Other research claims that the adoption of new Islamic dress codes is an expression of 'Islamic modernism' in response to Western modernism (Salehin, 2010). Moreover, many scholars of Islam (e.g. Esposito, 1994; Roy, 1996) go beyond the dress code and argue that the resurgence of 'Islamic sociability'[1] in Muslim societies around the world needs to be 'understood as an expression of *resistance* against western politico-cultural domination as well as a form of social protest against the failed modernization project of postcolonial Muslim regimes' (Mahmood, 2005, p. 24, emphasis in original).

Along with patriarchy and the veil, issues related to relationships between men and women, discourses about purity and sexuality, and marriage, appropriate behaviours of women in Islam require appropriate attention in dealing with women in Islam (Ahmed, 1992). Yet these issues spark controversy among scholars. Ahmed (1992) shows that women are not very gendered or sexualized in the Quran, but a widely used message of al-Tabari shows that

> Female sexual desire is a potential source of danger to men; it will cause them to sin, because it will come between them and God. It must, therefore, be punished. Only when satisfied within the bonds of marriage is female sexual desire redeemable, and, indeed, rewarded bringing happiness and sons to man. What more could a good woman want?
>
> (al-Tabari, cited in Leo, 2005, p. 137)

Man thus takes over the authority to control female sexuality which is more to do with the local cultural practices and interpretations of Islamic texts than with the text of the Quran itself. For example, female circumcision to control female sexuality, as practised in many Islamic countries, is a pre-Islamic local cultural tradition which is absent in the Quranic text (Leo, 2005, p. 136). Regarding marriage and divorce, Ahmed (1986, p. 678) argues that Quranic verses do recognize women's right to equality in marriage, and provide direction on how to initiate divorce or stipulate marriage conditions. In the case of child-bearing, Wadud (1999, p. 64) argues that there is no term in the Quran which indicates that child-bearing is 'primary' to a woman. In this context Ahmed (1986, p. 687) refers to a Quranic verse which reads: 'they [wives] have rights corresponding to those which husbands have, in equitable reciprocity'. Thus Engineer (2004, p. 13) argues,

> If the ulama still resist change in certain Shari'ah edicts concerning women such as polygamy, evidence, divorce, etc it is not because they are based on Qur'an and *Sunnah* ... but because societies are still male dominated and it hurts the pride of men to accept change.

With this background to the debate on gender issues in Islam, the following section will explore how development discourse and practices conceive of Islam and gender issues with a particular focus on Islamic NGOs in Muslim societies.

### *Islam, gender and development discourse*

With the return of religion in development practices since the 1990s there has been increasing interest and subsequent publications about religion and development in general, while gender in the context of Islam in development practices has been left relatively unexplored. Although women's empowerment has become one of the most important goals and programme agendas in the development practice of NGOs, they have failed to incorporate the local traditional and religious dynamics of a particular country, and hence prescribe a Western model of emancipation for women (for example, in Bangladesh). On the other hand, the inherent tendency in orientalist scholarship to see Islam as problematic and an obstacle to development, particularly with regard to gender relations, has led development practitioners to conceive of Islam as inherently patriarchal and an impediment to progress. This is, as I contend, due partly to the fact that the secular–liberal hegemonic discourse which dominates development practice, and partly due to the incapacity and/or subordination of academic scholarship in the Muslim world to this dominant discourse. At the same time, the evidence of involvement of some Muslim charity organizations (for example, from the Gulf region) in funding terrorist activities has provoked negative reactions, as is evident in Bosnia-Herzegovina in the first half of the 1990s (De Cordier, 2009, p. 608). On the other hand, local religious elites' and Mullahs' endeavours to defend Islam and women against NGOs and Western donors (as in Bangladesh) and the subsequent clashes between the two, also made scholars readily assume that the religious elites were reactionary and Islam hostile to women and development.

However, it is now obvious that humanitarian and development agencies have become more aware of the role and significance of religion in the lives of their development partners – their beneficiaries in developing societies. For example, the engagement of several organizations such as UNFPA, DFID, UK and many other national and community organizations have a religion-based approach to women's rights and empowerment.[2] On the other hand, there is an increased prominence of religion- or faith-based organizations in development practices around the world. Among the faith-based organizations, international Islamic NGOs such as Islamic Relief Worldwide and Muslim Aid UK have made significant contributions to development in Muslim as well as in other countries. What is not clear in the development practices of Islamic NGOs, as well as NGOs that incorporate Islam into their development practice, is their stance on women and gender empowerment. While some Islamic NGOs adopt a more liberal stance regarding women, others are more conservative. Using the example of development practices of Islamic NGOs such as the Union for Islamic Development and Culture in the Samolyan region in Bulgaria, Ghodsee (2007, p. 541) argues that Islamic NGOs 'advocated for more orthodox forms of Islamic practices, forms that challenged local Muslim traditions and advocated for explicit male authority over women'. Seeking to spread the 'correct' or 'true' Islam, these NGOs are promoting new dress codes and conservative Islamic gender roles, since Bulgarian culture in general and Pomak's (Bulgarian-speaking Muslims) practice of Islam was often incompatible with 'true' Islamic practices as understood by the Islamic NGO, the Union for Islamic Development and Culture (UIDC) in Bulgaria.

Contrary to Ghodsee (2007), Harmsen (2008) shows how different types of Muslim faith-based organizations such as politically unaffiliated and conservative Muslim NGOs (e.g. the Islamic Welfare Society of Salt, the Islamic Anwar Al-Huda Welfare Association) and Progressive Muslim NGOs in Jordan (e.g. the Al-Faruq Welfare Society for Orphans, the Khawla' Bint Al-Azwar Association) approach women's empowerment issues in different ways. Thus, for progressive Muslim NGOs such as the Al-Faruq Welfare Society for Orphans in Jordan, to promote human welfare means fostering the empowerment of the targeted people through the (re)interpretation of religion, in terms of a vision of human progress and development (Harmsen, 2008, pp. 231–232). Therefore, the power of religious discourse to legitimize a framework for gender relations is well manifested in the practices of Muslim NGOs. The Al-Faruq Welfare Society in Jordan, and its use of the Quranic principle, connects with 'the modern language of rights, by interpreting religious duties as a call for people to respect one another's rights' (Harmsen, 2008, pp. 241–242). For example, they use the Quranic language and principles such as *rahma* (compassion), *tasamuh* (forgiveness and tolerance) and *sabr* (patience) to counter the practice of verbal and physical abuse against women (Harmsen, 2008, p. 377).

In the context of women's rights and empowerment, the regulation and control of women's reproductive rights and sexuality through practices such as female genital mutilation (FGM), particularly in many parts of Muslim African societies, and the regulation of female sexual behaviour/chastity through the inscription of *fatwa* in Bangladesh, use religious discourse to legitimize their actions against women. Therefore, many faith-based organizations and activities (for example, the Fankanta project in Senegal, implemented by a German–Senegalese cooperative), or UNFPA's programme in Africa and the Middle East, engaged local Imams to end the practice of FGM (Kirmani and Phillips, 2011, p. 92). Bangladeshi Islamic NGOs like MACCA engage local Imams and other faith leaders to make communities aware of HIV/AIDS prevention in Bangladesh.

## Religion and gender in Bangladesh

A significant number of studies (e.g. Abecassis, 1990; Banu, 1992; Devine and White, 2009; Hashmi, 2000; Landell Mills, 1992; Naher, 2005; Rozario and Samuel, 2010; White, 2009) argue that religion and Islam in Bangladesh represent the 'inner core' of rural people (Mesbahuddin, 2010). The practice of Islamic discourse has huge implications for women's lives, particularly rural and already marginalized women. Islamic discourse in Bangladesh, as Hussain (2010, p. 326) suggests, 'highlights the prerogatives of men and legitimizes the authority of men over women'.

Many authors suggest that Bangladesh is both 'more modern' on the one hand and 'more Islamic' on the other (White, 2009, pp. 1–3; 2012, p. 23). For example, in the context of patriarchy and the prominence of the Islamic way of life, a large segment of women have adopted the 'modern' (Western) lifestyle (as manifested in their dress code; for example, wearing jeans and shirts), while another section of women have been caught in the web of 'Islamic modernism'. An increasing number of 'mobile women' in the urban areas (for example, university student, garment workers) of Bangladesh are increasingly visible with a new 'modern' Islamic dress code (for example, the *burqa* or *hijab* (veil)) (Rozario, 2006; Salehin, 2010). Hussain (2010, p. 326) also provides the same insight, as she suggests:

> while previously physical veiling was perceived as absence of modernity and mostly practiced by rural middle class and illiterate women, in the present context wearing the *hijab* by educated, urban, middle class, young women exhibits their wealth and piety without losing modernity. Adoption of this Islamic dress code and activism is seen as a reaction against western modernism.

Islamists in Bangladesh consider Western concepts of women's rights as an 'imposed social order' by the West, causing damage to the social fabric of Islamic society (Hussain, 2010, p. 326). This antagonistic relationship between the West and religious leaders conceived as the efforts of secular NGOs to empower women was seen as a representation of the West. Naher (2010) also analyses gender, religion and its relation to development practices of NGOs in rural Bangladesh. This analysis has a particular focus on the emergence of rural women as the centre of contention between NGOs and Islamic 'fundamentalists'. For Naher (2010, p. 316), the 'deeply rooted patriarchal values and notions held by all classes of men made it easy for the "Islamist" opponents of NGOs to bring the issue of women's participation in development activities in the forefront'. To understand Islam and women in Bangladesh better, it is pertinent to focus on the politics of religion and Islamic identity, in particular, which allowed room for the 'Islamist' or 'fundamentalist' to rise and oppose women's rights and freedom.

### *Islamism and the reconstruction of gender identity in Bangladesh*

As discussed in Chapter 3, Islam, which is embedded within people's beliefs and minds, was used both by the politicians and Islamists to redefine Bangladeshi national identity and gain political legitimacy. Military ruler Zia lifted the ban on the religiously based political parties and allowed the return of the Jamaat-e-Islami leaders and war criminals into the country.[3] General Zia's successor General Ershad (1982–1990), through the Eighth Amendment to the Constitution of Bangladesh on 7 June 1988, declared Islam as the state religion of Bangladesh (Article 2, Clause A) with the provision that other religions may be practised in peace and harmony in the Republic (Government of Bangladesh, 1991; Islam, 2001; Mohsin, 2004). Bringing Jamaat-e-Islam (a rightist conservative Islamist political party) back into Bangladeshi politics was a major shift in the political spectrum and increased the visibility of Islam in the public sphere.

The return of Jamaat-e-Islam to politics and the subsequent electoral victory of 18 seats in the National Parliament in the 1991 general election made it possible for Jamaat to have a huge impact on public policy. The return of Jamaat and its leader in Bangladesh has had an impact upon women's psyche, particularly through one of its leaders Delwar Hossain Saydee through his *waz mahfil* (public preaching). Shehabuddin (2008a, pp. 598–599), a US-based Bengali scholar, argues that

> Jamaat continues to cast women in a subordinate role in society ... insist on a strict form of *pudra* ... it adopts male-biased positions on issues with immediate implications for women such as family law; and finally, it refuses to field female candidates for parliament.

Along with the prominence of Islam in Bangladeshi politics, the Tabligh movement,[4] as Jahangir (1990) argues, is an important factor in the revival of Islam and its practice in Bangladesh. Although non-political in nature, the activities of Tabligh Jamaat, namely to refine Islam through the observance of Islamic practice, are now the major source of construction of 'pious Muslim' in Bangladesh. Moreover, the gender ideology of Tabligh 'is not very different from the politically oriented religious groups' (Naher, 2010, p. 317); hence its contribution to redefine Muslim womanhood through the practice of piety in both private and public spheres, for instance, their appearance in public wearing a *burqa* (veil). Moreover, the politicization of Islam in Bangladesh also explains why the Bangladeshi state could not make its position clear regarding women's issues; rather it provided contested policies that largely influence women's subjugation. Thus the official Bangladeshi state narrative on gender issues requires a critical examination for understanding the role of the state in addressing gender issues (for example, *fatwa*, violence against women).

### *Contested state: laws,* fatwas *and women*

Guhathakurta (1985) has considered Bangladesh as a 'soft state'. This 'softness' of the state is revealed through its inability to 'firmly institutionalize its own statist interests and thus caters to diverse, fragmented, and often contradictory interests' (e.g. international capital, donor governments, the rural rich, the urban middle class, and certain state functionaries such as the army and the police force) (Guhathakurta, 1985, cited in Chowdhury, 2011). In the same vein, Bangladesh, as White (1999) argues, represents a weak state in a strong society to indicate that the state has failed to infiltrate many societal issues; for example, the implementation of an anti-*fatwa* law for women. Therefore, the Bangladeshi state has shown many shifts and contradictions regarding its position on gender relations since it became independent in 1971. These 'shifts and contradictions within state policy are possible only because the state itself regards the issue of women's rights in essentially instrumentalist terms' (Kabeer, 1988, p. 115). One of these issues is the *fatwa*.[5] Although Bangladesh has a secular legal framework, in the name of Islamic jurisprudence the *fatwa* has been widely practised, particularly in rural areas. It has been used primarily to regulate women's lives through inflicting physical and psychological punishment, in particular to prevent 'illicit' sexual behaviour. The punishment as prescribed by *fatwas* and instituted through *shalish*[6] varies in nature and degree over time and from place to place (Shehabuddin, 1999, p. 1017; 2008b, pp. 97–98), ranging from stoning to death, lashing and public shame. In 2001 the Bangladesh High Court declared all *fatwas* 'unauthorized and illegal' and a 'punishable offence' (*Daily Star*, 7 January 2001). Despite this, the practice persists today, and around 503 women were victims of *fatwas* between 2001 and 2011 (*Daily Star*, 2011). On 12 May 2011 the Supreme Court reiterated that '[n]o punishment, including physical violence and/or mental torture in any form can be imposed or inflicted on anybody in pursuance of fatwa'. The Court further held that *fatwas* may be issued only by 'properly educated persons', and clarified that even where they were issued, they are not binding and cannot be enforced (Human Rights Watch, 2011). Although many see this as a victory for women, it still maintains a loophole for Islamists to exploit the verdict until it is banned. Moreover, practising *fatwa* also contradicts the secular legal system where the 'legal system of Bangladesh empowers only the courts to decide all questions relating to the legal opinions on the Muslim and other laws as in force in Bangladesh'[7] (*Daily Star*, 2011).

Besides, women's lives are regulated by a pluralistic legal framework where the principles of *shari'a* through Muslim personal law along with the general law, which is secular in its character, adhere to the British colonial legacy. Muslim personal law covers the fields of marriage, *talaq* or divorce, maintenance, guardianship of children and inheritance. The general law covers the rights under the Constitution, penal codes, civil and criminal procedure codes, evidence acts and so on (Kamal, 1988). It is worth mentioning that Bangladesh inherited the Muslim Family Law Ordinance 1961 from Pakistan, which along with other codes and laws has become a source of conflict among Islamists and secularists in Bangladesh to regulate and reform gender relations. Whereas Islamists contend that the entire system must be Islamic, secularists argue that existing laws are already too grounded in Islamic law and deny women the equity granted by the Constitution and international conventions such as the Convention to Eliminate All Forms of Discrimination Against Women (CEDAW). Most importantly, as Sultana Kamal (1988, p. 4) mentions, the legal status of Muslim women in Bangladesh is 'in the context of these two sets of law as in both cases women are supposedly fortified with theoretical legal rights, but there is a gulf of difference existing between theory and its actual application'.

Although there is a significant amount of research on gender and religion in Bangladesh, most approach the subject in a relatively simple and reductionist manner (Samuel and Rozario, 2010). Therefore, more rigorous scholarship is required to understand the role of religion in women's lives and the subsequent socioeconomic development of Bangladesh. A recent special issue of the journal *Women's Studies International Forum* (vol. 33, 2010) has meticulously depicted the nexus between religion and gender in Bangladesh, focusing on issues such as the moral regulation of women as a state project (Feldman, 2010). It also examined the conflict between Islamists and NGOs over gender roles (Naher, 2010), women's increased involvement in the Islamist movement (Hussain, 2010) and the nexus between rural women's religious lives and the sustainability of the village community (Rozario and Samuel, 2010). Yet, despite these efforts, the role of Islamic NGOs in the construction of Islamic women's identity and the regulation of women's lives in rural Bangladesh has not been addressed. This is despite the increased visibility of Islamic practices as reconfigured by Islamic NGOs.

## NGO-led development discourses in Bangladesh: gender empowerment and disempowerment

The main objectives of the development practices of NGOs emphasize the issue of empowerment of rural poor women in Bangladesh. Even the Bangladeshi state, under military leadership, also capitalized on the 'Women in Development' (WID) paradigm to gain development dollars and legitimacy from Western democracies. Thus gender empowerment turned into a prime focus of development in Bangladesh. Empowerment, as conceptualized in the NGO-led development discourse in Bangladesh, has produced debate and contradiction (Kabeer, 2001, p. 63; Mahmud, 2003, p. 582; Parmar, 2003, p. 426; Selinger, 2008, p. 28). A simplistic understanding of empowerment tends to focus on particular indicators; for example, participation in economic activity, decision-making powers to score on an 'empowerment index' – an index which measures empowerment. Yet the notion of empowerment has been changing. For Sen (1993), empowerment is about 'altering relations of power ... which constrain women's options and autonomy and adversely affect health and well-being'. Kabeer (1999, p. 437) considers empowerment in terms of agency, since it is 'the expansion in people's ability to make strategic life choices in a context where this ability was previously denied to them'. Using eight different indicators of women's empowerment (e.g. mobility, women's ability to make purchases, the ownership of productive assets, decision-making powers, freedom from family domination, political and legal awareness, and participation in public protest and political campaigning), Hashemi *et al.* (1996, pp. 638–639) found that Bangladeshi rural women's participation in NGO microcredit programmes was a tool for empowerment. For them, one of the important non-economic aspects of women's empowerment is that those women had now built a network outside of their family and 'learned to talk' in public (Hashemi *et al.*, 1996, p. 648). Access to credit, for them, was found to be associated with the reduction in incidences of violence against women. They cited one of the beneficiaries:

> In the past my father-in-law would never stop my husband from beating me. But after I joined Grameen Bank he said to my husband, 'You had better stop beating and scolding your wife. Now she has contact with many people in society. She brings you loans from Grameen Bank.'
>
> (Hashemi *et al.*, 1996, pp. 648–649)

In the same way, Amin *et al.* (1998, p. 225) argue that 'by providing women with control over material resources, microcredit programs may increase women's domestic prestige and their importance in the eyes of their husband'. Other research findings also suggest that women's access to microcredit has made substantial changes in the empowerment process. Pitt and Khandker (1995), for example, argue that women's preferences carried greater weight in determining decision-making outcomes in households where they received a loan, compared to households where either the men received loans or in households where no loans had been received. Mahmud (2003, p. 577) emphasizes the notion of women's choice and active agency in the attainment of greater well-being. Therefore, empowerment for her is the 'process of gaining power over those strategic life decisions through expansion of women's choice and increase in women's agency in order to increase welfare, both absolute and relative, and reduce subordination to men' (Mahmud, 2003, p. 586). She argues that access to microcredit has strongly increased women's ability to exercise agency in intra-household processes and, hence, increases women's welfare and reduces male bias in welfare outcomes (Mahmud, 2003, p. 76).

However, contrary to the positive arguments regarding women's empowerment through microcredit, a large number of (influential) studies argue that access to microcredit reinforces patriarchal norms of women's subordination, and hence worsens gender relations and disempowers women in rural Bangladesh (Goetz and Gupta, 1996; Karim, 2008; Montgomery *et al.*, 1996; Parmar, 2003; Rahman, 1999). One of the most important works on microcredit is the ethnographic study on Grameen Bank beneficiaries by Rahman (1999), who critically examines the narratives of NGO-led empowerment programmes for women in rural Bangladeshi villages. Using 'hidden' and 'public' transcripts (Scott, 1990, pp. 42–44), Rahman (1999) reveals the ideological justification[8] that hides the true basis for why Grameen Bank almost exclusively provides loans to women, arguing that women are accepted into credit programmes due to their 'positional vulnerability'[9] in rural society. Women are targeted by NGOs such as Grameen Bank since they are an easily manipulated population (Selinger, 2008, p. 33). Rahman (1999, p. 69) quotes one of the respondents who works with Grameen Bank:

> Women in the village are easily traceable. They regularly attend more group meetings than men. Women are reliable and more disciplined (passive/submissive) than men. Working with women is easier than working with men.

He also argues that women borrowers are not direct benefactors of the loan; rather, they mediate

> between their male household members and the Bank. Thus, the lending institution invests loans in the village society to generate profit, but it uses the prevailing patriarchal norms of the society and the positional vulnerability of women (immobile, shy, passive) for timely repayment and distribution of new loans.
>
> (Rahman, 1999, p. 23)

Whatever the reasons for targeting women in microcredit programmes, the huge growth in the number of women beneficiaries must have some positive economic impacts. However, it is important to ask, as Goetz and Gupta (1996, p. 47) suggest, 'How far have women been able to convert access to credit, and membership of credit organizations, into a process of "empowerment"; in what way does women's access to credit affect gender relations?' Hence, they conclude that the women who receive loans from NGOs have no control over those loans (Goetz and Gupta, 1996, p. 45). However, it is not just about control over credit; rather that credit imposes a burden upon women. This burden is two-dimensional: the woman's husband pressures her to obtain credit from the NGO on the one hand and on the other hand the NGO pressures her to repay the loan every week. Although the woman has no control over the credit, she is the one who has to face all the hurdles in repaying the loan, whether it is from the bank or from her peers. As Rahman (1999, p. 72) puts it:

> When a woman fails to make her instalment on time, she experiences humiliation through verbal aggression from fellow members and bank workers in the loan centre.... In an extreme case peers may take the defaulter to the Bank office.

Moreover, although women are considered to be an important part of the NGO-led participatory development discourse of empowerment, research shows that they are often excluded from this process. Therefore, when NGO workers 'take the empowerment of women into their own hands, women's struggle to end sexist oppression is hijacked' (Parmar, 2003, p. 466). In the context of Bangladesh, NGO-led programmes, whether microcredit or health, or something else, a prescribed version of social change is imposed upon women which is not grounded in the women's own experiences. In the context of microcredit programmes, Fernando (1997, pp. 156–157) has argued:

> the beneficiaries of credit programs do not participate in the planning, implementation, or evaluation connected with the micro-enterprises in any meaningful or systematic way. These policies are decided by highly centralized administrations primarily accountable to respective donor of NGOs.

Although women's empowerment has become one of the most important goals and programme agendas in the development practices of NGOs, they have failed to incorporate the local traditional and religious dynamics of the particular country and hence prescribed a Western model of emancipation for women; for example, in Bangladesh. As a result, a confrontation has developed between the secular NGOs and the rural religious elite on these activities, particularly those that challenge and change the traditional gender roles.

## *Religion, secular NGOs and women: the conflicting schema*

Bangladesh, as many authors suggest, is representing 'the increased visibility of religion (Islam) with globalized modernity' and capitalism (White, 2009, pp. 6, 23). Yet the activities and programmes of mainstream secular NGOs have unconsciously or wilfully avoided including Islam and cultural values particularly related to gender and women's empowerment in their programmes, and hence have witnessed a backlash against them.

Yet there are many explanations for such a conflict between secular NGOs and religious elites over gender issues. In interpreting this backlash, NGOs were accused by the Mullah of conducting anti-Islamic work by charging interest (which is strictly prohibited in Islam) on microcredit, by bringing women outside of their homes, thereby making them shameless, which violates the norms of *purdha* (veil/seclusion) and breaks up the traditional family system of the village (Naher, 2005, p. 147). On the contrary, pro-secular, pro-modernist or the liberal intelligentsia and the NGOs have treated the religious Right, which comprises the Islamists and their allies, as 'backward', 'traditional' and 'reactionary', and the main impediment to development (Shehabuddin, 1999, p. 1026; Wood, 2009), and hence has produced a backlash. Yet, Karim argues that NGOs with neoliberal and modernist agendas have ignored the role of religion, manipulated rural women's beliefs, and exploited women's constructions of shyness and *purdha*[10] which is better explained as the 'economy of shame' (Karim, 2008, p. 7). Thus, both NGOs and the religious elites or the Mullahs in the rural areas were in conflict with each other, mainly to establish their authority over gender roles in rural Bangladesh. In this context, the emergence of Islamic NGOs as new service providers for women needs critical analysis to examine their efforts regarding empowerment and gender issues. Despite the fact that gender empowerment has been widely discussed in academic scholarship, an in-depth examination of gender within Islamic development discourse, has yet to be undertaken. Thus, in the following section, I deal with Islamic development discourse with women and Islamic NGOs at the centre of my analysis.

## Change and resistance in gender relations: do Islamic NGOs make a difference?

Gender equity and women's empowerment is the third of eight Millennium Development Goals (MDGs), and it is undeniable that Bangladesh has made significant progress in gender empowerment. NGOs were part and parcel of the empowerment process which reflects on the 'cherished goal of the NGOs' (Abed, 2000, p. 7). Yet I mentioned in the above discussion many negative consequences of NGO intervention in gender issues; for example, women's control over economic assets and knowledge of social issues. In the section that follows I explore the way in which Islamic NGOs make a difference to gender empowerment. The Islamic NGOs included in this book, as stated in their mission statements, are designed and function using the teachings of Islam. Therefore, the programmes of these NGOs reflect the core values of Islam as understood by the NGO. Along with the microfinance programme of these NGOs, they also offer religious and moral education to members of the *samity*.[11] Moreover, when I attended some weekly *samity* meetings, I noted the observance of Islamic rituals at the beginning of the meetings. Usually the meeting starts with the recitation from the Holy Quran followed by a predesigned discussion on moral and religious issues; for example, how to recite the Quran properly, instructions on how to offer prayer, how to be happy in conjugal life, how to maintain *purdah*, etc. After collecting the weekly instalments, the meeting ends with the *monajat*.[12] Women's participation in Islamic NGO/*samity*, and the weekly meetings of these *Islami samity* in particular, forms a critical focus of my analysis in the chapter, which influences both the personal as well as the public sphere of women.

### *From personal life/private sphere to social life/public sphere of women; from symbolic opposition to engagement*

With modernity and increased urbanization, changes are also occurring at the rural level and in community life in Bangladesh. However, in contrast to the modernist identification of religion with a distinct area of life, for most of my respondents in all of the three study areas, religion is embedded in their everyday understanding of life, livelihood, death and survival. Moreover, certain everyday activities that go beyond formal religious rituals, what Ammerman (2007) calls 'everyday religion', have a profound impact upon women's lives. Therefore, it is imperative to examine the use of religious references of Islamic NGOs, to see how they structure and change women's everyday lives, in both the personal and social realms, in a way that informs women's symbolic opposition to 'secular NGOs' and their engagement with Islamic NGOs.

Several studies have found that 'one of the most significant accusations' (Naher, 2005, p. 151; 2010) against NGOs (e.g. Grameen Bank, BRAC) was that they sought to break up traditional family order by targeting women through the provision of microfinance (White, 2009, p. 17). In this sense, these programmes would have limited effects on women's empowerment (Mahmud, 2003, p. 577). The perception of the women whom I interviewed in rural areas about secular NGOs confirmed these previous findings. In my study areas, women beneficiaries of Islamic NGOs repeated popular sayings to me about secular NGOs: *Sahmir Kotha Shunbo na/Shusilon charbona* ('We won't listen to what our husbands say/we won't leave the Shusilon[13]), *Shami boro na 'Sir'*[14] *boro, 'Sir' boro 'Sir' boro* ('Is the husband greater, or is the "sir" greater? "Sir" is greater, "sir" is greater). White (2012, p. 11) argues that these sayings represent the replacement of '*domestic* patriarchy by *development* patriarchy[15] – or the local by the global; or the (Islamic) universal by the (Western? modern? secular?) particular' (emphasis in original). During my fieldwork with Islamic NGO beneficiaries, I found that many of them had never joined the secular NGOs. Among the reasons stated by both men and women for refusing to participate in the programmes of these NGOs were the recipients' fears that women would be urged to behave immodestly in the public sphere. As one of my respondents from Manikganj replied:

> I can't be shameless, unveiled for money. Those who joined Grameen Bank do physical training (PT) and parade in front of the strangers, unveiled their head and tied the sari into their hip that once covered the head. Now you tell me, should a woman behave like this.
>
> I found the same kind of sentiment at Shyamnar when I interviewed Shafiqul Islam, a beneficiary of an Islamic NGO, who told me:
>
> I try my best to feed and maintain my wife in such a way so that I can keep myself accountable to Allah. I can't send my wife on the street outside of my home just for the sake of the money, that she would earn 500 Taka if she goes outside.

Therefore, men's unwillingness to send their wives outside the home, where they might meet strangers, also reflects on the 'desire' of men who don't want their wives/daughters to mingle with other non-kin males. This desire of men is achieved through women's subjugation to men who exercise authority over them. What has become interesting with regard to Islamic NGOs is that when the women attend the Islamic NGOs, as my male respondents argue, it doesn't break the norms of *purdha.* Then I asked why. One of the male respondents at Sharonkhola told me: 'Yes, my wife goes to *Islami samity* maintaining *purdha,* she learns many Islamic rules and etiquette [*nyeom-kanun abong adob-kayda*]. This is a path of religion [*deen er rasta*]. And those who come to conduct the meeting are also *hojur* [religious Mullah].' I put the same question to female beneficiaries after my female respondents claimed that they cannot go outside to meet strangers (secular NGO workers). Then I asked Zerin (at Manikganj) whether she still appeared before the non-kin male strangers (workers) of Islamic NGOs. She simply replied, 'Yes, I go, but not without the veil. And the people from our NGOs ask us to maintain the veil as well as proper manners.' As the discussion proceeded she referred to Ayesha, one of the wives of Prophet Muhammad, who took part in fighting against non-Muslims. She said:

> If *bibi* [wife] Ayshea [of the Prophet] can leave the house and fight alongside the Prophet, why can't we? We are fighting for our development and to maintain *taqwa.*[16] But we are fighting to maintain our religious belief [*iman*] and practice [*amol*].

This is the way women are redefining their identity in the public sphere, which corresponds to the reconstruction of *purdah* by some Islamic NGOs; as these NGOs maintained, 'women can go outside but have to maintain *purdha'.* Therefore, Islamic NGO beneficiaries also hold the same view on the reconstruction of the norms of *purdha.* One of my respondents claims,

> We are Muslim; we have more or less some knowledge of *shari'a.* What our government says, then we are bound to follow this, but our mentality does not allow us to follow this. We also want women's development. [I asked him how and he replies] Leaving them in the home, they can still develop. You can buy her a sewing machine, or chickens or you can buy two goats for her.

Therefore, the efforts of secular NGOs to empower rural women go against their norms of everyday practices of religion, as many respondents claim. Whenever I asked beneficiaries of Islamic NGOs about their perceptions of the activities of non-Islamic NGOs (e.g. BRAC, Shushilan, Grameen Bank), issues related to their mobility (for example, joining an NGO rally or procession) some of the respondents at Satkhira replied: 'they [other NGOs] are ill-mannered and the devil'. However, when I asked these women why they considered these NGOs to be the devil, the women replied: 'other NGOs bring women to the procession on the street, and make them not follow *purdha*'. This opposition to secular NGOs represents rural women's 'desire' to be guided by the norms for *purdha*. Shajia, an Islamic NGO beneficiary, when asked how she feels when they see other women going out freely and without the veil replied, 'We feel rather bad when we see other woman not maintaining *purdha*' and those who don't maintain *purdha* 'forgot that they will have to die one day and give account to Allah for being *purdha*-less [*bae-purdha*]'. Therefore, their commitment towards Islamic practices, as they argue, is not hampered if they are with Islamic NGOs. Rather their opportunity to become pious has been increased which leads them to be considered as 'pure Muslims' by the *samaj* (society). It is unequivocal that Islamic NGOs have an obvious impact upon women's piety which subsequently influences women's private and public spheres. Therefore, the existing public mood on the veil and traditional boundaries (for example, staying at home) are rightly appropriated by the Islamic NGOs and thus reflect these feelings and desires of rural women throughout their activities and programmes.

Islamic NGOs or *Islami Samity*[17] have succeeded in influencing the personal behaviour or private sphere of women by mobilizing them to participate in NGO programmes, such as Islamic microfinance and Islamic/moral education which inform the women's code of conduct in the public sphere. One of the female beneficiaries of IBF at 'Shajalal Model Village' at Shrankhola said: 'According to religion, a woman has to obey her husband, take care of her children and follow the rules of seclusion. Then there will be peace in the family and society will treat me as a "good woman".' Yet this reading of religion is not very different from the views held by the males of the society. Although the notion of the 'good woman' may be debated, in the everyday practices of rural Bangladeshis it corresponds to piety, modesty in dress code (maintaining *purdha*) and behaviour.[18]

For most of the women beneficiaries, as they told me, their participation in the weekly *samity* meeting helps them to reduce conjugal fighting which leads to a happy conjugal life. Zhinu, a 30-year-old woman who has been a member of MACCA for the past five years, explained how MACCA has changed her conjugal life:

> When I was with other *samity*, I used to have continual fights with my husband … especially if we couldn't manage our weekly credit instalment. Now it is better than before. There is no fighting. We follow the methods they [MACCA] showed us. We observe and listen to them and therefore offer prayers every day. Look, though we cannot manage the time to pray five times a day due to our work load, we (my husband) must pray the *Jumma* [Friday prayer] now. We have learnt how to be patient [*sabur*], what are the rights of husband and wife, and we try to follow them. We live happily.

Another important factor around the construction of the notion of the 'good woman' lies in the naming of every *Islami samity* (in the case of the IBF) after the names of the Prophet Muhammad's family members and his companions; for example, *hazrat* Fathima (daughter of the Prophet) or Aysha (wife of the prophet). For example, center no. 33 of IBF at Sharankhola is named '*Ma Fathima*',[19] which uses the image of a pious woman as a model for women to follow. The extent to which this is successful is clear in the 'desire' of rural women to lead a pious life.

However, this is also clear in the rhetoric of the Islamic NGOs' mission. As one mission statement of an Islamic NGO states: 'our programme aims not only to empower economically but to make people pure Muslims'.[20] At the same time, the operation manual of the *Fael Khair* programme of the IBF[21] explains the duties and responsibilities of the project's programme officer, which states, 'Alongside investment, you [programme officer] will have to teach religious education to live as a pure Muslim and inspire them to perform.' Although it would be an issue of debate whether we should, and how we could, define someone as a 'pure' or 'impure' Muslim, Islamic NGOs endeavour to make 'good women' and 'pure Muslim' men.

During my interview one of the respondents, who is head of a programme of an Islamic NGO, told me a story about one of his clients which portrays their efforts to understand the construction of 'good women'. This is the story of Ayshea, a woman beneficiary of their *shari'a*-based microfinance programme which he 'would remember forever':

> My husband did not like me at all. He did not want to look at me at all. Repeatedly he used to behave badly with me. It was such a situation that he used to tell me, 'you leave my house', 'don't come in front of my eyes'. Now, my parents are poor, do they want me to go back to them? But I could not understand why he does not like me, why he is always angry with me. I used to think what my fault is. When I wanted to be a member of *Fael Khair*, he did not want to allow me. However, when he saw my neighbours were becoming members and getting money from *Fael Khair*, he allowed me. After joining here, I came to know the duties of wives to their husbands. There were many discussions in our meetings on different topics. In such a discussion, I heard that debating with a husband, quarrelling with a husband, always searching for his faults, annoying him, criticizing him and demanding something beyond his ability, or embracing him by always asking for this or that, is not right. Our sirs say, 'when your husband is back from work, he is tired, sweaty, and already agitated by working under the sun, so your responsibility is to receive him wearing nice clothes, fan him, present food in front of him, attend him during the meal and see if he needs something'. They [sirs] taught us to look at these issues and follow these instructions. They told us to wear good clothes and be always fresh by avoiding dirty clothes that spread the smells of the sweat. Then he [the husband] will not look at other women. If he [the husband] is not satisfied inside the home he would say, oh hell! I am not satisfied with the wife at home, women outside are very beautiful. I wish my wife is such a beauty! In this way his

> [husband] *iman*[22] is getting affected. They [sirs] said, 'you [the beneficiary] may be very good, but you are not well decorated, so he [the husband] would see you are disastrous and might think other women are more attractive. Therefore, you need to take care of these issues and you have to try to make them [husbands] satisfied. According to Islam you have to please your husband.' After listening to this, I found myself not doing these things. When I have started to practise these, I saw my husband had started becoming gentle towards me and my relation with my husband became good.

These practices, my respondents claim, would ultimately lead them to enter into *jannat* (heaven) easily. Therefore, the motivation behind the participation in Islamic NGOs, as my respondents stated, was not just to get an 'interest-free loan', but was also manifest in their desire to 'gain the eternal life'. Yet the prescription to be pretty and present themselves in front of their husbands as well as to serve their husbands (*shami-sheba*) is a very rural, traditional and patriarchal interpretation of the responsibilities of a woman which ultimately depicts her as a good and devoted wife. Therefore, the issue of women's empowerment, still a grey area in Islamic NGOs, requires a rigorous explanation.

## The Islamic way of women's empowerment: Muslim women's agency in rural Bangladesh

In order to analyse Muslim women's agency, it is imperative to decide whether agency needs to be understood as the capacity to resist domination (Butler, 1993), or whether it is embedded in a particular historic, cultural, social and economic context (Mahmood, 2001). My understanding of Muslim agency stems from Saba Mahmood's (2001, p. 203; 2005, p. 168) conceptualization of agency as 'a capacity for action' which actively shapes women's 'desire through embodied practices linked to piety under Islam' (Korteweg, 2008, p. 438). Therefore, women who are rural, mostly with little or no education and who live within the context of an unequal, patriarchal social system, are able to attain and engage their capacities (as Islamic NGO beneficiaries and 'good women'), to resist the 'development patriarchy' of the mainstream secular NGOs as well as to challenge 'traditional patriarchy'. Women's involvement with Islamic NGOs therefore represents a resistance towards secular NGOs that become a financial burden and an obstacle to piety. All the respondents who were formerly members of secular NGOs are now unable to bear the financial burden imposed upon them because of the high rates of interest charged by secular NGOs. Therefore, women's participation in Islamic NGOs should not be portrayed as the victimization of women by 'development patriarchy'. Rather, it represents women's desire for liberation and freedom within the setting of a society where *dharma* is still important.

In the areas that I researched, many women do not join secular NGOs due to the perception that these organizations encourage women to go outside of the home, thereby going against the norms and everyday practice of *dharma*; thus these women join Islamic NGOs instead. Joining Islamic NGOs, as the women beneficiaries suggest, does not go against the norms of *purdha* and their practice of *dharma.* Rather, it encourages Islamic practices. As one of the respondents at the *Hasana* programme at Manikganj put it: 'I used to wear my sari with a single swathe,[23] but I now understand that after joining the *Islami samity*, I did not do the right thing.' Therefore, Muslim women's bodies here represent a site for contestation and for exercising their agency to decide what to wear and not wear. This was reinforced through their participation in Islamic NGOs in making an explicit distinction between '*halal*' (approved) and '*haram*' (prohibited) deeds. Through this ordinary and everyday 'embodied practice', as McGuire (2008) suggests, people, both individually and collectively, literally live their religion and 'serve to express and support their efforts for social change'.

In terms of assessing the effectiveness of women's empowerment programmes, it is imperative to discern the changes that occur in women's lives when they participate. Participation in Islamic NGOs did bring some economic improvement[24] for their families. To understand these economic changes I asked my respondents to relate some measurable indicators of those changes. One of the most common answers was the increase in their monthly income (which almost doubled), an increase in the number and amount of assets (e.g. cattle, grocery shops, land), an increase in consumption (e.g. food and non-food items) and children's education. The unit-in-charge (manager) of the IBF at Sharonkhola explained to me the changes he observed among his beneficiaries after participation in their programme when I asked him to give me some concrete indicators of changes:

> I know a member from South Kadomtola who doubled her income with the loan from us. Initially we gave her 10,000 Taka and training by the government officials. With the money she has bought an ox and fattened it. Within one year she sold this ox for BDT24,000. With this money she bought a cow again and used some portion of her money for her family. The smile I saw on her face tells me how happy she is now. Now she is making money from battle leaf culture. Therefore, within two years we gave her four loans and she had a very good agricultural harvest.

Like the IBF, Muslim Aid emphasizes the self-reliance of women. When I asked one of the high officials of Muslim Aid how they measured whether their female members had become self-reliant, he told me:

> We consider a woman self-reliant and making progress when we see that her family income has at least doubled from her business (e.g. beef fattening, handicrafts making) and has a sustained flow of income. She does not need to borrow from money lenders or other NGOs, and she has a voice in decision making in the family. We also take other issues into consideration, such as children's schooling, improved access to health and sanitation.

Thus it is obvious that Islamic NGOs, like their secular counterparts, also emphasize transforming women into entrepreneurial *Homo economicus*, from housewife to a highly motivated rational economic being. Many of them, as Islamic NGOs argued, are now self-reliant, owning a small or medium enterprise and capital. Yet, it is imperative to mention that control and use of the money, in some cases, is still in the hands of male members of the family. However, in many other cases, as some female respondents told me, they control the money and make their husbands listen to their decisions. For example, if her husband wants to expand his grocery shop he needs to consult his wife first to get the necessary financial help, as my respondents from Tala told me.

As empowerment is about self-esteem and increased dignity (Rowlands, 1997), Islamic NGOs beneficiaries see their involvement with these NGOs as enhancing their dignity. When I asked how it has helped them to increase their dignity, they referred to the reduction in or absence of conjugal fighting and domestic violence as a measure of dignity. Since they bring money to the family on the one hand, and maintain a peaceful life following Islamic principles on the other, they are helping their husbands to consider them worthy and they respect them. As my respondents claimed, they know what the rights and duties of a man towards his wife are. When they return from the *samity* meetings, many of them inform their husband what they have learned; for example, a husband has to return *mohorana* (bride-money) to his wife, otherwise he will have to be accountable to Allah after his death. At the same time, they are now more aware of their Islamic rights. However, as Mokul, an IBF member, said, 'those (husbands) who are educated realize this quickly, but it's hard for those husbands who are obstinate. They [their husbands] say you want to understand this, so just you understand this. Don't try to teach me!'

In addition to dignity and the economic implications of participation (for example, increased access to and ownership of assets), women's participation in the weekly *samity* meeting provided opportunities for women to discuss, share, learn and teach each other about Islamic *dharma*. In certain cases some of the respondents referred to the *samity* meeting, as they are attending a *Talim.*[25] This illustrates the increased opportunities available to women who were once outside the NGO web and subject to the patriarchal norms of society. As part of these opportunities, *samity* meetings help those making choices over financial transactions; for example, which business is profitable, which is not, how to use the money efficiently and so on. One of my respondents at Sharonkhola, who is the centre leader of the IBF, told me how participation in NGOs even strengthens their knowledge of agriculture, since they provide practical training in agricultural activities.

Moreover, during my participation in several *samity* meetings at different locations, I noticed that some women who were not members of the NGO attended the weekly meetings. I asked them why they came to the meetings if they were not members of the NGO. They told me that they had come to listen to the *boyan* (speech) from the *hojur.*[26] This gave women who had never been in contact with NGOs the opportunity to meet with other women as well as with *hojurs*. Therefore, participation in Islamic NGOs provides increased visibility of women in the public sphere, particularly for those women who were left out of the NGO web. There are many women who never became a member of any NGO but who are now members of Islamic NGOs.

However, it is imperative to mention that participation in the *samity* meeting is not only a vehicle for religious and moral education but it also makes a space for mutual assistance, sharing pain and pleasure and figuring out solutions together, and hence forming positive social capital for them. Therefore, unlike the secular NGO-led group approach, the Islamic NGO-led group approach created strong bonding among members in order to respond to any misfortune or crisis together, while secular NGOs produced negative social capital. Zinia, a centre leader of the IBF at Shajalal Model Village, told me why the bonding is stronger among them:

> You will see in my centre, there is no repayment-related strife [*jaghra-bibad*]. Even if anyone can't repay, we together would pay. But, *Alhamdu-lillah* (Praise to God), within the last two years I haven't seen any such trouble.

In the case of MACCA's IDEAL village programme, this bonding is even stronger. Since this is an integrated approach ranging from credit, medication, to all aspects of social life, members are dependent upon each other and well integrated. For example, if they or their cattle get sick, their first point of contact is either the group leader or *Hasana* leader who arranges any necessary treatment or help. Although it seems to me overstated, MACCA beneficiaries claimed that they are so connected with each other that they never experienced conflict among themselves.

It is imperative here to mention that all the Islamic NGOs as with their secular counterparts take dowry and child marriage seriously and consider these as symbols of oppression and the indignity of women. Islamic NGOs are thus raising female beneficiaries' voices against the issue of dowry and child marriage in their community. What makes them different from secular NGOs is their emphasis on how Islam treats dowry and child marriage, as well as their emphasis on the engagement of the Imam to eliminate dowry and child marriage. For example, during my interview, one of the officials from MACCA read out the following statement regarding their stand on child marriage and dowry:

> With a view to promoting the culture of cooperation and respectfulness in the family MACCA propagates for 'Marriages without Dowry'. While marriage is blessed by the Almighty, dowry is prohibited by Islam and thus in the name of dowry any kind of repression on women is strongly condemned. MACCA supports to organize the marriage functions of the poor women and also provides some financial support in kind to make a livelihood for the new couples. So far it organized approximately 70 marriages without dowry. MACCA follows up the couples and assists them on various occasions especially during floods and other natural calamities.... It also plans to sit with women's organizations and activists to share their concerns and

> to advocate subsequently mainstreaming the issue of women in the light of Islamic interpretation for translation into the policy environment.

Yet, during my field visit in Shyamnagar, some participants were not members of Islamic NGOs. They disliked Islamic NGOs because of their focus on the rich rather than on the poor. Jalil and Harun expressed this concern when I asked about women's empowerment by NGOs like BRAC, and Jalil argued how BRAC ruined women. He stated:

> They [NGO officers] don't call us. When the NGO officer comes they ask, 'Where is she? Where is *umok* (pseudo name). Where is *tumok* (pseudo name). I can't say my wife's name, but you [NGO official] can. When I said, 'NGOs are empowering women. Isn't that a good thing?' Both of them reluctantly answered after a long pause. 'Yes, good!' They are doing such a deed … that they won't talk to you, they talk to women and when women return home they have an attitude and talk back to us. It's like they [women] have become president. Men don't have any value. Women don't listen to anything. If I ask to go for a shower, they would wander around the garden.

Although the statements made by Jalil and Harun at times reflect their frustration over women's empowerment this reflects the desire of a husband in a traditional patriarchal social system. Thus it is imperative to focus on some of the contradictions among gender issues within Islamic NGOs.

## Contested gender relations and Islamic NGO discourse

Although Islamic NGOs in Bangladesh work mainly with women, their agendas on women's empowerment is not clear enough and the notion of women's empowerment among Islamic NGO officials is different from the mainstream secular NGOs. As one Islamic NGO staff member said: 'We also support women's empowerment, but in a different way. They can be empowered while they are in *purdha*, maintaining *purdha* does not mean to be confined at home, but they can move around while in *purdah*.'[27] This idea of empowerment relates to the orthodox Jamaat's concepts of empowerment described earlier in this chapter. While secular NGOs have become a strong advocate for women's empowerment, Islamic NGOs link the idea of empowerment with family or household empowerment. I asked the official to explain the main ideals of family empowerment. He told me:

> Allah created all human beings in pairs and the Quran promotes the concept of family empowerment emphasizing both men and women as equal in terms of work and financial rewards. Allah declared in the holy Quran: 'And covet not that whereby Allah has made some of you excel others. Men shall have a share of that which they have earned, and women a share of that which they have earned.'

Yet, on the contrary, my field data suggest, in some contexts, that some officials of Islamic NGOs personally believe in men's superiority and women's subordination.[28]

However, Hussain (2010, p. 330) argues that 'when the mainstream NGOs campaign for women's empowerment, Islamic NGOs reconstruct their gender discourse, as according to them, women can work outside under the veil and can be empowered as long as they remain *subordinate to men*' (emphasis added). This, as Karim (2004, p. 300) argues, has created a positive ground for minimizing 'the resentment of the clergy who were refused before by the Western donor funded NGOs to be included in their system of patronage'. This is also true in my cases. For example, during my fieldwork I met with Chand Miah, a 55-year-old Imam of a local mosque at Chandirchar. He is president of all eight *Hasana* of MACCA. When I asked him who and how he was selected as the president of *Hasana* he replied,

> For the effective management of their programme, Masjid Council was needed of an Imam. I am the Imam of this area. So they [MACCA] selected me as the president, and the members of MACCA also supported me. I help members to refrain from paying interest, I push them towards prayer.

Another example of such engagement is also apparent in Muslim Aid, as I found in Shronkhola where the person in charge of the Rainbow Family programme is a local *Madrasah* (Islamic school) teacher. Moreover, the founder of MACCA clearly illustrates the importance of engaging the faith leaders (for example, Imams) for a better development outcome. He argues:

> We wanted to make the faith leaders the ambassadors and champions of development for the poor people of the country, overcoming the traditional perception that faith leaders often create hindrances to development activities.[29]

Therefore, the engagement of local clergy in the development practice of Islamic NGOs would minimize the resentment of the clergy and any backlash.

Yet the inclusion of the issue of women's empowerment and gender relations in the programme, mission and objectives of Islamic NGOs varies from one to another. For example, the web page and official documents[30] of the Islami Bank Foundation did not include the issue of women's empowerment, even though they work to empower women from an Islamic perspective. Other NGOs like Islamic Relief aim to:

> Root out gender-based discrimination by striving for a society in which women and men are able to live equally fulfilling lives ... in line with Islamic principles as outlined in the Qur'an and Sunna, as well as in accordance with international human rights and development norms.
>
> (Islamic Relief, 2008, p. 5)

For MACC, 'gender equity and women empowerment is one of the priority areas of MACCA. The program primarily focuses on the issues that stand as hindrances to women empowerment' (Masjid Council for Community Advancement, n.d., p. 12).

It is worth mentioning that it is the women who themselves resist the hegemony of secular development discourse through joining Islamic NGOs and rejecting secular NGOs. Since Islam and religion in general is an integral part of the social and political fabric, and represents the everyday practices of the people of Bangladesh, there is a need to engage Islam and religion in the development practices of NGOs. However, both the progress of Islamic NGOs in engaging religion in development practice and the subsequent impact on gender ideology need to be critically understood to identify further potential implications in society. Although some may contest the extent of the influence of Islamic NGOs on the lives of rural women in Bangladesh, my research findings suggest that through integrating religion in development practices and the careful engagement of Islamic NGOs (keeping them accountable) will produce better development outcomes for women in Muslim-majority countries like Bangladesh. Therefore, Chapter 6 focuses on the potential of Islamic NGOs as alternatives to the coercive practice of secular NGOs in Bangladesh.

## Notes

1 Mahmood (2005, p. 24) used the term 'Islamic sociability' to include women's body performance (e.g. the veil), correct forms of performance of Islamic rituals and increased Islamic charity.

2 For details on DFID, UK's initiative on Islam, gender and development, see DFID's project on Women's Empowerment in Muslim Contexts (WEMC) at www.dfid.gov.uk/R4D/Project/60091/Default.aspx. For UNFPA's engagement, see the United Nations Fund for Population Activities (2004) *Culture Matters: Working with Communities and Faith-based Organisations. Case Studies from Country Programmes*. New York: UNFPA.

3 Golam Azam, the central figure of Islamists in Bangladesh and convicted war criminal, was allowed to return to Bangladesh on 11 July 1978 on a Pakistani passport under a two-week visa to see his sick mother. Even though his visa had expired he was allowed to stay at his residence in Dhaka. Since his return, the work of rebuilding the Jamaat continued faster than ever before. It formally re-emerged as a political party at a convention in Dhaka on 25–27 May 1979 (Islam, 2001). Golam Azam was secretly made Ameer of Jamaat while Abbas Ali Khan was made the officiating Ameer. In 1991, Golam Azam was declared Ameer of Jamaat (Karlekar, 2005).

4 Tabligh Jammah is the international piety movement originally conceived by Maulana Muhammad Ilyas (a Deoband-educated Muslim scholar) in 1927 in Mewat, south of Delhi in India (Ali, 2003, p. 175). Its followers get together in the *Bishwa Ijtema* (Global Congregation or Meeting) held every year in Dhaka, Bangladesh. This is now considered the largest Muslim congregation of Muslim after Hajj in Mecca. As I have observed in Bangladesh, people seem to consider attending *Bishwa Ijtema* as equal to attending Hajj for those who cannot afford the pilgrimage to Mecca.

5 See Shehabuddin (1999, 2008); Riaz (2004); *fatwa* is a religious decree practised mainly by the local Imams in conjuction with other *alem* (religious scholars) and Mullahs mainly in rural Bangladesh.

6 *Shalish* is an informal and traditional arbitration system widely practised in Bangladesh, particularly in rural settings. However, recently, *shalish* has become more formal with the introduction of an alternative dispute resolution (ADR), particularly the NGOs.
7 Mohammad Gholam Rabbani and Nazmun Ara Sultana, the judges of the Bangladesh Supreme Court, High Court Division in the landmark 2001 judgment on *fatwas*.
8 In his ethnographic work entitled 'Women and Microcredit in Rural Bangladesh' (1999, he provides both the NGO workers and the borrowers testimony in this regard.
9 Positional vulnerability is understood in relation to culturally and religiously patterned behaviour of women which is associated with limited physical mobility, 'submissiveness', 'modesty', 'purity', 'respectability', 'shyness' and *purdha* (Rahman, 1999, pp. 73–75).
10 Translation of the Bengali word *purdha* into English is 'veil' or 'seclusion'. However, in the everyday practice of religion in Bangladesh, *purdha* represents social control, but also women's honour, status and condition in society. For details, see Feldman and McCarthy (1983).
11 As per the guidelines of credit disbursement, all NGO beneficiaries are grouped around certain *samity* (association in English). Every *samity* has around 30 to 40 members who are divided into groups of five or six members to ensure maximum accountability and loan repayment. *Samity* is usually located in any of the beneficiaries' houses/premises known as a centre. In every *samity* there is a centre leader and deputy leader.
12 *Monajat* is an Islamic tradition to ask for mercy and forgiveness of God.
13 *Shusilon* is a national NGO working with biodiversity, conservation, gender issues and alternative dispute resolution (ADR). This and other chants is also related to other, larger NGOs (e.g. BRAC, Grameen Bank) (see Naher, 2005; White, 2012) which I have also found in other areas under study.
14 The NGO officials who collect the weekly instalments and hold meetings are known as 'sir' and the manager of an NGO branch office is known as 'boro' (greater) 'sir'.
15 Development patriarchy, as used by White (2012, p. 11) to indicate the power and control of women's lives by the NGO. Although she did not elaborate on the term, I use it to explain competing powers and the tendency of NGOs to exert their power and influence to govern the life of rural women along with other actors (e.g. the rural religious elite, husbands and male family members).
16 *Taqwa* comes from the word '*waqiya*', which means to protect. It is protection from the anger of Allah and His punishment. This is why *Taqwa* is used to describe the performing of actions, which pleases Allah, and abstaining from all actions that displease Him.
17 It is important to note that for all Islamic NGOs under study, beneficiaries and even non-beneficiaries refer to them as *Islami Samity*, without knowing the real names of these NGOs.
18 See Rozario (2006) for a detailed discussion on the issue of Muslim women, the veil and empowerment in Bangladesh and which provides details on the issue of 'good women'.
19 *Ma* in Bengali means mother. The use of examples of Fathima as the daughter of the Prophet Muhammad is widely practised in the everyday life of Muslim women in Bangladesh.
20 During my interview with a high official of IBF, he provided me with some documents that stated their mission and modus operandi, though official published material was not available at the time of my visit.
21 *Fael Khair Prokolpo Manual* (in Bengali) was collected during my interviews with the high official of IBF at Dhaka office. This manual provides a comprehensive guide for those involved in the project. This specifically mentioned 28 duties and responsibilities of a programme officer.

22 In Islam, *iman* refers to a believer's faith in the metaphysical aspects of Islam (i.e. belief in the six articles of faith) which must be accompanied by righteous deeds. If a Muslim does not believe in any one of the six pillars of *iman* then they are not a true Muslim.

23 Women in rural Bangladesh used to wear the sari in many cases with a single twist that sometimes exposed their shoulder.

24 The accounts on their economic development were visible during visits to their home, which showed some of their assets, including cows, fishing equipment and agricultural inputs. However, in this book I do not emphasize the economic aspects of Islamic NGOs intervention.

25 *Talim* is commonly used to mean a congregation of Muslim women in a certain place where a female preacher (sometime called *Amma Hojur*) makes a speech on the Quran and *Hadith*-related issues and topics. It is becoming very common among urban and educated women. Yet it is not uncommon in rural areas.

26 Usually meaning religious speaker or Mullah; in this case they refer to the fieldworkers of Islamic NGOs who collect the weekly instalments and who also have a background in religious education.

27 During the interview with one of the high officials of Muslim Aid who explains what women's empowerment means to him.

28 Although some of the officials expressed their personal opinion regarding gender relations, this did not necessarily represent the organization they belonged to.

29 Opening speech of *Moulana* Abul Kalam Azad, Chairman of MACCA in the Annual Report 2009–2010.

30 During my interview with the high official of the *Fael Khair* programme, he handed me a short resumé of the foundation.

## References


Abecassis, D. (1990). *Identity, Islam, and Human Development in Rural Bangladesh*. Dhaka: The University Press.

Abu-Lughod, L. (2002). Do Muslim Women Really Need Saving? Anthropological Reflections on Cultural Relativism and its Others. *American Anthropologist, 104*(3), 783–790.

Ahmed, L. (1986). Women and the Advent of Islam. *Signs, 11*(4), 665–691. doi: 10.2307/3174138.

Ahmed, L. (1992). *Women and Gender in Islam*. New Haven, CT, and London: Yale University Press.

Ahmed, L. (2011). *A Quiet Revolution: The Veil's Resurgence, from the Middle East to America*. New Haven, CT, and London: Yale University Press.

Ali, J. (2003). Islamic Revivalism: The Case of the Tablighi Jamaat. *Journal of Muslim Minority Affairs, 23*(1), 173–181.

Amin, R., Becker, S. and Bayes, A. (1998). NGO-promoted Microcredit Programs and Women's Empowerment in Rural Bangladesh: Quantitative and Qualitative Evidence. *The Journal of Developing Areas*, 221–236.

Ammerman, N. T. (2007). *Everyday Religion: Observing Modern Religious Lives*. New York: Oxford University Press.

Badran, M. (2001). Understanding Islam, Islamism, and Islamic Feminism. *Journal of Women's History, 13*(1), 47–52.

Banu, U. A. B. R. A. (1992). *Islam in Bangladesh*. Leiden, The Netherlands: E. J. Brill.

Barlas, A. (2002). *'Believing Women' in Islam: Unreading Patriarchal Interpretations of the Qur'ān* (1st edn). Austin, TX: University of Texas Press.

Butler, J. (1993). *Bodies that Matter: On the Discursive Limits of 'Sex'*. New York: Routledge.

Chowdhury, H. (2011). Revisiting Globalisation Perspective Bangladesh. *India Quarterly: A Journal of International Affairs, 67*(3), 245–262.

*Daily Star*. (2011). Ban Fatwa, Make it Punishable Offence. *Daily Star*, 14 February. Available at www.thedailystar.net/newDesign/news-details.php?nid=174163 (accessed 14 June 2012).

De Cordier, B. (2009). Faith-based Aid, Globalisation and the Humanitarian Frontline: An Analysis of Western-based Muslim Aid Organisations. *Disasters, 33*(4), 608–628.

Devine, J. and White, S. (2009). *Religion, Politics and the Everyday Moral Order in Bangladesh*. University of Birmingham. International Development Department. Religions and Development Research Programme.

Engineer, A. A. (2004). *Rights of Women in Islam* (3rd edn). New Delhi: Sterling Publishers.

Esposito, J. L. (1994). *The Islamic Threat: Myth or Reality*. New York: Oxford University Press.

Feldman, S. (2010). Shame and Honour: The Violence of Gendered Norms under Conditions of Global Crisis. *Women's Studies International Forum, 33*(4), 305–315. doi: 10.1016/j.wsif.2010.02.004.

Feldman, S. and McCarthy, F. E. (1983). Purdah and Changing Patterns of Social Control among Rural Women in Bangladesh. *Journal of Marriage and Family, 45*(4), 949–959.

Fernando, J. L. (1997). Nongovernmental Organizations, Micro-credit, and Empowerment of Women. *The ANNALS of the American Academy of Political and Social Science, 554*(1), 150–177.

Fernea, E. W. (1998). *In Search of Islamic Feminism: One Woman's Global Journey*. New York: Doubleday.

Ghodsee, K. (2007). Religious Freedoms versus Gender Equality: Faith-based Organizations, Muslim Minorities, and Islamic Headscarves in the New Europe. *Social Politics: International Studies in Gender, State and Society, 14*(4), 526–561. doi: 10.1093/sp/jxm022.

Goetz, A. M. and Gupta, R. S. (1996). Who Takes the Credit? Gender, Power, and Control over Loan Use in Rural Credit Programs in Bangladesh. *World Development, 24*(1), 45–63.

Government of Bangladesh. (1991). *The Constitution of the People's Republic of Bangladesh*. Dhaka: Government of Bangladesh.

Guhathakurta, M. (1985). Gender Violence in Bangladesh: The Role of the State. *Journal of Social Studies, 30*, 77–90.

Harmsen, E. (2008). *Islam, Civil Society and Social Work: Muslim Voluntary Welfare Associations in Jordan between Patronage and Empowerment*. Leiden, The Netherlands: Leiden University Press.

Hashemi, S. M., Schuler, S. R. and Riley, A. P. (1996). Rural Credit Programs and Women's Empowerment in Bangladesh. *World Development, 24*(4), 635–653.

Hashmi, T.I. (2000). *Women and Islam in Bangladesh*. Basingstoke and London: Macmillan.

Helie-Lucas, M.-A. (1994). The Preferential Symbol for Islamic identity: Women in Muslim Personal Laws. In V. Mogadham (ed.), *Identity Politics and Women: Cultural Reassertions and Feminisms in International Perspective* (pp. 391–403). Oxford: Westview Press.

Hessini, L. (1994). Wearing the Hijab in Contemporary Morocco: Choice and Identity. In

F. Gocek and S. Balaghi (eds), *Reconstructing Gender in the Middle East: Tradition, Identity, and Power* (pp. 40–56). New York: Columbia University Press.

Human Rights Watch. (2011). Bangladesh: Protect Women Against 'Fatwa' Violence: Despite Court Orders, Government Has Failed to Intervene. Available from www.hrw.org/news/2011/07/06/bangladesh-protect-women-against-fatwa-violence (accessed 14 June 2012).

Hussain, N. A. (2010). Religion and Modernity: Gender and Identity Politics in Bangladesh. *Women's Studies International Forum, 33*(4), 325–333. doi: 10.1016/j.wsif.2010.02.006.

Islam, S. S. (2001). The Politics of Islam in Bangladesh. In S. C. Saha and T. K. Carr (eds), *Religious Fundamentalism in Developing Countries*, pp.167–185. London: Greenwood Press.

Islamic Relief. (2008). *Islamic Relief Worldwide*. Dhaka: Islamic Relief.

Jahangir, B. K. (1990). Fundamentalism in Bangladesh. In B. K. Jahangir (ed.), *Violence and Consent in a Peasant Society and other Essays*. Dhaka: Centre for Social Studies.

Kabeer, N. (1999). Resources, Agency, Achievements: Reflections on the Measurement of Women's Empowerment. *Development and Change, 30*(3), 435–464.

Kabeer, N. (2001). Conflicts over Credit: Re-evaluating the Empowerment Potential of Loans to Women in Rural Bangladesh. *World Development, 29*(1), 63–84.

Kamal, S. (1988). Laws for Women in Bangladesh. *WLUML Dossier, 4*(August/September), 4–8. Available at www.wluml.org/node/248 (accessed 3 November 2011).

Karim, L. (2004). Democratizing Bangladesh State, NGOs, and Militant Islam. *Cultural Dynamics, 16*(2–3), 291–318.

Karim, L. (2008). Demystifying Micro-credit: The Grameen Bank, NGOs, and Neoliberalism in Bangladesh. *Cultural Dynamics, 20*(1), 5–29. doi: 10.1177/09213740070 88053.

Kirmani, N. and Phillips, I. (2011). Engaging with Islam to Promote Women's Rights. *Progress in Development Studies, 11*(2), 87–99. doi: 10.1177/146499341001100201.

Korteweg, A. C. (2008). The Sharia Debate in Ontario: Gender, Islam, and Representations of Muslim Women's Agency. *Gender and Society, 22*(4), 434–454.

Landell Mills, S. P. (1992). *An Anthropological Account of Islamic Holy Men in Bangladesh.* Unpublished Ph.D. thesis, University of London.

Leo, E. S. (2005). Islamic Female Sexuality and Gender in Modern Feminist Interpretation. *Islam and Christian–Muslim Relations, 16*(2), 129–140.

MacLeod, A. E. (1992). Hegemonic Relations and Gender Resistance: The New Veiling as Accommodating Protest in Cairo. *Signs, 17*(3), 533–557.

Mahmood, S. (2001). Feminist Theory, Embodiment, and the Docile Agent: Some Reflections on the Egyptian Islamic Revival. *Cultural Anthropology, 16*(2), 202–236.

Mahmood, S. (2005). *Politics of Piety: The Islamic Revival and the Feminist Subject.* Princeton, NJ: Princeton University Press.

Mahmud, S. (2003). Actually how Empowering is Microcredit. *Development and Change, 34*(4), 577–605.

Masjid Council for Community Advancement. (n.d.). *Annual Report 2008*. Dhaka: Masjid Council for Community Advancement.

McGuire, M. B. (2008). *Lived Religion: Faith and Practice in Everyday Life*. New York: Oxford University Press.

Mernissi, F. (1992). *The Veil and the Male Elite: A Feminist Interpretation of Women's Rights in Islam*, trans. M. J. Lakeland. New York: Basic Books.

Mesbahuddin, T. (2010). Religion in Development: An Islamic Model Emerging in Bangladesh. *Journal of South Asian Development, 5*(2), 221–241.

Mir-Hosseini, Z. (1996). Stretching the Limits: A Feminist Reading of the Shari'a in Post-Khomeini Iran. In M. Yamani (ed.), *Feminism and Islam: Legal and Literary Perspectives* (pp. 285–320). London: Ithaca Press.

Moghadam, V. M. (2004). Towards Gendered Equality in the Arab/Middle East Region: Islam, Culture and Feminist Activism. *Occasional Paper: Background Paper for HDR 2004*. New York: United Nations Development Programme.

Moghissi, H. (1999). *Feminism and Islamic Fundamentalism. The Limits of Post-modern Analysis*. London: Zed Books.

Mohsin, A. (2004). Religion, Politics, and Security: The Case of Bangladesh. In S. P. Limaye, M. Malik and R. G. Wirsing (eds), *Religious Radicalism and Security in South Asia* (pp. 467–488). Honolulu, HI: the Asia-Pacific Center for Security Studies.

Montgomery, R., Bhattacharya, D. and Hulme, D. (1996). Credit for the Poor in Bangladesh. In D. Hulme and P. Mosley (eds), *Finance against Poverty* (pp. 94–176). London: Routledge.

Naher, A. (2005). *Gender, Religion and Development in Rural Bangladesh*. Ph.D thesis, Heidelberg University, Heidelberg.

Naher, A. (2010). 'Defending Islam and Women's Honour against NGOs' in Bangladesh. *Women's Studies International Forum, 33*(4), 316–324. doi: 10.1016/j.wsif.2010. 02.005.

Parmar, A. (2003). Micro-credit, Empowerment, and Agency: Re-evaluating the Discourse. *Canadian Journal of Development Studies/Revue canadienne d'études du développement, 24*(3), 461–476.

Pitt, M. and Khandker, S. (1995). *Household and Intrahousehold Impacts of the Grameen Bank and Similar Targeted Credit Programmes in Bangladesh*. Paper presented at the Credit Programmes for the Poor: Household and Intrahousehold Impacts and Programme Sustainability, Dhaka, Bangladesh.

Rahman, A. (1999). Micro-credit Initiatives for Equitable and Sustainable Development: Who Pays? *World Development, 27*(1), 67–82. doi: 10.1016/s0305–750x(98)00105–3.

Rowlands, J. (1997). *Questioning Empowerment: Working with Women in Honduras*. Oxford: Oxfam Publications.

Roy, O. (1996). *The Failure of Political Islam*, trans. C. Volk. Cambridge, MA: Harvard University Press.

Rozario, S. (2006). The New Burqa in Bangladesh: Empowerment or Violation of Women's Rights? *Women's Studies International Forum, 29*(4), 368–380. doi: 10.1016/j.wsif.2006.05.006.

Rozario, S. and Samuel, G. (2010). Gender, Religious Change and Sustainability in Bangladesh. *Women's Studies International Forum, 33*(4), 354–364. doi: 10.1016/j.wsif.2010.02.009.

Salehin, M. (2010). *Refashioning Islamic Dress Code in Bangladesh: A New 'Islamic Modernism' against Western Modernism*. Paper presented at the ISA World Congress of Sociology, Gothenburg, Sweden.

Samuel, G. and Rozario, S. (2010). From Village Religion to Global Networks: Women, Religious Nationalism and Sustainability in South and Southeast Asia. *Women's Studies International Forum, 33*(4), 301–304. doi: 10.1016/j.wsif.2010.02.003.

Scott, J. (1990). *Domination and the Arts of Resistance: Hidden Transcripts*. New Haven, CT: Yale University Press.

Selinger, E. (2008). Does Microcredit 'Empower'? Reflections on the Grameen Bank Debate. *Human Studies, 31*(1), 27–41.

Sen, G. (1993). Women's Empowerment and Human Rights: The Challenge to Policy. In F. Graham-Smith (ed.), *Population, the Complex Reality: A Report of the Population*

*Summit of the World's Scientific Academies* (pp. 363–372). London: Fulcrum Publishers, Royal Society.

Shaheed, F. (1994). Controlled or Autonomous: Identity and the Experience of the Network, Women Living under Muslim Laws. *Signs, 19*(4), 997–1019.

Shehabuddin, E. (1999). Contesting the Illicit: Gender and the Politics of Fatwas in Bangladesh. *Signs, 24*(4), 1011–1044.

Shehabuddin, E. (2008a). Jamaat-i-Islami in Bangladesh: Women, Democracy and the Transformation of Islamist Politics. *Modern Asian Studies, 42*(2/3), 577.

Shehabuddin, E. (2008b). *Reshaping the Holy: Democracy, Development, and Muslim Women in Bangladesh*. New York: Columbia University Press.

Wadud, A. (1999). *Qur'an and Woman: Rereading the Sacred Text from a Woman's Perspective*. New York: Oxford University Press.

White, S.C. (1999). NGOs, Civil Society, and the State in Bangladesh: The Politics of Representing the Poor. *Development and Change, 30*(2), 307–326.

White, S.C. (2009). Beyond the Paradox: Religion, Family and Modernity in Contemporary Bangladesh. *Religions and Development (RaD) Research Programme*. University of Bath, UK.

White, S.C. (2012). Beyond the Paradox: Religion, Family and Modernity in Contemporary Bangladesh. *Modern Asian Studies, FirstView*, 1–30. doi: doi:10.1017/S0026749X12000133.

Winter, B. (2001). Fundamental Misunderstandings: Issues in Feminist Approaches to Islamism. *Journal of Women's History, 13*(1), 9–41.

Wood, G.D. (2009). Clashing Values in Bangladesh: NGOs, Secularism and the Ummah. In F. C. Khan, A. Ahmad and M. Quddus (eds), *Recreating the Commons? NGOs in Bangladesh* (pp. 43–80). Dhaka: The University Press.

# 6 Coercion in development practice

## From negative social capital to Islamic alternative

Since the NGO sector in Bangladesh is predominantly microfinance orientated, there is considerable evidence of NGO coercion, particularly related to repayment of loans. Yet contradictions from both sides – NGOs and academic research – exist over the coercive nature of NGOs. Moreover, there is a lack of empirical research on the coercive practices of NGOs in Bangladesh. Therefore, the main aim of this chapter is to provide an overview of NGO coercion, particularly over the repayment issues of the microfinance programmes of the mainstream or secular NGOs, on the one hand and the possibility of an Islamic alternative to it, on the other. Since most of the beneficiaries of microfinance programmes of NGOs are women, coercion needs to be closely analysed to depict the vulnerability of women in NGO development practices. In this book, NGO coercion has been defined as the intended or unintended practice of NGOs, in which beneficiaries are forced or compelled to behave in ways that may harm their physical, mental and social well-being. It may involve the physical, mental or social infliction of pain and injury. This chapter looks in particular at the construction of shame (*lazza/apoman*), honour (*samman*) and social collateral, i.e. peer pressure in group-based lending processes at the centre of NGO coercion, which ranges from verbal aggression, starvation, forced sale and economic vulnerability to suicide. The coercive practices of NGOs produce negative social capital and are inevitably related to the mode of vertical power relations between the beneficiaries and the NGO. This chapter, therefore, explains how what may be understood as positive notions of social network and connectedness, within and among group members, are transformed into negative social capital that may result in shaming and suicide, women's suffering and economic vulnerability. The chapter then proceeds to explain why NGOs become coercive, and finally assesses the possibility of Islamic NGOs as an alternative to such coercive practices.

### People's experience of NGO coercion: the nature and extent of coercion

As described by Qazi Kholikuzzaman Ahmad, Chairman of PKSF (Palli Karma Sahayak Foundation) in Bangladesh, microfinance is a 'death-trap' for poor people (Melik, 2010). The present centre-left government in Bangladesh led by Sheikh Hasina is very critical of microcredit, particularly of Grameen Bank, and has termed it the 'bloodsucker of the poor'. The overt conflict between Grameen Bank and the government is now well manifested in the media, research and public discourse (Chakrabarti, 2011).[1] While there are contradictions in opinion, it is now well acknowledged that once they have entered into the microfinance net, women place themselves in a cycle of credit, making themselves even more vulnerable. Some researchers, such as Mayoux (2001, p. 439), have argued that the microcredit programme, instead of enhancing social capital as it purports to do, inflicts what she calls 'negative social capital'. By this she is referring to negative outcomes of social capital such as the distrust and strife that may emerge from a microcredit solidarity group. This section gives examples of practices used by NGOs to enforce loan and interest payments. These include verbal aggression, forced sale, starvation, and harassment by the police. Yet, many of the examples of coercion include suicides by female borrowers, forcing people to leave bodies unburied and making women sell *nakphul* or nose pins, which have symbolic meaning (e.g. of losing *nakphul*) and are associated with the loss of a woman's chastity and being a widow. While this is unusual and perhaps not the rule, popular hearsay about such practices creates an atmosphere of fear and potential shame, which enforces repayment at all costs.

### *Women borrowers, starvation and suffering*

As mentioned elsewhere in this book, the positional vulnerability of women for which the male (for example, mostly the husband and sometimes the father) and NGOs' use of women leads to the increased victimization of women through development practices. Poor people and particularly poor women are the main victims of such development practices, as has been found in the study areas. This section narrates some stories around the nature of such practices. Although the NGOs promise that they will alleviate aid recipients' poverty and hunger, many of the respondents still experienced significant difficulties. The overall impression of NGO activities or what Jalil at Shyamnagar refers to as *Samity* is such that 'due to these *samity* [NGOs] we cannot even eat in peace'. Shakila, a BRAC beneficiary at Shyamnagar, narrated her sufferings as follows:

> I took a loan of 15,000 Taka from BRAC. I could not repay the loan. So I went to the manager and asked him to give me work. I will repay the money bit by bit in exchange with this work. Since I have borrowed the money, I have to repay. If you let me work [BRAC's post-cyclone rehabilitation cash for work] in the project, I will be able to repay, as well my son can sit for the exam, and his problem will also be solved. He will sit for SSC [Secondary School Certificate exam, the largest public exam in Bangladesh]. It did not work … his exam is in 10 days [she takes a long breath]. Since I cannot repay, whenever the NGO worker comes to my home I request and beg them, I pay 50 Taka instalment instead of 200 Taka, but I pay. They use

> verbal aggression. At that time I felt like if I could get into the earth, then I could get rid of this. They said a lot. My kids are crying for rice on the one hand, BRAC is for money, this is such an anxious situation I can't finish telling you.

Karimun, a 50-year-old woman and a mother of six children from Tala, explained how she repaid the loan with the money that was supposed to be used to buy medicine. In the past she had been a member of four different NGOs, including Grameen Bank, Uttron, Unnyan Prochesta and Gagoroni Sangstha. She had been a member of Grameen Bank for 16 years. She claimed that Grameen Bank did not return her savings (DPS) and insurance money when she left Grameen Bank. Moreover, she told me her story of the harsh treatment of an NGO called Uttaran:

> My daughter got a heart disease [*ter hearte pani asche*] [her heart swelled] so her in-laws sent her back to my house. She needs medicine of 1,000 Taka every day. Once I borrowed 1,500 Taka from people to buy her medicine. But Uttaran came to my home and said they won't leave my home until I pay and used many harsh words. Thus they compelled me to pay their instalment with the money I was supposed to buy medicine for my daughter.

Zarina, a 40-year-old woman from Tala, was once a member of many NGOs but she could name only four of them (i.e. ASA, Grameen Bank, BRAC and Uttaran) during the interviews. She unfolded the story of coercive practices of all the NGOs she was involved with and how she lost her only available asset – her home – because of Grameen Bank and how she feels about BRAC, which cheated her. She took on a Grameen phone to establish a phone business, but she said that Grameen Bank charged her a much higher rate than she had anticipated. According to her count, the bill for the phone came to between 4,000 and 5,000 Taka, while for Grameen Bank it was 9,000 to 10,000 Taka. So she could not pay the money back and therefore Grameen Bank continually exerted pressure on her to repay the loan. Therefore, she borrowed money from other sources. However, she ended up borrowing from 16 different sources and was in debt to the sum of 300,000 Taka. Thus she had to sell her home and she became a street beggar. She also said that people started to hate her since she had 'become homeless and a beggar and started asking for money from everybody'. She considered BRAC to have cheated her. She had once been a member of BRAC and obtained 5,000 Taka as a loan. Since she could not repay the loan, BRAC proposed to her that if she payed back the previous loan of 5,000 Taka, they (BRAC) would grant her a further loan of 50,000 Taka. Therefore, she borrowed money from people to pay the loan back. But when she repaid the loan, BRAC denied granting her any further loan. This was just BRAC's strategy to collect the loan, and what she termed as BRAC's cheating.

### *Forced sale, economic vulnerability and public uprising*

One of the most common procedures to cope with the coercive repayment practices of NGOs is the forced sale of available assets, mainly household items such as cooking utensils, or agricultural inputs such as cattle, or personal belongings such as ornaments and clothes. It is apparent from the field that all the respondents who previously received microcredit from BRAC, Grameen Bank, Uttron and Gonomukhi and Unnyan Podekhep had been forced to sell certain of their assets to meet the repayment requirement. One of them was Hasina, a mother of six children, and the wife of a street hawker, Abul Hossain at Tala. She explained her mistrust of NGOs and their coercive repayment methods that led her not to be a member of any NGOs except one, namely Islamic Insurance. She continued:

> I used to be a member of BRAC and got a loan of 5,000 Taka. However, we lent this borrowed money to Ajit who could not repay us the money. Since we did not use the money and Ajit could not repay us, we have had to repay the money. But we were unable to repay the instalment. Then, every morning a BRAC worker used to come to my home and reproach me and used abusive words whatever comes in their mind. They also threatened me to take away my cattle. Then I had to sell the mango tree planted by my father-in-law to repay the loan.

There is numerous evidence of such forced selling to repay the loans that make already poor people more vulnerable in their lives and livelihoods. Karimun from Tala borrowed 15,000 Taka from Uttaran and she told me her story of how she repaid the loan.

> During my daughter's marriage I had to pay the dowry (hand and ear ornament for my daughter, and wrist watch, bicycle and ring for the groom). So I could not pay one of their instalments. So I told them my daughter got married and therefore I have a crisis with money. Since I could not pay, she [Uttran worker] stayed in my house until evening and told me she can't leave until I pay the money back. While sitting on my veranda, she started crying at some point. What can I do? I told her I have a pair of earrings and I will sell them tomorrow and pay the money back. Therefore, I repaid her money by mortgaging out my earrings.

Besides forced sales of items, respondents also explained their experiences of how NGOs took away their houses, or even roofs and clothes. Rahim Mia, a local Imam in Manikganj, said he knew of many such incidences of the NGOs forcibly taking the house away (*ghar-banga*). As he claimed: 'I saw many who took a loan from BRAC and built houses, but they had to repay the loan through selling that house otherwise BRAC took it away … so they turned into what they were before.'

### *Surveillance, policing and vulnerability*

Besides group surveillance, legal measures such as engaging the police or sending a summons from the local court have also been practised in the study areas and which caused anxiety, confusion and trauma for many. In many cases as the respondents suggest, they received a summons from the court to repay their loan. Since the rural beneficiaries of the NGOs are in the 'death-trap' and involved with several NGOs at a time to repay the loan this creates a vicious NGO cycle. They cannot escape from this cycle and turn from credit worthy to worthless. They become even more vulnerable when they encounter the state police and the court system. When peer pressure fails to reclaim the loan, NGOs tend to call or take their members into their office and won't release them until they pay the money, or someone from their family agrees to act as a guarantor to provide a statutory declaration that they will repay the loan within a certain period of time. Shaheda Khatun at Tala, who is now a member of the local government, explained how she encountered such trouble when she received a loan from BRAC and could not repay three consecutive instalments (*kistee*). In Shyamnagar, an Islamic NGO beneficiary called Romisa told me how Gonomukhi took her godmother (*Dharma Ma*) to their office since she could not repay their loan. When an NGO takes someone to their office for a loan default, it calls to mind a criminal being brought to account before the police. Thus, it is an issue of public shame and dishonour. Besides these coercive surveillance practices, NGOs tend to use courts and state police to recover their loans. Rural villagers, who are often illiterate and without assets that could be used for bribes, are often afraid of the courts and state police. There is an abundance of stories among the respondents from Shyamnagar of the fear of being caught by the police and subsequent imprisonment. For example, Hafez Md. Mohidul Islam, a 42-year-old male member of the Hazrat Abu Horaira centre of the IBF, narrated some stories regarding coercive practices of secular NGOs like BRAC, Grameen Bank and Gonomukhi.[2] He continued:

> Grameen and BRAC are very strict [*kothor*]. They called many people to their centres, and put someone in jail. Hannan, nephew of Atajoddin, was thrown into jail for three months. He received a loan from Gonomukhi, but did not pay the loan back. For the last five years he was a defaulter, did not contact Gonomukhi as he was afraid of their harsh treatment. However, finally he could not avoid this. Gonomukhi filed a case in the local court and subsequently he was caught by the police and was in prison for three months.

Nevertheless, Harun, at Shyamnagar, who was once a member of BRAC, received a summons from the court to repay his loan. He explained:

> I received a loan from BRAC, but became unable to repay and missed some instalments. After a few weeks I received a notice from the court to pay the

> money back; otherwise they would file a case against me. I then got so frightened that I had to repay their money immediately. When the court alerts us, we become frightened and are compelled to repay the loan to avoid the case against us.

Although using the state policing mechanism and subsequent imprisonment is not common to all the loan defaulters, it is clear that it had happened with some regularity in the study area, and that respondents were very aware of the possibility of it happening through heresay.

### *Between honour and shame: survival and suicide*

The virtues of modesty and purity are important signifiers for rural women's identity in Bangladesh (Kotalova, 1996). These virtues of modesty and honour (*somman* or *izzat*) are used by NGOs in lending practices and may be converted to shame (*lozza*) when loans are not repaid. For example, research (e.g. Rahman, 1999; Nahar, 2010; Karim, 2008, 2011) on microcredit programmes of NGOs like BRAC and Grameen Bank show how the discourse around *shame* is developed and maintained through lending practices in rural society. Earlier research on microcredit borrowers in Bangladesh shows the coercive treatment of NGOs and the subsequent suicide of a member. Rahman (1999, p. 70) narrates the following:

> Vanu gave an example from a neighbouring Grameen Bank branch where a woman failed to pay instalments for a few weeks and was brought to the bank office by her peers. The bank workers asked the woman to sit inside a room in the Bank and locked the door from outside. The woman felt so humiliated [*opomanito-hoy-se*] that she hanged herself from the roof-fan by using her own sari [women's clothing in rural Bangladesh].

The incidence of suicide due to defaulting on microcredit is very likely,[3] since there are news reports and other evidence of microcredit-related suicide in Bangladesh. For example, a rickshaw puller, Abdus Samad (55 years old) and his wife Zarina Bibi (45 years old), a domestic worker at Balahar village in Niamatpur under Naogaon District, borrowed all together 1 *lac* Taka (US$1,200) from Grameen Bank and Astha and was unable to repay the loan. The pressure of meeting the repayments, as the local police believe, led them to commit suicide. Daily Prothom-Alo reported on another incident of microcredit-related suicide on 18 June 2012.[4] According to this news report, Abdus Samad from the village of Mominpur in Tangail District took out BDT81,000 as a loan from four NGOs in five terms. He had to pay BDT1,800 in weekly instalments. He tried to manage instalments by selling his last remaining asset, his six decimal homesteads, yet no one wanted to buy his homesteads. Since he could not pay the instalments, officers from four NGOs used abusive words and threatened him. Having no alternative, he committed suicide by consuming poison.

Other recent stories of microcredit-related suicide unveil the same incidents of coercive practices of NGOs. The *Daily Independent* reported the suicide of a female member of the Society for Social Service (SSS) and Grameen Bank named Hasna Begum on 17 February 2012[5] in Tangail. She received 15,000 Taka as a loan from the SSS and a small amount from Grameen Bank. But she could not repay the loan, despite reminders from the NGOs. She borrowed a further 60,000 Taka from a village money lender at a high rate of interest. She hired a tailoring shop for her son with the borrowed money, but it was not enough to cover the large instalments she had to pay. Thus friction mounted between the parents and their son over the issue and led a frustrated Hasna to commit suicide.

The incidents of the suicide of a van driver, Jashim in Barishal and Abudus Salam from Jaalokhati, tell the same story of NGO coercion. The most recent incidence of suicide during my research occurred on 23 July 2012,[6] when a day labourer, Abul Hashem Mizi from the village of Sreepur in Haziganj Upazila of Chandpur District, committed suicide. He took out a 15,200 Taka loan from one NGO and then a further 23,000 Taka from another NGO. Altogether he had to pay 1,125 Taka in weekly instalments. He was unable to pay and he could not sleep at night due to anxiety over the repayment. He hanged himself from a mango tree by a nearby pond.

The incidence of suicide, of course, reflects upon the coercive nature of NGOs in development practices. A recent report on Grameen Bank from the Government of Bangladesh says: 'The borrowers are harassed in the name of loan recovery in Grameen Bank. There exists instances of such families who have become penniless; some borrowers even committed suicide having failed to repay the loan.'[7]

Yet, most of the NGOs will defend this, claiming that suicide doesn't occur because of their coercive practices.[8] Against the NGO officials' claim, it is found that microcredit default suicides are not limited to Bangladesh, and there is evidence of microcredit-related suicide around the world (for example, in Andhra Pradesh in India, and in Africa). In India, the BBC reports how two borrowers of microcredit died due to pressure from the microcredit provider.[9] As suicide may involve many other social factors, it is also possible that the microcredit burden could lead beneficiaries to commit suicide. During the field visit in Satkhira, respondents told me about a woman who committed suicide in a neighbouring village. One of the respondents claimed that she knew of three such cases of suicide related to microfinance. Moreover, during participation in a centre meeting with an IBF beneficiary, I was told by respondents that they knew Monju, the wife of Bazlu from a neighbouring village called Islam Kathi, who used to be in the same group with one of my respondents and who died drinking *andrin* (a type of insecticide). In response to questions regarding causes of Monju's suicide, they mentioned some reasons including Monju's inability to repay the loan. Zarina, one of the respondents, added: '*Apoman soite na pare* [she could not bear the humiliation].' Then I asked Zarina, what sort of humiliation? She replied: 'Who likes to face NGO workers as an everyday presence in the household and be pressured for loan recovery and their use of abusive words [*gali-galaj*] and *vater khota* [shaming for eating]?' She told me that when she could not repay the loan, the NGO worker humiliated her, saying, 'You can eat rice, but cannot pay; you should be ashamed that you are eating and not paying the money back.' Thus the issue of *apoman* (humiliation) and *lazza* (shaming) constitutes the strongest narrative in coercive practices of NGOs in development discourse. Every woman whom I interviewed expressed her concern over the behaviour of the NGO officials and of being humiliated (*apomanito*) by the NGO workers. In most of the cases it was verbal humiliation through using abusive words (*gala-gali*) and *khob bajye bhabohar* (very harsh behaviour). One such victim, Pervin, who was once a member of BRAC and ASA, told me:

> We had a poultry farm, but we encountered losses of 85,000 Taka due to the *Gambura* virus for which all of the 1,100 chicken in the farm died. Since then, we have had difficulties repaying our loan to BRAC. My husband also got kidney disease. We suffered a lot to repay the loan. I need 1.5 kilos of rice every day for my family, but I could buy only half of it to feed my family. I myself worked hard to maintain my family. Once, I could not pay one instalment of BRAC, they came to my home and charged me. They told me it's a BRAC rule that even if someone dies, and the dead body remains on the veranda, you have to pay the money. They also used many other words. I told them, look, I never missed the instalment. But now I am in trouble … you have to give me some time. But they said they can't allow me any more time to repay. They pressured me a lot. Then my husband requested one month to repay, in order to get a loan from others and buy chickens for the farm to repay. But they didn't agree. Sometimes I could not buy rice to feed my family but pay the instalments for BRAC. I told BRAC that I could not even buy rice for my family, how I could pay. But they used such abusive words, that I decided that I'd rather starve and pay them the money back.

When I asked her to tell one of the abusive words used by BRAC, she replied, 'they used many words that I can't even utter them in my mouth in front of you'. I asked her to tell me some of their words that could be used in front of me. She replied: 'they told me you have to pay me the money back by selling your blood. It's not my job to see whether you can buy rice or not, you have to pay.' Although she could not tell me the abusive words used by BRAC, I had to imagine what such abusive words could be, since she told me that she had to flee from home to avoid such shaming by the NGO workers.

Therefore, whether myth or fact, such examples from the beneficiaries of NGOs reflect the coercive nature of NGOs and the endeavour of women to protect their honour from these NGOs, through leaving such organizations, or in extreme cases committing suicide. Although none of respondents attempted suicide, it is undeniable that NGOs have been playing with the lives of their members, as NGOs pose a coercive power within the vertical power relations between NGOs and rural women.

Zhinu, for example, a MACCA beneficiary at Manikganj, had once been a member of three different NGOs to obtain a loan, including BRAC, Grameen Bank and ASA. However, she left BRAC and Grameen Bank after a few years. The obvious reason for leaving these NGOs was the high rate of interest they charged. Yet the instalment collection techniques were very harsh for Zhinu, as she explained: 'we had to pay them the instalment leaving a dead boy at the country yard'. Although metaphoric, it represents the vertical power relationship between the patron and the client where the instalment collectors exercise their coercive authority over their beneficiaries. This is not the end of the nature of the harsh treatment from NGO officials to collect the repayments. She explained how a group of five or six BRAC officials came to her home on motor bikes to collect the instalment. She continued her story on what she did to repay Grameen Bank's credit instalment:

> When I was with Grameen Bank, I could not pay my weekly instalments back due to sickness. Since they forced me to pay the instalment, I had to sell my cooking utensils. As I was in trouble, I had to sell them cheaply to repay their loan…

I needed to know whether she informed the Grameen Bank officials about her sickness and inability to repay. She replied: 'Doesn't matter whether I am sick or not. They said, didn't we give the conditions that you have to pay your instalment even if you have a dead body inside the house? Since I was insolvent at that time, I had to agree with their conditions.' If the same condition was imposed upon a male member, the scenario could be different; that is, because he would have more options available to respond to the NGO; for example, he could leave home, argue with officials or simply ignore the harsh treatment. Yet because of women's positional vulnerability (for example, they are less mobile), NGO workers exercise greater disciplinary powers over women, and in most cases these powers end up being coercive.

The story of respondents leaving dead bodies at home in order to repay loans is of great significance to beneficiaries. When someone dies in a family, they will mourn and perform many rituals for the funeral. If an NGO has scheduled an instalment collection on that day, how could a member of the mourning family attend the meeting to repay the loan? The rhetoric of 'leaving dead bodies' thus implies that mourners must leave a dead body and related funeral activities in order to repay the loan, and that NGO officials will not leave the mourners' house until they repay the instalment. This has become a common allegation against development NGOs. While many of the respondents had not experienced such treatment themselves, they said they had heard of someone in another village who had faced this situation. Other respondents, like Jalil, although he did not experience such treatment, strongly believed that 'since they [BRAC] don't leave the beneficiaries' veranda without our instalments, this must be true'. Whether or not this happens regularly or is a tale told regularly in rural villages, the story of 'leaving dead bodies' reflects perceptions of the coercive practices of NGOs.

Some coercive practices carried out by NGOs also have deep symbolic meanings within rural society. For example, many women reported that they themselves and many others had to sell their gold nose pins (*sonar nakphul*) to repay their loan. Although selling a nose pin does not bring much money to the family to repay the loan, the symbolic value is much higher. Usually in Bangladeshi cultural practice, the groom has to give a nose pin to his bride that she has to wear until her husband dies. Therefore, for rural women, wearing a nose pin symbolizes their marital status. Losing a nose pin, therefore, symbolically means being divorced or widowed. Moreover, losing *nakphul* has also been associated with losing women's chastity and being raped (Riaz, 2004, pp. 55–56). During the political transition after the 2001 general elections in Bangladesh, stories of gang rapes of minority women reveal the deeper meaning behind losing a nose pin where they narrated their rapes, the worst experience a woman can undergo, through using a euphemism – loss of *nakphul* [nose pin/ring]' (Riaz, 2004, p. 54). One such victim of gang rape narrates:

> Jesmin ran to a nearby paddy field submerged in water. But the attackers found her, dragged her out, and repeatedly asked 'where is your daughter?' As she declined to divulge the whereabouts of her young daughter, the ruffians beat her, hacked her indiscriminately with a machete, and finally snatched away her *nakphul*.

The story of another gang rape victim, Laxmi, conveys the same meaning. As she narrates:

> They grabbed both of us – my daughter-in-law and me – and forcibly dragged [us] to a nearby empty house. The seven gangsters dragged my daughter-in-law to the kitchen and looted her *nakphul*, and they did the same thing to me.

Women are forced to sell their nose pins to repay their loans. When respondents in Shyamnagar told the story of women selling their nose pins due to their debt to the NGOs, they gave a glimpse of their sense of honour and their strong emotional attachment to that bodily ornament. Shafiqul Islam, a beneficiary of IBF and *moazzen* (who calls for prayer) at the local mosque told the story of selling nose pin:

> They [NGO workers] used very harsh words, and behaved badly. I have seen many women members fleeing from their home. Whenever the women see the NGO officer coming to their home, they flee to protect themselves from the worker's abusive words … whatever the way, either selling their nose pin or something else, they must pay their loan, and they have to pay their loan back. Sometimes, the women are called upon by the NGO to attend their office and to defend their default payment.

The selling of one's nose pin is not a common practice adopted by the defaulting members of any NGO if they could avoid it through arranging an alternative way to repay the loan. Yet the experiences of fleeing from home to escape the harsh treatment of NGO workers and avoid the shaming are abundant.

Based on the above discussion, this book argues that secular NGOs' microcredit programmes have resulted in many coercive practices, most of which are related to loan repayment. As has already been mentioned, the group-based approach of microcredit is used to ensure the financial stability of NGOs rather than the welfare of the beneficiaries. Although this group-based approach (in theory) aims to generate or strengthen social capital (for example, creating trust, networks and solidarity) among the women borrowers, ultimately it turns into negative social capital (distrust, strife and segregation) among such women. The following section mainly discusses how positive social capital turns into negative social capital as a manifestation of women borrowers' vulnerability.

## Social capital and its vulnerability

To understand how positive social capital leads to negative social capital through coercion and violence against women requires an explanation of positive and negative social capital. The term 'social capital' is contested and its interpretation differs among scholars. For Putnam (1993, 1995), social capital implies a set of horizontal networks among people and related norms that influence the productivity of the community. For Coleman (1988, p. S98):

> Social capital is defined by its function. It is not a single entity but a variety of different entities, with two elements in common: they all consist of some aspect of social structures, and they facilitate certain actions of actors – whether persons or corporate actors – within the structure.

Yet social capital in general is conceived of as networks, forms of associational activities and development agencies aimed at ensuring the participation of their beneficiaries in these vehicles to hold society together (Molyneux, 2002, pp. 171, 175, 176). The emerging literature, in addition to capturing the positive associations of social capital, has also examined the negative aspects of social capital (Mayoux, 2001; Portes, 1998, 2000). Portes (1998) meticulously explains the positive and negative consequences of social capital, portraying how one can gain (i.e. positive consequences) or lose (i.e. negative consequences) in a transaction (i.e. through membership in networks and other social structures) mediated by social capital. He identifies at least four different ways in which negative social capital may be produced. One is through the exclusion of outsiders, which is clearly demonstrated in the group-based approach of the microfinance industry. The other three include excessive claims on group members (e.g. by the group leader, centre chief and NGO workers), restrictions on individual freedoms and downward levelling norms.

Mayoux (2001, pp. 436, 450) uses the term 'negative social capital' to portray the inherent complexity of social capital in poverty alleviation through microfinance mechanisms. Although she agrees that microcredit can make a significant contribution to poverty alleviation as well as women's empowerment, 'serious questions need to be asked about what sorts of norms, networks and associations are to be promoted, in which interests, and how they can best contribute to empowerment, particularly for the poorest women'. With Portes (1998) and Mayoux (2001) in mind, this book is concerned with the negative or less desirable consequences that emerge from social capital. This book thus focuses on the ways in which NGO-led microfinance uses 'social collateral' such as surveillance and policing to ensure individual accountability and the ways in which this may become a source of conflict (*jaghra-bibad*) and develop into coercive practices.

As social capital works as a kind of social glue that holds society together and enables poor and marginal people to organize themselves to increase solidarity and social cohesion (Smets and Bähre, 2004, pp. 217–218), so development NGOs, use the social capital framework to empower women through participation in their programmes, such as the microfinance programme in Bangladesh. Microfinance-oriented development practices in Bangladesh, as pioneered by Grameen Bank, have been using a group approach to manage the microfinance programmes of NGOs. The microfinance industry targets those poor who certainly lack regular and sufficient income and financial collateral, such as land or any other assets, to gain credit from the formal sources of credit from government banks and credit institutions. Thus the conventional collateral has been replaced with the idea of group collateral or social collateral. Social constraint mechanisms lie at the heart of the social collateral system through which organized pressure from group members ensures the repayment of the loan. Usually every centre of microfinance in a village consists of five or six groups. Each group consists of five female beneficiaries, where there is a group leader for each group and a centre leader for each centre. Each group must take responsibility to ensure the weekly repayment of the credit of the default member. Thus group members impose surveillance on each other to safeguard the repayments. Although social capital is regarded as glue for social cohesion and a tool for the poor to organize themselves, it is important to understand how such a group approach could turn into negative social capital.

Group-based microcredit programmes of NGOs have generated the idea that through participation in regular meetings, marginalized women are able to develop new social networks and support bases in times of need (Dowla, 2006). Yet this group-based approach or social collateral reinforces conflict among the group members. As the main mechanism for the successful recovery of a microfinance loan is peer pressure through exploiting social norms, it often ends in conflict. One of my respondents from Shyamnagar who was a member of BRAC and Grameen Bank for many years explained how social collateral escalates conflict among members:

> One of our group members Rasida was not able to repay her loan during the weekly meetings as a result of which sir [NGO official] halted granting our

> loans. She did not come to our weekly meeting. Therefore, sir asked us to bring her to the meeting or pay the loan ourselves. We sent one of our group members to her house and she refused to come to the centre. Along with our sir and centre chief we went to her house again after the meeting. She knew that we would come again so flew from home. However, after waiting for an hour in her home, sir left her house asking us to bring her to the office the next day. When sir left, she suddenly appeared with her husband and started using abusive words against us, asking whether sir is our husband [*vatar*] or not and why did we bring him to her house. Then, since we could not tolerate such words, strife began with her and her husband.

Other respondents also told me that the same sort of strife was related to microcredit repayments, as they suggested that 'strife has now mixed with our blood'. This contradicts the claim that credit programmes enhance group solidarity and subsequently social capital. There is a lot of evidence of escalated domestic violence against women borrowers, particularly by the husband, and unequal power relations among beneficiaries (Rahman, 1999).

It is also clear from the field that though there is a promise of empowerment and strengthening relations through increasing social solidarity and social cohesion, microcredit rather enhances patronage relationships and unequal power relations among members. It also increases a vertical power relationship between NGO workers and their clients, leading to the NGO worker exerting a control mechanism over the client. Therefore, the NGO official is able to play on these unequal power relations and the lack of group solidarity in order to get the women to do what he needs them to do, i.e. to turn against each other to get the woman who owes money to pay up. He attempts to shame the woman in front of her peers and gets the women in the group to do his work for him. One of the respondents at Shyamnagar explained this process:

> If any woman of our group wants to get credit [*reen*], the very first process is to give a credit proposal [*reen prostab*]. For this proposal to be valid, sirs compel us to organize two other members' signatures along with the signature of the group leader. As a result, three persons, including the centre's chief [*kendra prodhan*] get involve in that woman's loan. Now if that woman fails to repay the instalments (*kistee*) all these people pressure her to pay the instalment. Sometimes, male members of these women's family get involved too. As a result it leads to strife and brawls [*jaghra-bibad*] for most of the time, when the woman doesn't want to pay. Sometimes, the centre leader negotiates and conducts arbitration [s*halish kore*] among these members. As a result, our sirs do not need to do anything, as he has already turned other women against that woman. Sir must get his instalments at the end. Do you now understand [asking me], our sirs are very good at frying fish in its own oil [*macher tele mach vaja*].

Moreover, some of the previous research on microfinance programmes in Bangladesh (e.g. Rahman, 1999; Karim, 2008, 2011) shows that women are subject to domestic violence from their husbands due to missing family chores (e.g. cooking), since these women get delayed in the centre meetings, and this sometimes creates disorder in the undertaking of household chores. Consequently women become the victim of physical violence or verbal aggression from their husbands. As a result there is a decrease in attendance at *samity* meetings in the case of secular NGOs, and thus many members, as one of my respondents told me, just send their instalments through their husbands or sons, or other members, which does not fulfil the basic premise of the social capital approach. The social capital approach involves the beneficiary attending centre meetings, participating in discussions to build networks and create new opportunities, and having an understanding of collective action. Thus it is clear that a group-based approach in the credit delivery system, instead of creating a social network, solidarity and trust, produces negative consequences for the women as they are shamed and humiliated by other women in the group as well as by NGO staff. As a result, one of my respondents is afraid of group strife [*jaghra-bibad*] and abusive treatmentfrom the NGOs as she told me: 'I would rather starve than join an NGO'. In the context of the coercive treatment of NGOs, is there any possibility that the beneficiary could rise up against the NGOs? In the section that follows, I explore the issue of people's uprisings against the NGOs' coercive treatment.

## Resistance and uprising against NGOs

As a result of the sufferings of borrowers, there are incidences of people's uprisings against BRAC and Muslim Aid in Shyamnagar and Sharonkhola. Occasional uprisings among the rural community are not uncommon in Bangladesh. During the 1990s, rural religious elites rose up against the secular NGOs, particularly with regard to their role over women's empowerment issues, though it is not common (Shehabuddin, 1999, 2008). There were other stories of uprisings against NGOs which are 'suitcase' or 'fake' NGOs and which appropriate poor people's initial savings or deposits and then go into hiding. In addition, the same kinds of NGOs cheat job seekers and loot huge amounts of money. It is hard to find evidence of mass people's resistance against mainstream NGOs, though it is not entirely absent in the study areas. For example, one of the employees of a local NGO explained what happened to BRAC:

> One BRAC worker took away some clothes from the clothes line that was placed in the yard for drying. Since that woman from Koikhali village could not pay the loan a BRAC worker took away these clothes. However, the villagers did not like it. They chased the BRAC worker and caught him and punished him [*dhore petiche*]. Then his co-worker and manager came to Koikhali to rescue him.

It is not uncommon for people to protest against treatment by Islamic NGOs. For example, at Sharonkhola one of the key informants, Jalauddin, who is also a beneficiary of Muslim Aid, informed me that people had demonstrated against

Muslim Aid due to the NGO not following its promise of giving them 120,000 Taka to build their houses. Yet Muslim Aid gave them 90,000 Taka, so the people had to spend more money to build their houses. In order to get the additional money, they borrowed from the local usurers and other NGOs. This ultimately caused many of them to get into debt.

Although people rising up against NGOs is not common, one of the respondents, who is also a member of the local government and beneficiary of certain secular NGOs, claims that rural women are more aware of the coercion and would not allow the coercion to go unchallenged. She explained why people could rise against NGO coercion:

> NGOs came to our area for the last 20 years. Our people are now very used to NGOs and they are not afraid of NGOs' treatment. Now we can choose better NGOs from many options. As well, we know many loopholes in the NGO business.

Yet it is problematic to generalize such a view, as most of the other respondents think they cannot go against the NGOs, though they have some options to make complaints to their *boro* sir (NGO branch manager). Yet they rarely make any complaint. Although many women from the secular NGOs (e.g. BRAC and Grameen Bank) are critical of the NGOs' treatment, particularly in relation to credit instalments or repayment policies, none of them showed their anger or dissatisfaction with NGO officials in front of them while they participated in the *samity* meetings. They called these NGOs *rokto chusa* (bloodsucker) *samity* and *shudkhur* (usurer) *samity*. These forms of resistance, following Scott (1985, p. xii), could be termed passive resistance, which is hidden and has a very low profile. In everyday life, a 'subordinate group creates, out of its ordeal, a hidden transcript that represents a critique of power spoken behind the back of the dominant' (Scott, 1985, p. xii). Yet it is crucial to know why they participated in these NGOs despite the coercive practices and consequent grievances. The main response was 'there is no other way, but to join them'. One of the respondents and a BRAC beneficiary explained: 'We are poor, nobody likes the poor. If I do not go to the *samity*, who will give me the money … will you [pointing towards me]?' Therefore it may be argued that the empirical evidence from the fieldwork indicates people's subordinate position to the increasing involvement of NGOs in development practice in rural Bangladesh, and the incapacity or lack of solidarity to rise up against the oppression of the NGOs. This is embedded in asymmetrical or vertical power relations between the NGO as patron and its beneficiaries as dependent clients. This also reflects the NGOs' power to deny the fact of people's uprising. For example, the Islamic NGO officials both at their local office and head office denied any demonstration against them in Sharonkhola.

## Why does the development model become a coercive model?

There are several explanations for the coercive nature of NGOs and hence it is important to explore some of the possible causes of such coercive practices in Bangladesh. During the fieldwork, people (secular NGO beneficiaries and key informants) tend to think that NGOs in rural Bangladesh are nothing more than for-profit business organizations, as Shamim Miah, a MACCA beneficiary at Manikganj, explained about the coercive repayment practice of Grameen Bank while his wife was a member. Moreover, his construction of the idea of mainstream NGOs also reflects the perceptions of members of Islamic NGOs in the study areas. For him, 'they [mainstream NGOs] have come to make a profit, we do not have any benefit, it is their benefit. They [mainstream NGOs] have come to do business, and they [MACCA] came here to preach the words of *deen* [religion] and serve [*sheba*] humans.' Moreover, the research has shown that NGO staff members adopt the same attitude; as one of the Managers of Grameen Bank said: 'Why are you surprised? Grameen Bank is a business and not a charity' (Karim, 2008, p. 20). Moreover, workers at Islamic NGOs also perceive NGOs that charge high interest as profit-making institutions rather than as NGOs. The coordinator of NGOs in Sharaonkhola considered microcredit NGOs such as BRAC as '*nubbo mohajon*' (neo-money lenders/usurers) with the effect that 'there was no change in people's livelihood, rather they become further impoverished'. The same comments on microcredit operations of NGOs came from another rights-based NGO, Progoti at Shyamnagar, who claimed that he does not 'seek funding from those donors who provide microcredit which is a mechanism of exploitation'.

This perception of NGO beneficiaries and staff members led to the argument that NGOs, then, are not considered as third-sector organizations, but rather as business organizations that count on cost–benefit analysis and turn into a profit-making machine, and subsequently become a corporate success (for example, the success of Grameen Bank and BRAC in the telecommunication industry, food, fashion and crafts industry and the education industry). This successful nature of NGOs has also been found in other studies (e.g. Karim, 2008). Therefore, NGOs need to ensure profit maximization and the smooth operation of their programmes by putting their staff in the field under tremendous pressure to recover loans. This pressure is also associated with job insecurity, promotion and transfers of NGO workers. Research has shown that in spite of certain rules and regulations on promotions and transfers, they (the NGO fieldworkers) are unable to take any action against decisions, as they reported: 'What can we do when our superiors do not follow the rules? We cannot go on strike or afford to go to the courts' (Khan, 2003, p. 184). This pressure on NGO staff led them to adopt any means to recover the loans from poor people. Many of the respondents in the study who received coercive treatment from the NGOs told me that when NGO workers reach the beneficiary's home, they consistently exert pressure on them to collect the money. Khaleda, one of the respondents in Tala, talked about the agony of a BRAC fieldworker who came to her home to collect the instalment:

'If we cannot collect your instalment, the manager will humiliate me. If I don't get your money, he won't allow me to enter into the office.'

On the other hand, NGO staff members are also under pressure for loan disbursement leading to granting loans to people who are already members of many other NGOs. One Islamic NGO branch manager claimed that the NGO head office had set a target for loan disbursement. Therefore, to achieve that target, he provides the loans without taking into consideration the circumstances of a particular client. For example, one of the NGO fieldworkers reported that a NGO manager receives a target to disburse 40 *lac* BDT (US$50,000) in one month, so what can he do? He grants loans without regard for the capacity of the client to repay the loan. The client has the capacity of 5,000 Taka and he grants him 15,000 Taka, leading to an increased default rate and subsequent coercive practice to recover the loan. Moreover, if he cannot achieve the target disbursement and recovery he will have to face a forced transfer or he will be sacked. Therefore, in the study areas most of the women are members of more than one NGO at the same time. In extreme cases, as one of the beneficiaries claimed, she borrowed from 16 sources. Since women cannot pay one NGO loan, they get involved in another to recover the previous loan, leading to the trap of microcredit. This leads ultimately to a loan default and the subsequent adoption of coercion by the NGO to recover the loan.

In the various study areas some of the respondents also explained why the women become defaulters. Among many reasons, some respondents expressed their concern over the control and pattern of the use of loans by the male members of their family. Some agreed that they just borrowed the money on behalf of their husbands. In most cases women are just the official borrowers, but the money is actually spent by their husband. Bithi, one of the respondents from Sharonkhola, explaied why some women cannot repay their loans:

> There are many Grameen Bank borrowers who borrowed the money and the husband took that money, got married with someone else and left the woman. What can this woman do? Since the money is in her name, the NGO charge her. Since there is no income from her husband how will she repay the money?

Thus there are some clients, as one respondent claimed, who are so reluctant to pay the money that NGO workers have no alternative but to be coercive. It is also important to mention that in the context of poverty, women borrowers who do not use their money for economic activities, but rather spend it on consumption or social activities (for example, meeting dowry demands) become loan defaulters, which leads to their coercive treatment from NGOs.

When a poor woman becomes a member of any NGO to receive a loan, she needs to follow certain disciplinary rules to obtain the loan. Therefore, any member of a group receiving a loan means that other members agree to repay and recover the loan for any defaulting member. Research has shown that the practice of group or social collateral for the poor can turn out to be a coercive measure for the surveillance and policing of members by their peers, which significantly reduces the operational costs for such NGOs (Karim, 2008) and increases the recovery rate. This social collateral then becomes negative social capital, leading to regular credit-related conflict between the member and her immediate family.

Although NGOs opt for women's empowerment, their policies and practices reveal the gender vulnerability. Research has shown that their theoretical construction of womanhood in rural Bangladesh is not reflected in the NGOs' practice, or what Rahman (1999) explains in terms of a 'hidden script' and a 'public script'. It is apparent that NGOs target women in their programmes due to the positional vulnerability of women and, subsequently, these women are an easily manipulable population. Thus, NGO workers know that they can exploit the norms of shame and honour of these rural women, to discipline them in the NGO principle. This disciplining mechanism of NGOs leads to effective management of the recovery of the loan. Thus shaming women for becoming defaulters of loans, by calling them to their office or by repeated visits of NGO workers to the women's homes, ensures that women are vulnerable to the coercive practices of NGOs.

## Islamic NGOs: can they be an alternative?

The coercive practices of secular or mainstream NGOs and the non-coercive nature of Islamic NGOs have thus led to an explanation as to why these Islamic NGOs behave differently. Yet it is not very easy to assume whether Islamic NGOs will be the alternative to such coercive practices of mainstream NGOs, but they could make a difference, as Islamic NGO staff members and beneficiaries believe. None of the respondents from the Islamic NGO beneficiaries talked about the harsh treatment from the NGOs to which they belong, although a few respondents told us about the public demonstration against one Islamic NGO. However, all the Islamic NGOs involved in microfinance use the same group-based approach and social collateral used by secular NGOs for providing loans to rural women. One branch manager of an Islamic NGO, however, agreed that they chose women as their beneficiaries since they are easily accessible and there are more chances of repayment than if the beneficiaries were men. However, at the same time they also use the male guardian of the family, in the initial stage, to establish contact with the female and use both the husband's and wife's photos in their borrower's book.

As has been discussed elsewhere in this book, Islamic NGOs have a very soft attitude towards the repayment of credit. They avoid being coercive to their beneficiaries. Thus all of the NGO officials both at the field office and at head office explained why they have a very soft attitude towards loan repayments. The NGO officials from the field claimed repeatedly that they do not have any pressure from their head office for repayment of the loans. Thus, this absence of pressure from head office led them to avoid coercive measures in loan repayment. Moreover, the Islamic NGO staff at their head offices claimed that they were not here to *make business* but to serve humanity. In the case of Muslim Aid, they referred to the *humanitarian* teachings of *Islam* as the main ideology for their work. They referred to the Quranic verse 'And whosoever saves the life of one, it shall be as if he had saved the life of all of mankind' (Quran 5:32), which demonstrates the value of each individual life and is the ethos by which they operate. In addition, the sources of funding determine the nature of the activities of these organizations. When the funding comes from the Muslim diasporas in the form of *zakat* or *sadaqah*, the religious obligation attached to it dictates the nature of the treatment of beneficiaries. Major funding for one of the NGOs discussed in this book comes from its parent organization based in the UK, making it easier not to be coercive with their beneficiaries. For example, in the case of the Muslim Aid microfinance programme, they have received a quarter of their funding from Muslim Aid UK which is interest and service charge free, while the remaining funding for the programmes is managed locally from the Islamic Development Bank (through *Fael Khair*) and their internal source. Therefore, the particular source and nature of the funding has helped Muslim Aid to grant interest-free loans and to become non-coercive.

Although it is very hard to understand the real goals of Islamic or any other NGOs, what may be understood is their ideological standpoint, which could explain why they behave in a certain way. For the Islamic NGOs, their commitment to certain Islamic ideologies (for example, the humanitarian values of Islam and its principles of social justice) has made them follow non-coercive practices. As Muslim Aid[10] describes, the difference between the faith-based and secular NGOs in development practices reveals their strong commitment to Islamic teachings for serving:

> However, despite these similarities faith-based NGOs can be differentiated from secular organizations in certain respects. Being motivated by faith, they have a committed support base and a constituency that responds to humanitarian concerns. People who believe in an established faith or those who are not fully committed to formally believing in a set of beliefs feel it is their duty to cater for those in need. Muslim Aid, for instance, is guided by the teachings of Islam and strives to alleviate poverty and its causes by finding long term solutions that are innovative and sustainable. Thus, even though the expression of faith is manifested in different religions in various forms, it remains a strong motivator of humanitarian activities.

In the context of Bangladesh, it became clear that Islmic NGOs refer repeatedly to their stance on compassion and empathy for fellow Muslims, leading them to adopt non-coercive practices to Muslims and non-Muslims. MACCA (n.d., pp. 1–3), for example, includes the following in the introduction to its *Hasana* programme booklet:

> The position of Islam in regard to helping the poor people and working for the greater development is very sturdy and apparent. The Quran in Surah

> Al-Mau'n narrates, 'Have you seen him who denies the Recompense? That is he who repulses the orphan (harshly), And urges not the feeding of Al-Miskeen [the poor]'.

Therefore, if some NGOs use *zakat* or any other form of Islamic alms giving as their source of funding, there is even less chance to be coercive in their development practices due mainly to their commitment to Islamic religious practice. This is also reflected in the rhetoric of Islamic NGOs as they claim 'we are not here to oppress [*Julum*],[11] but to serve [*sheba*] the poor and bring social justice'.

One of the field supervisors of an Islamic NGO narrates the context of being non-coercive towards their beneficiaries:

> Until now none of our beneficiaries could say that we have misbehaved with them. We used to give sufficient time for collection. If they [other NGOs] cannot recover the money in the morning, five to six people went in the afternoon to pressure the defaulter and collect the money. They [BRAC] become coercive in recovering the money. They have offices in every union and the office in charge looks after the instalment collection. So if one field-worker cannot collect the instalments, he gets charged by his superintendent officer. We have even heard that if, at the end of a month, there are still some instalments unrecovered, then the salary of the related field officer is stopped until he can recover the default money, or the default amount of the instalments is deducted from the respective fieldworker's salary. This is what we call *zulm* [oppression or injustice] inflicted on them, and as a result these fieldworkers oppress [*zulm*] their members. But we did not have such pressure from the head office. Since we were not pressurized by our head office, we did not oppress our beneficiaries. If we are oppressed, maybe we would have to adopt such oppressive behaviour, because at the end of the month if I don't get my salary, I have to recover that default money by any means because I have a family to support from this salary. Either I have to leave the job or recover that default money to get my salary. But we have not had such problems in our programmes. If anyone could not pay, we have extended our compassion. One reason for such compassionate behaviour is that unlike other NGOs, we don't have strict dictation from the head office. Since I am a local person, I personally did not like to behave harshly. Specially, since this is known as Islamic *samity*, it was impossible to be oppressive and use abusive words and become oppressive. Since I belong to an *Islami Samity* and I go there wearing cap [*topi*] I cannot *zulm* [oppress] them.

It is also important to note that, though some of the respondents mentioned their involvement with Islamic NGOs because of their political identity (for example, Jamaat-e-Islam), none of the members mentioned any discussion on the political issue of voting preference of the Islamic NGO towards any particular political parties in Bangladesh. What is important to mention here is that many of the beneficiaries of Islamic NGOs in the study areas are the supporters of Jamaat-e-Islam. For example, in Shyamnagar, one of the respondents claimed that 80 per cent of the members of his *samity* support Jamaat. In Tala, one of the respondents argued that it was obvious that people who support Jamaat are also members of *Islami samity*, since he claimed that 80 per cent of the villagers are supporters of Jamaat. During the interview with grassroots political leaders, one of the respondents who is secretary of a ward,[12] Awami League at Sharonkhola, alleged that 'in this area they [*Islami samity*] selectively gave credit to those who are the supporter of Jamaat. They did not give any credit to me.' The same allegation was also found during an interview with the vice-president of Sharonkhola Upazila and secretary of the Upazila Awami League. Yet the supporters of the Bangladesh Nationalist Party, who are close allies of Jamaat, denied this allegation. The allegation has also been made by some other local leaders who told me that they suspect the Islamic NGOs have a preference for Jamaat supporters. In the case of Islamic NGOs in the study areas, though they did not say anything about the future of a *shari'a* state, many of the workers of Islamic NGOs and beneficiaries believe that one day they will be able to build an 'ideal society' (*adarsha samaj*) where justice, honesty and compassion will prevail. Therefore, it could be sympathy from the Islamic NGO for the beneficiaries to behave in a non-coercive way for a greater political end – to establish an 'ideal society'. This fellow-feeling works through the Islamic rhetoric of working for the Muslim *umma* (community). This community obliges its members to stand together and show solidarity, i.e. to support one another, meaning that Muslims should engage in the provision of aid to the poor, because they are part of the same religious community, the *umma*, and, as such, are obliged to help one another. This is apparent in the programme and mission of Islamic NGOs. One of the Islamic NGOs mentioned on its website the obligations of the community: 'The Prophet [PBUH] is reported to have said "if any individual of any village wakes up in the morning having passed the night starving, Allah [SWT] does not take the responsibility to sustain the village" [Musnad-EImam Ahmad]' (MACCA, n.d.).

Another important aspect which needs an explanation in order to understand how Islamic NGOs are becoming distinctive from the mainstream secular NGOs, (and which has led them to be non-coercive) is the beneficiaries' firm commitment to their Islamic beliefs. During the interviews, I asked the women who were once members of BRAC and Grameen Bank, and who could not repay their loan while with these NGOs, how they were now able to pay them on time. All of the respondents agreed that this was due to the interest-free nature of the loan, the extended grace period during the loan repayment and, most importantly, blessings (*barkat*) from Allah. They see that there is *rahmat* (clemency) from Allah for them because they are following Islam and using *valo taka* (good money) or *Islam er taka* (money of Islam). Thus in borrowing money from Islamic NGOs, which aim for Islamic development, there is *barkat* from Allah on the money (*eai takai barkat ache*) and the borrowers are, for this reason, able to repay the loans. Thus a strong commitment to the religious belief which is reinforced by the Islamic NGOs has also led them to repay their loans regularly and therefore provides no place for coercion.

Christian NGO-led development intervention (for example, CARITAS in this research) shares the same kind of mandate for development with that of Islamic NGOs. According to the philosophy of CARITAS, 'while many times development, as such, can tend to lead people away from God and Religion, authentic development will lead people to God and Religion, i.e., to that love for God and for all humanity' (CARITAS, n.d.). Like Islamic NGOs they also use the concept of *sheba* (service) to be at the heart of the programme. This is also manifested in their philosophy which claims that

> CARITAS is for *sheba*, i.e. service in a spirit of religious devotion. Involvement in CARITAS should be seen as a calling from God to offer one's life for others and to see others as precious gifts of God in our lives. It is not only work but life itself that is offered; and it is mutually offered, for as we serve we are in turn served by a friend, by a brother or a sister. Both CARITAS personnel and those benefiting from CARITAS programs should have this same spirit of *sheba*.
>
> (CARITAS, n.d.)

This philosophy was also echoed in conversations with me while I interviewed CARITAS officials at Shyamnagar.

It is also important to mention that some people who are not members of Islamic NGOs alleged that Islamic NGOs had a preference for the richer client and ignored the real poor. It is true that, during my visit to their many houses the centre leaders of Islamic NGOs gave me the impression that they are well off, better off than many others in society. Examining the socioeconomic conditions of some of the centre leaders could validate this claim. For example, one of the centre leaders of the IBF at Sharonkhola is Zinia, and she claims her economic conditions are better than other people's and that she holds some power over others, which makes such women listen to her commands. Her husband is a reporter/journalist on a national daily newspaper. Most of the centre leaders whom I met gave me the impression of having relatively better economic conditions than others. Some of the respondents from Shyamnagar claimed that *Islami Samity* do not give credit to the poor. During the interviews, whenever I asked why they are not members of an Islamic NGO, Jalil reported, 'but *Islami samity* is giving to the rich. Who are with these NGOs, who have 50 acres of land … whenever *dumba's* [Arabian lamb] meat [Qurban or sacrificial meats from the Middle East] come, they will distribute them among themselves, they won't give it to us.' In response to such claims, a local member of an Islamic NGO in the same area explained that this meat was only for members of the Islamic NGOs, and that was why other poor people did not get the meat. At the same time, one of the Islamic NGO officials believed that 'to be honest, it is difficult to give credit to those who are absolutely penniless, taking into account their ability to return the money'. Moreover, in the case of Islamic NGOs, some of the respondents have been reluctant to discuss issues of coercion. This is, I assume, because they are Muslim and they may not want to admit that Islamic NGOs could commit acts of coercion. In the case of Christian NGOs, some of the respondents (for example, Jalil, Harun and Rokshana at Shyamnagar) told me that they know at least one field officer who received bribes (*gush*) from beneficiaries to deliver aid following cyclone *Aila*. Besides, one of the respondents (who did not want to be identified as the field official of a Christian NGO) in Shyamnagar claimed that the Father of a local church has a huge influence on the programme of CARITAS in that area and gave preference to the local *Munda* tribe. This preferential treatment to this marginal tribal group reflects a hidden agenda, he claims, to gain converts to Christianity.

Poor people's vulnerability has been manifested through the coercive practices of NGOs in rural Bangladesh. This does not necessarily mean that Islamic NGOs could be an alternative option in this regard. What is clear in the study areas is that the non-coercive treatment of Islamic NGOs is contrary to their secular counterparts' behaviour in the service delivery. Yet it has become apparent that Islamic NGOs have been accused by some of the respondents regarding their preference towards a particular political party (for example, Jamaat-e-Islam) and bias towards richer clients. It is imperative for these NGOs to avoid any political and economic preference in beneficiary selection which can lead to the exclusion of many other potential beneficiaries. Like secular or mainstream NGOs, the use of women members in their programmes to safeguard their investment does not make them distinct in development practices. It is also imperative for Islamic NGOs to consider the sustainability and transparency of their funding in order to sustain their non-coercive practices.

## Notes

1 The conflict between Grameen Bank and the present Bangladesh government is currently very explicit. There are people for and against, governments claim. The Norwegian documentary arguing that money had been siphoned off by Yunus of Grameen Bank to another account ignited the strife. There are many explanations of the government's attitude towards Grameen Bank, one of which argues that

> Politicians led by Hasina have attacked [Grameen Bank] because of their own perceived lack of importance in world opinion compared to Yunus and it is probably more envy generated than anything else. Not having done much to alleviate poverty, they are critical of a loan system.... Some people are quite simply, uncomfortable with Yunus' success and have taken it out. Most are quite unfamiliar with the loan system but have criticised so one must assume a level or animosity not explained by reason.
>
> (Chowdhury, 2010: see 'Grameen Bank: Why People are Critical and What it Tells about Us', available at http://opinion.bdnews24.com/2010/12/21/grameen-bank-why-people-are-critical-and-what-it-tells-about-us/ (accessed 24 July 2012)

2 Gonomukhi (official name: Nowabenki Gonomukhi Foundation), a local NGO based in Shyamnagar, Satkhira is mainly a microcredit NGO.

3 See Bdnews24.com on 'Microcredit Troubles Drive Couple to Suicide', 4 July 2009 (www.bdnews24.com/details.php?id=137107&cid=2).

4 See 'Eker pore k rin, pore athmahothma' (Loan One after Another, then Suicide), *Daily Prothom-Alo*, 18 June 2012, available at www.prothom-alo.com/detail/date/2012–06–17/news/266514 (accessed 25 July 2012).

5 See 'Woman Commits Suicide Failing to Repay Loan', *Independent*, 18 February 2012, available at www.theindependentbd.com/national/95490-woman-commits-suicide-failing-to-repay-loan.html (accessed 25 July 2012).

6 See 'Riner Chintay Athmahonta' (Suicide from Credit Anxiety), *Daily Prothom-Alo*, 24 July 2012, available at www.prothom-alo.com/detail/date/2012–07–23/news/275960 (accessed 25 December 2012).

7 See 'Summary of the Review Committee Report on Grameen Bank', available at www.mof.gov.bd/en/budget/pr/gp_press.pdf (accessed 23 July 2012).

8 After every microcredit-related suicide, when the journalists interviewed the respective local officials, they denied their connection between coerceive repayment practice and incidences of suicide. See *Daily Prothom-Alo* (18 June and 24 July 2012), *Daily Independent* (18 February 2012).

9 See 'India's Micro-finance Suicide Epidemic', available at www.bbc.co.uk/news/world-south-asia-11997571 (accessed 10 July 2012).

10 See 'Are International NGOs Truly International: How Diverse are the Faith-based NGOs?', available at www.muslimaid.org./index.php/what-we-do/research-development/750-diversity-of-faith-based-ngos (accessed 3 July 2012).

11 The Arabic *Zulm* is used to mean cruelty or unjust acts of exploitation, oppression and wrongdoing, whereby a person either deprives others of their rights or does not fulfil his or her obligations towards them.

12 Union Parishd, the lowest tier of local government, comprise several wards consisting of one or two villages in each ward.

## References


CARITAS. (n.d.). Philosophy of CARITAS Bangladesh (1994). 2.

Chakrabarti, S. K. (2011). Bangladesh's 'Banker to the Poor' Faces a Political Battle to Survive. *Time*. New Delhi: Time Inc.

Coleman, J. S. (1988). Social Capital in the Creation of Human Capital. *American Journal of Sociology*, 95–120.

Dowla, A. (2006). In Credit we Trust: Building Social Capital by Grameen Bank in Bangladesh. *Journal of Socio-Economics*, *35*(1), 102–122. doi: 10.1016/j.socec.2005.12.006.

Karim, L. (2008). Demystifying Micro-credit: The Grameen Bank, NGOs, and Neoliberalism in Bangladesh. *Cultural Dynamics*, *20*(1), 5–29. doi: 10.1177/0921374007088053.

Karim, L. (2011). *Microfinance and its Discontents: Women in Debt in Bangladesh*. Minneapolis: University of Minnesota Press.

Khan, M. M. (2003). Accountability of NGOs in Bangladesh: A Critical Overview. *Public Management Review*, *5*(2), 267–278.

Kotalova, J. (1996). *Belonging to Others: Cultural Construction of Womenhood in a Village in Bangladesh*. Dhaka: The University Press.

Mayoux, L. (2001). Tackling the Down Side: Social Capital, Women's Empowerment and Micro-finance in Cameroon. *Development and Change*, *32*(3), 435–464.

Melik, J. (2010). Microcredit 'Death Trap' for Bangladesh's Poor. *Business Daily, BBC World Service*. London: BBC.

Molyneux, M. (2002). Gender and the Silences of Social Capital: Lessons from Latin America. *Development and Change*, *33*(2), 167–188.

Naher, A. (2010). Defending Islam and Women's Honour against NGOs in Bangladesh. *Women's Studies International Forum, 33*(4), 316-324. doi: 10.1016/j.wsif.2010.02.005.

Portes, A. (1998). Social Capital: Its Origins and Applications in Modern Sociology. *Annual Review of Sociology, 24*, 1–24.

Portes, A. (2000). The Two Meanings of Social Capital. *Sociological Forum, 15*(1), 1–12.

Putnam, R. D. (1993). The Prosperous Community. *The American Prospect, 4*(13), 35–42.

Putnam, R. D. (1995). Bowling Alone: America's Declining Social Capital. *The City Reader*, 120–128.

Rahman, A. (1999). Micro-credit Initiatives for Equitable and Sustainable Development: Who Pays? *World Development, 27*(1), 67-82. doi: 10.1016/s0305-750x(98)00105-3.

Riaz, A. (2004). *God Willing: The Politics of Islamism in Bangladesh*. Lanham, MD: Rowman & Littlefield.

Scott, J. C. (1985). *Weapons of the Weak: Everyday Forms of Peasant Resistance*. New Haven, CT: Yale University Press.

Shehabuddin, E. (1999). Contesting the Illicit: Gender and the Politics of Fatwas in Bangladesh. *Signs, 24*(4), 1011–1044.

Shehabuddin, E. (2008). *Reshaping the Holy: Democracy, Development, and Muslim Women in Bangladesh*. New York: Columbia University Press.

Smets, P. and Bähre, E. (2004). When Coercion Takes Over: The Limits of Social Capital in Microfinance Schemes. In H. Lont and O. Hospes (eds), *Livelihood and Microfinance: Anthropological and Sociological Perspectives on Savings and Debt* (pp. 215–236). Delft, The Netherlands: Eburon Publishers.

# 7 Conclusion

This book contributes to our understanding of the compatibility between religion and development in general and Islamic religious practice and neoliberal governmentality in particular, through an exploration of the activities of NGOs and, in particular, Islamic NGOs in Bangladesh. The book analyses how new charitable practices (for example, Islamic NGOs), institutions and subjectivities are rearticulating the hegemonic, secular development discourse in Bangladesh. In the domain of the hegemonic secular development practices of NGOs, Islamic NGOs have emerged as a new frontier of development in Bangladesh in the 1990s. This has produced a hybrid form of neoliberalism. This form of social regulation produces and reproduces subjectivities, particularly Muslim (women) subjectivity, and has combined religious and economic rationality, and has further complicated the boundaries and the relationship between Islam, modernity and development. Thus, the book argues that Islam and the activities of Islamic faith-based organizations are not antithetical to neoliberalism; in fact, neoliberalism works even better with faith-based organizations.

The main aim of this book has been to explore the role of Islamic NGOs' development practices in the absence of the state and to understand the problems of secular NGOs in service delivery in rural Bangladesh. An exploration was undertaken of the *shari'a*-based microfinance programmes of Islamic NGOs, as compared to microcredit programmes provided by secular and non-Islamic NGOs. The research included an exploration of humanitarian aid (e.g. shelter, microfinance) to see whether this made a difference. I have endeavoured to understand the activities of NGOs; for example, microfinance in conjunction with the idea of neoliberalism, with particular emphasis on neoliberal governmentality as embedded in a Foucauldian conceptualization.

As I extended neoliberal governmentality into the domain of religion, I explored the conceptualization of pious governmentality or pious neoliberalism to see how Islamic NGOs use a discursive combination of Islamic rhetoric with the procedures, and the techniques of neoliberal governmentality to govern the population for successful and pious private entrepreneurial beings based on economic rationality and calculative reasons. Thus the book has explored how the assemblage of the techniques and practices of governance integrate with the neoliberal principles of accountability and transparency, as well as 'personal responsibility' and 'self-care' by the entrepreneurial, competitive and rational economic individual with that of religious values and piety.

This book is based on a qualitative study informed by interpretivist methodology. I used in-depth interviews, FGDs and participant observation as my methods of study. Published and unpublished documents, including NGO and government reports, were used to supplement the primary data. I drew upon grounded theory and thematic analysis for my data. My research shows that secular NGOs in Bangladesh emerged in the context of post-war reconstruction of the Bangladeshi state and nation-building in the 1970s and gained prominence in the 1990s. With the spread of neoliberalism, NGOs moved from conscientization to service delivery and thus particularly captured the rural economy. Globalization, as my research found, is working through these NGOs at the grassroots level, thus contradicting Appadurai's (2001) conceptualizations of grassroots globalization which 'proceed independently of actions of corporate capital and the nation-state system'. These NGOs played a significant role in the de-clientelization of the rural poor away from the model of the exploitative patron (e.g. *mohajon*/usurer), yet reproduced a new small money lender group comprising mainly well-off NGO recipients including rural Muslim women. This expansion of NGOs in the service delivery role was used to govern their subjects in a way that conformed to the norms of the market.

Based on my research findings it is apparent that there has been an emergence of a new form of governance in rural Bangladesh which combines the principles of Islam with economic rationality through the practice of Islamic NGOs. This research has identified the transformation of Islamic charity or the emergence and expansion of Islamic NGOs related to many factors which I discuss in Chapter 2. One factor is the transformation of Bangladeshi society over the past 30 years, when Bangladesh adopted neoliberal structural adjustments leading to a shrinking of the state's social safety nets. This was accompanied by increased unemployment in the rural economy and a spread of non-state actors who assumed the role of provider to the abandoned state social services. This decade is marked by the emergence of the privatization of the economy, an emergence of ready-made garment factories and subsequent rural–urban migration and social problems (e.g. family disintegration). An increase in the number and prominence of Bangladeshi Muslim diasporas, particularly in the West, helped the Islamic charities to grow and be sustained. Another factor is related to the social structure of Bangladesh where Islam is embedded in everyday aspects of life (for example, from eating habits of the people to state legitimacy). The politics of secularism and Islamism in Bangladesh allowed space for the growth of the Islamic NGOs, even the radical ones (e.g. Revival of Islamic Heritage Society (RIHS), Al Harmain Islamic Foundation (AHIF), and the Benevolence Society based in Kuwait, Saudi Arabia, Libya and Pakistan). Moreover, NGO-led development space is a competitive one, and the shortcomings of secular NGOs in providing services to the rural people, particularly microcredit (due to the high rate of interest), allowed space for Islamic NGOs to emerge as successful competitors in which they blended piety with entrepreneurialism through providing interest-free credit.

In this form of governance, as this book argues, Islamic identity largely shapes economic practice. This book has considered those organizations as Islamic NGOs whose mission, vision (either latent or manifest) and activities are based in the teachings of Islam, including any subsect of Islam. As I discuss in Chapter 3, Islamic ideological orientation of these NGOs informs the development practices of Islamic NGOs in particular to develop and adopt certain ways to act, run and implement their programmes among rural people, whether through naming a particular village in an Islamic way, or using an Islamic ideal-based financial system (for example, *shari'a*-based microfinance) or a *zakat*-based programme. All the Islamic NGOs in the areas studied emphasized Islamic principles and idioms on naming; for example, the names of the NGOs themselves and their programmes' activities, including the Shajalal Model Village and the *Fael Khair* programme, and the centres named after the Prophet's companions and family members. The most significant component is their use of *shari'a* ruling in their programme of activities; for example, the prohibition of charging interest (*shud*), which is *haram* (strictly prohibited) in Islam as well as the adoption of *shari'a*-based financing; for example, *Quard-Hasana, Murabha* and *Musharaka*. During their programme of activities they refer to the teachings of Islam as prime movers; for example, the *zakat*-based *hasana* programme where Islamic NGOs frequently refer to the Quranic injunction as the basis of their programme. Islamic NGOs provide religious and moral teachings in the *shari'a*-based microfinance or *Hasana* programme with the aim of making their beneficiaries *khati Musulmaan* ('pure Muslim') through encouraging piety. This is also evident in the everyday practice of Islamic NGO officials, as many of them consider serving in the Islamic NGOs and not just working for the organization but *Ibadat* (worship) that would bring rewards for them in the life hereafter. Both Islamic NGO workers and their beneficiaries consider Islamic NGOs to be unique, due to the fact that they are the source of *mukti* or salvation, both from the oppression of the high interest rates of secular NGOs and from the sin (due to getting involved in interest or *shud*). Moreover, Islamic NGO workers, as they argue, conduct themselves in an honest and dedicated manner, making these organizations the least susceptible to corruption. This contradicts Ahmad's (2009) finding of corruption in religious NGOs. During my research I also found that some respondents alleged that religious NGOs were involved in bribery and corruption, particularly in relation to the distribution of disaster aid.

This book has shown that Islamic NGOs in some contexts hold a comparative advantage in their operations due to their Islamic identity. This illustrates the idea of the cultural proximity of Islamic NGOs with the Islamic culture of rural Bangladesh. As the respondents acknowledge, they can readily identify and feel more comfortable working with Islamic NGO officials. They therefore consider that joining Islamic NGOs does not go against the norms of *purdha* and Islamic teachings. Yet Islamic identity, which is evident from their symbols, activities and programme propaganda, is much more complicated. Islamic NGOs are keener to show their non-discrimination policy rather than being called religious or Islamic NGOs. This research has found that the crisis of identity in the Islamic

NGO, which I discussed in Chapter 3, lies in the national discourse on the politics of secularism and religious nationalism that divide the people into two categories aligned with two political parties; for example, the Awami League as champions of secularism and Bangalee nationalism, and the BNP as champions of pro-Islamic politics with Bangladeshi nationalism.

A significant insight into the crisis of identity of Islamic NGOs also emerged from the field which is related to the war crimes tribunal. At least some of the main figures in the Islamic NGOs in my study (for example, the founder of MACCA, one trustee of Muslim Aid) are accused of having either a direct connection with war crimes in Bangladesh in 1971 or a perceived connection with Jamaat; hence the subsequent strict state surveillance of Islamic NGOs. The country-wide terror bombing in 2005 by the Islamists, and their alleged connection with some of the Islamic charities, particularly after the centre-left political party assumed state power in 2008 and instituted strict state surveillance, became a source of insecurity for many Islamic NGOs in Bangladesh. This strict state surveillance is also a result of the terrorist attacks of 9/11 and subsequent war on terror which created a pressure on the so-called 'moderate Muslim country'; for example, Bangladesh to comply with the Western (USA) war against terrorism in Muslim countries. As a result, Islamic charities, as Benthall (2003) argues, have faced increasingly intense controls for alleged links with extremist groups such as Al Qaeda. As a result, some Islamic charities had their assets frozen and were kept under strict surveillance, and some were banned (Petersen, 2012, p. 131). Moreover, in the Western media and discourse, what was often misunderstood and disregarded were the differences between active *dawa* and terrorism. Hence, there is a tendency to brand all the Islamic NGOs as terrorist or 'religiously militant' and extremist (Appleby, 2000; Benthall, 2003; Ghandour, 2003). Thus this book also found a tendency among the media, and some centre-left governments and *shushil samaj prothinidi* (representatives of civil society), to equate all Islamic charities with the rise of Islamic militancy, thus resulting in strict surveillance.

It is apparent from the field that Islamic NGOs face a crisis in their identity, or at least do not want to be called Islamic. Yet it was clear that they used religious principles to govern the people, an issue which I discussed in Chapter 4. Like the secular NGOs they emphasized the principles of accountability, transparency and empowerment, with development and efficient management practice. They achieved this, but in a different way; i.e. they coupled Islamic principles with neoliberalism to encourage entrepreneurial *Homo economicus* which, following Atia (2012), could be called pious neoliberalism. Grameen Bank, BRAC and other secular NGOs in the study uphold the idea of the individual entrepreneur who, with the help of microcredit, becomes self-employed, owns private property (e.g. cattle, grocery shop), thus cultivating the subjectivity of a rational economic being. This also produced and reproduced a social identity (i.e. access to and membership of a formal organization and the consequent identity of self-maximizing women as successful entrepreneurs as well as employees of NGOs) (Mayer and Rankin, 2002, p. 806). Yet people's participation in such activities is a governmental strategy through which NGOs accomplish the desired restructuring 'consistent with the financial stability of the lenders and an ideal of self-regulating markets' (Rankin, 2001, p. 28). Therefore, as Muhammad Yunus argues, 'not only capitalism is good for the poor, "the poor are good for capitalism"' (Yunus, 2007, cited in Karim, 2008, p. 14). Yet these beneficiaries, mostly women, are obliged to act in accordance with the values of 'discipline, efficiency and competitiveness' (Karim, 2008, p. 6). In this system, as Rose (1996, p. 338) argues, 'each individual is solicited as an ally of economic success through ensuring that they invest in the management and success of their own economic capital'.

This book considers charity as an economic practice and as an act of governing subjects (e.g. rural men and women). These Islamic charities or NGOs have applied Islamic rhetoric in the procedures, applications and techniques of neoliberal governmentality, to enable the population to live successful and pious private entrepreneurial lives based on economic rationality and calculative reasons. As I explained in Chapter 4, all the Islamic NGOs in their published and unpublished reports provide case studies of success stories of women borrowers and how they had transformed rural housewives into successful entrepreneurs by providing *shari'a*-based microcredit. This is the same as the picture I found in the field, one which exclusively emphasizes the self-reliant and productive, rational, economic being.

What is distinctive in the application of Islamic principles is their practice. For example, they integrate neoliberal principles of accountability and transparency, and 'personal responsibility' and 'self-care' with those of religious values and piety. Contrary to secular NGO beneficiaries who use the money for usury, consumption or for unapproved business or activities, Islamic NGO beneficiaries cannot use the money for usury or unapproved activities. Since they (both the NGO and the beneficiary) are not only accountable to each other, but also to Allah, the surveillance of Allah keeps both of these groups on the right path of economic and pious development practice. This book has shown that Islamic NGOs with their emphasis on *halal vs. haram* (approved vs. prohibited), submission to Allah, avoidance of sin (for example, through avoidance of usury or *shud*), regular prayer and modesty, as well as rewards in the life hereafter, help to sustain neoliberalism at the grassroots level which I detailed in Chapter 4. Becoming successful in their business, respondents believe, is because 'this money [of *Islami samity*] has blessings [*barkat*] from Allah' as they follow the Islamic way of doing business and avoid getting involved in *shud*. Therefore, by using Islamic rhetoric in economic practices, Islamic NGOs become successful in controlling the behaviour of their beneficiaries, which is indeed government strategy.

Arguing this way, I do not claim that only Islam is uniquely suited to neoliberal governmentality; rather other faiths have the same potential (for example, Christianity). Therefore, Islamic NGOs or FBOs in general govern the neoliberal subject both through their service provision (for example, *shari'a*-based microfinance and humanitarian aid in my research) and Islamic teachings. As with secular NGOs, they use accountability, transparency and management practice in their operations. They consider accountability to the donors and beneficiaries to be important, as it makes them transparent. At the same time, both the NGOs and the beneficiaries of Islamic NGOs consider that their accountability to the transcendent (i.e. Allah) guides them to behave in a certain way which helps beneficiaries repay the loan and to do *halal* business as well as dedication and transparency in the work of the officials. One way to blend neoliberal principles of empowerment in order to transform Muslim housewives into entrepreneurial beings is through the blending of the traditional notion of *purdha* with economic activities.

NGO-led development discourse is predominantly women oriented; i.e. it targets women for empowerment. Islamic NGOs also aim to empower rural female beneficiaries through programme participation. As I discussed in Chapter 5, many women did not join secular NGOs due to their fear of breaching the norms of *purdha* and instead joined Islamic NGOs. Joining Islamic NGOs, they claim, does not breach the practice of Islam but rather encourages them to be pious in their private and public lives. Many of these women, as they themselves and the community understand it, are now successful pious entrepreneurs. This participation of women in Islamic NGOs reflects their desire to do so, as well as a resistance towards the secular NGOs in Bangladesh. Several studies found that 'one of the most significant accusations' (e.g. Naher, 2005, p. 151; 2010) against secular NGOs (e.g. Grameen Bank, BRAC), particularly by the religious elite, was that they sought to break up the traditional family order, by targeting women through the provision of microfinance, through which secular NGOs practise a 'development patriarchy' (White, 2009, p. 17; 2012), while Islamic NGOs encourage family empowerment. Thus beneficiaries of Islamic NGOs tend to view the activities of non-Islamic NGOs (e.g. BRAC, Shushilan, Grameen Bank) as ill-mannered and Satanic.

This opposition to secular NGOs represents rural women's 'desire' to be guided by the norms for *purdha.* Moreover, at a personal level they are now more aware of their rights and obligations as wives and mothers, as well as the formal practice of religion in everyday life, including what kind of dress would be *shari'a* approved. Their participation in Islamic NGOs, they claim, has reduced conjugal fighting due to a decrease in *kistee* (instalment)-related conflict and increased observance of Islamic rituals in family life. Participation in these *samity*, which I detailed in Chapter 5, has increased their self-esteem and dignity as economically successful wives. The practice of piety has ultimately increased their social status as a 'good woman' in the family and in the *samaj* (society). These women now believe they are more aware of their rights and duties as wives and mothers in the light of Islam and are able to exercise authority in household decision making (e.g. on the use of money, children's education).

In contrast in my study, secular NGOs emerged as coercive actors in development, particularly regarding women. These NGOs, as I discussed in Chapter 6, used social constructions of shame (*lazza/apoman*), honour (*samman*) and social collateral (i.e. peer pressure) in group-based lending processes which resulted in coercion ranging from verbal aggression (from NGO workers as well as peers), starvation, forced sale and economic vulnerability, to suicide. The symbolic meaning of certain forms of coercion such as to lose one's nose pin (*nakphul*) (due to forced sale) or taking someone to the NGO office (to compel them to repay the loan) was seen as a loss of one's chastity and social honour and status respectively. NGOs are well aware of such social constructions of humiliation (*apoman*) and exploited this to ensure the repayment of credit instalments. This emerged particularly in the context of the inability of the microcredit borrowers to repay the instalments (*kistee*). These NGOs, the research found, used a group-based approach to ensure the surveillance and policing of one woman by another. This, though it slashed administrative costs, ultimately produced negative social capital (i.e. distrust among members), and hence strife (*jaghra*) became part of the everyday life of borrowers. Therefore, it undermined the supposed benefits from social networks and connectedness. The main argument for the use of social collateral was the strengthening of financial stability and the exercise of authority over the beneficiaries of these NGOs rather than the production of social capital. Thus NGOs are now able to exercise arbitrary power over their rural, marginal subjects and in particular over their women beneficiaries. Thus it is not inevitable that NGOs with microcredit emancipate women; rather they convert them into docile agents upon which NGOs survive.

It is apparent in the field that Islamic NGOs have emerged as the least coercive development practitioners. The main reason for becoming non-coercive is, as local officials argue, the absence of pressure from their head office. This, I found, is due to the different sources of funding from which Islamic NGOs can provide interest-free credit. As there is no interest, they are less likely to become coercive in collecting the repayments. In addition, as the research has found, Islamic NGOs expressed their commitment to the principles of justice, *sheba* (service) and responsibilities to the orphan, the penniless and the poor as instructed in the Quran and *Hadith*. They construct their commitment not to make any profit out of their programme of activities but to serve those in need, which comes from, these NGOs claim, the humanitarian spirit of Islam.

Thus this research has found that development discourses and their related technologies (of accountability, self-reliance and entrepreneurship) have penetrated the charitable landscape of Bangladesh, but these discourses are now coupled with the Islamic tradition of justice, compassion and religious obligation to help the poor. Thus Islamic charities or NGOs are still charities and Islamic, but they are increasingly transforming themselves into agents of development. Neoliberal principles (e.g. rational economic beings, individualization of responsibility, self-help, accountability, managerialism) have become the so-called solution to poverty in rural Bangladesh, with the introduction of religious principles creating a hybrid form of neoliberalism. While the idea of neoliberalism as occupied within secular mainstream NGOs has produced negative consequences, Islamic NGOs emphasize the economic activities for success in this world leading to success in the life hereafter. This research therefore contradicts the orientalist discourses that highlight a binary opposition between Muslims and the West. Thus I have shown how Islam works hand in hand with neoliberalism. Arguing this way, I am not saying that Islamic NGOs and related ideas of pious neoliberalism are an alternative to neoliberalism; rather I have explained how neoliberal logic works with Islam and Islamic NGOs in the context of Bangladesh. In doing so, I am aware of the many different shortcomings of Islamic NGOs.

One such problem is with the issue of funding. It is evident in my research that Islamic NGOs are providing better service and are less coercive than secular NGOs. Hence, Islamic NGOs could be an alternative to the mainstream secular NGOs in development practice in the Muslim majority countries like Bangladesh. But one of the obvious reasons for Islamic NGOs to be non-coercive is their source of funding. Since most NGOs use an informal source of funding (i.e. donations in the form of *zakat, sadaqa* from institutions and individuals), the question remains: Who are these funders and from where is the funding coming? Is there any political agenda (e.g. Islamism) in the funding issues? However, this book does not aim to trace the sources of funding; rather I have explained the discourse on the funding of Islamic NGOs and found that people in the rural areas regard the money they receive from Islamic NGOs as the money of Islam (*Islam er Taka*). They also make an imagined connection with some rich, kind-hearted Muslim in *bedesh* (a foreign country), i.e. Saudi Arabia or Kuwait. They are not sure about the sources of the funding but they do consider themselves as part of an imagined Muslim community or *ummah*. Therefore, in this context we need to conduct further research on the issue of funding which would help us to find any ulterior motives in altruism.

It is also important to note that Islamic NGO beneficiaries, even if they experience coercive treatment from Islamic NGOs, may not share this knowledge with me due to the fact that they are receiving loans from their fellow Muslim brothers or like-minded – either political (e.g. Jamaat) or ideological (e.g. Islamic) – people or NGOs. There are other contradictions in the intervention of Islamic NGOs (e.g. women's empowerment). Although this research found that women's participation in Islamic NGOs represents their desires and liberation, I am critical of their approach to empowerment (explained in Chapter 5) which in some cases represents a traditional and patriarchal view of Jamaat's ideology on empowerment in some points. The practice of Islamic discourse in the Islamic NGO, therefore, has huge implications for women's lives, particularly for the rural and already marginalized women, as Islamic discourse in Bangladesh, Hussain (2010, p. 326) suggests, 'highlights the prerogatives of men and legitimizes the authority of men over women'. If this is the real intention of the empowerment project of Islamic NGOs, as it is always hard to know, it may adversely affect the empowerment of women. Yet I must contend, even in this approach to empowerment, rural women, as they claim, are more comfortable, since they don't have to break with the traditional norms of *purdha* as well as the everyday practice of religion. It is also noteworthy that many women consider participation in the *Islami samity* equal to that of *talim* (a congregation of Muslim women in certain places). Thus participation in *samity* meetings serves both the economic/financial requirements as well as transcendent/spiritual/

religious purposes, through which they achieve *dunier santi* (peace in this world due mainly to economic improvement), and *ekherater love* (rewards in the life hereafter). It is an undeniable fact that although Islamic NGOs intend to empower the rural and most vulnerable segment of the population as they claim, their main purpose, namely to select the women beneficiaries, also reveals the same motivation as secular NGOs who use women's positional vulnerability to ensure the timely return of repayment.

This book argues that Islamic NGOs have enormous potential to grow in the context of a Muslim majority country through blending Islamic principles with economic rationality and a liberal approach to development. Yet it is important to address certain issues for the sustainable and effective impact of Islamic NGOs in Bangladesh. First, Islamic NGOs' endeavour to prove their transparency through providing their balance sheets and account statements in their annual report is not enough. They also need to show all their sources of funding, including individual and institutional donations, to make it more transparent. At the grassroots level Islamic NGOs should provide sufficient and consistent information regarding their sources of funding so that people can readily assume from whom they are receiving the funds and for what purposes. Thus it is imperative for Islamic NGOs to be more transparent to gain trust and avoid surveillance over their activities by the state. Second, gender and empowerment constitute a major component of development in rural Bangladesh; Islamic NGOs need to make it clear regarding their position on gender. Islamic NGOs themselves, as well as their officials, must avoid a rigid interpretation of Quranic verses on women's issues to restrict their physical and social mobility and hence to confine women behind the *purdha*. Finally, one of the major complaints against Islamic NGOs is their preferential treatment in selecting the beneficiaries that include a bias towards rich clients (due to their ability to repay) which I discussed in Chapter 6. Other complains include a religious bias towards Muslims and a political bias mainly towards Jamaat-e-Islam-minded people which I discussed in Chapter 3. Therefore, to make development more equitable and just, Islamic NGOs must avoid these and any other kinds of preferential treatment in providing services to the public.

Religion in general and Islam in particular is part of the social and political fabric of Bangladesh, and represents a way of life for the majority of Bengali Muslims in the country. Thus, Islamic NGOs have become successful in mobilizing people to be pious as well as successful entrepreneurs. Rigorous research is required to identify the possibility of the adoption of charitable donations in the form of *zakat* and *sadaqa* as required for a systematic and effective distribution. Research is also needed on how state and non-state actors can effectively use these sources of funding for development where there will be no fear of sin and consequent coercion related to credit repayment. It is also important to conduct in-depth research on the Bangladeshi Muslim immigrants of the diasporas, particularly those living in Western countries, about their role in rearticulating Islamic discourse in Bangladesh, either through funding and/or transforming ideologies. Moreover, it is also important to conduct further research on the issue of the political economy of the Islamization of aid; the banking and financial systems as well as services (e.g. health care, education) in Bangladesh to explore the politics of Islamism and its consequences for the Bangladeshi sociopolitical and economic system.

## References

Ahmad, M. M. (2009). For God's Sake: The Religious Non-governmental Organizations in Bangladesh. In F. C. Khan, A. Ahmad and M. Quddus (eds), *Recreating the Commons? NGOs in Bangladesh* (pp. 183–206). Dhaka: The University Press.

Appleby, R. S. (2000). *The Ambivalence of the Sacred: Religion, Violence, and Reconciliation.* Lanham, MD: Rowman & Littlefield.

Atia, M. (2012). 'A Way to Paradise': Pious Neoliberalism, Islam, and Faith-based Development. *Annals of the Association of American Geographers, 102*(4), 808–827.

Benthall, J. (2003). Humanitarianism and Islam after 11 September. In M. Joanna and H. Adele (eds), *Humanitarian Action and the 'Global War on Terror': A Review of Trends and Issues* (pp. 37–48). London: HPG.

Ghandour, A.-R. (2003). Humanitarianism, Islam and the West: Contest or Co-operation? *Humanitarian Exchange, 25*, 14–17.

Hussain, N. A. (2010). Religion and Modernity: Gender and Identity Politics in Bangladesh. *Women's Studies International Forum, 33*(4), 325–333. doi: 10.1016/j.wsif.2010.02.006.

Karim, L. (2008). Demystifying Micro-credit: The Grameen Bank, NGOs, and Neoliberalism in Bangladesh. *Cultural Dynamics, 20*(1), 5–29. doi: 10.1177/0921374007088053.

Mayer, M. and Rankin, K. N. (2002). Social Capital and (Community) Development: A North/South Perspective. *Antipode, 34*(4), 804–808. doi: 10.1111/1467–8330.00273.

Naher, A. (2005). *Gender, Religion and Development in Rural Bangladesh.* Ph.D. thesis, Heidelberg University, Heidelberg.

Naher, A. (2010). 'Defending Islam and Women's Honour against NGOs' in Bangladesh. *Women's Studies International Forum, 33*(4), 316–324. doi: 10.1016/j.wsif.2010.02.005.

Petersen, M. (2012). Islamizing Aid: Transnational Muslim NGOs After 9.11. *Voluntas: International Journal of Voluntary and Nonprofit Organizations, 23*(1), 126–155. doi: 10.1007/s11266–011–9185–5.

Rankin, K. N. (2001). Governing Development: Neoliberalism, Microcredit, and Rational Economic Woman. *Economy and Society, 30*(1), 18–37.

Rose, N. (1996). The Death of the Social? Re-figuring the Territory of Government. *Economy and Society, 25*(3), 327–356. doi: 10.1080/03085149600000018.

White, S. C. (2009). Beyond the Paradox: Religion, Family and Modernity in Contemporary Bangladesh. *Religions and Development (RaD) Research Programme.* University of Bath, UK.

White, S. C. (2012). Beyond the Paradox: Religion, Family and Modernity in Contemporary Bangladesh. *Modern Asian Studies, FirstView*, 1–30. doi: doi:10.1017/S0026749X12000133.

# Appendices

## Appendix 1 Programme and activities of Muslim Aid Bangladesh

| *Activities/programme* | *Aims and target group* |
|---|---|
| **Disaster management and climate change**<br>Emergency response<br>Preparedness and response<br>Capacity-building for disaster risk reduction | Protecting lives and assets of disaster-affected community by ensuring food security to the affected and vulnerable communities during emergency situation in a timely manner that fosters livelihood recovery, reduces vulnerability and upholds dignity. |
| **Microfinance and SME**<br>General microfinance<br>Microfinance for the poor<br>*Fael Khair*<br>SME (small and medium enterprise)<br>Hardcore poor loan | Facilitating people's access to resources and there by accentuating equitable and justifiable resource distribution and social development following Islamic principles. |
| **Education of women and children's affairs**<br>General formal education support<br>Technical and vocational education<br>Non-formal education (NFE) | Providing education to marginalized children; skills training and post-training support to underprivileged and unemployed youth, encouraging socially disadvantaged youth into self-employment and involving them in mainstream development initiatives of the country. |
| **Health service**<br>In-patient service and out-patient service<br>HIV and AIDS prevention<br>Maternal and childcare, nutrition<br>Community programmes | Bringing health services to the doorsteps of the general population through providing preventive, curative and operative services at affordable costs. |
| **Food security and nutrition programme**<br>Enhancing resilience<br>Emergency food for flood victims<br>School feeding/food for education<br>Protecting and promoting food security and nutrition | Working towards building a hunger-free healthy nation by ensuring the availability, accessibility and utilization of food for the resource-poor and disaster-hit people. |
| **Agriculture and livelihood programme**<br>Supporting landless, marginal and small farmers<br>Yield maximization of oilseed crops<br>Strengthening household access to resources | Greening fields and greening lives by providing input and capacity-building of farmers as well as research on augmenting food production in the country. |

Source: Muslim Aid Annual Report (2011).

## Appendix 2 Programme and activities of the IBF

| *Activities/programme* | *Aims and target group* |
|---|---|
| **Income-generating programmes**<br>Rickshaw project<br>Poultry project<br>Rural health worker training project<br>Milk cow-rearing project<br>Self-employment project<br>Small business project<br>Small industry project, etc.<br>Sewing training project | To make unemployed youth self-reliant. |
| **Educational programmes**<br>Adrasha Forquania Maktab<br>Scholarship for poor and meritorious students<br>Scholarship for the students of higher studies<br>Financial support for educational institutions<br>Lump-sum grant for poor students, etc. | To improve the educational scenario of Bangladesh. |
| **Health and medicare programmes**<br>Establishment of medical centre supporting charitable dispensaries<br>Lump-sum help for treatment of poor patients<br>Tube well installation<br>Sanitary latrine construction, etc. | To provide better health and sanitation facilities for the poor. |
| **Humanitarian help programmes**<br>Establishment and operation of orphanages<br>Providing funds for the marriage of poor girls<br>Assist indebted people<br>Help distressed wayfarers and other similar activities | To provide humanitarian assistance to the needy. |
| **Relief and rehabilitation programmes** | To operate relief and rehabilitation activities during natural calamities like flood, tornado, tidal surge, river erosion, conflagration, etc. |
| **Literature, culture and publishing related activities**<br>Distribution of Islamic research magazines<br>Audio-video cassettes<br>Financial help to youth clubs and voluntary organizations<br>Taleemul Quran, etc. | To disseminate the true knowledge and teachings of Islam and to enlighten the common people as well as the elites, and to make them familiar with the concept of Islam. |

Source: IBF website available at www.ibf-bd.org/content.php?id=44&menu_id=1, and personal communication with the High Official of the IBF.

## Appendix 3 Activities of MACCA in Bangladesh

| *Programme* | *Aims and target group* |
|---|---|
| **Development programmes**<br>Mosque-based education<br>*Imam* training programme<br>Faith-based approach to HIV/AIDS prevention<br>Faith-based Integrated Development Education and Livelihood (IDEAL) village project<br>Income-generating project<br>Gender equity and women's empowerment<br>Faith institution-based development model | Comprehensive development of the ultra-poor. |
| **Complementary partnership for development**<br>Development education programme for faith leaders<br>Water and sanitation project<br>Pure drinking water supply project<br>Leaders of Influence (LOI)<br>BRAC wash programme | Development through cooperation with multi-level stakeholders. |
| **Humanitarian and emergency programmes**<br>Children Welfare Program (CWP)<br>Emergency responses<br>Free Friday clinic | To provide emergency support for the needy. |
| **Support of Election Commission**<br>Promotion of interfaith cooperation<br>Centre for Research on Society and Development<br>monthly 'Jiggasha' | Strengthening democracy. |

Source: MACCA Annual Report (2007 and 2008).

# Index

For Product Safety Concerns and Information please contact our EU representative GPSR@taylorandfrancis.com
Taylor & Francis Verlag GmbH, Kaufingerstraße 24, 80331 München, Germany

www.ingramcontent.com/pod-product-compliance
Ingram Content Group UK Ltd.
Pitfield, Milton Keynes, MK11 3LW, UK
UKHW022131190926
475702UK00013B/1752
* 9 7 8 1 1 3 8 3 4 7 5 5 7 *